The City and the Senses

# The City and the Senses

Urban Culture Since 1500

Edited by
Alexander Cowan and
Jill Steward

ASHGATE

Published by
Ashgate Publishing Limited
Gower House
Croft Road
Aldershot
Hants GU11 3HR
England

Ashgate Publishing Company
Suite 420
101 Cherry Street
Burlington, VT 05401-4405
USA

Ashgate website: http://www.ashgate.com

**British Library Cataloguing in Publication Data**
The city and the senses : since 1500. – (Historical urban studies)
  1.City and town life – Europe – History 2.Senses and sensation
  I.Cowan, Alexander II.Steward, Jill
  307.7'6'094

**Library of Congress Cataloging-in-Publication Data**
The city and the senses : urban culture since 1500 / edited by Alexander Cowan and Jill Steward.
    p. cm. – (Historical urban studies series)
  Includes index.
  ISBN 0-7546-0514-0 (alk. paper)
  1. Cities and towns – Europe – History. 2. Senses and sensation – Europe – History. 3. Sociology, Urban – Europe. 4. Europe – History – 1492-5. Europe – Social conditions. I. Cowan, Alexander. II. Steward, Jill. III. Series: Historical urban studies.

  HT131.C523 2006
  307.76094 – dc22
                                                                    2006003937
Reprinted 2008

ISBN-13: 978-0-7546-0514-0

Typeset by Express Typesetters, Farnham, Surrey.
Printed and bound in Great Britain by MPG Books Ltd, Bodmin, Cornwall

# Contents

**Part Three    Cultural Control and Cultural Subversion**

# List of Figures and Tables

# Contributors

**Ava Arndt** teaches eighteenth-century literature at the University of California, Irvine. She has published articles on circulation, economic history and William Harvey and female gamblers. She is in the process of completing a book on mobility and literary imagination entitled *Animating Subjects: The Rise of Capital, Object Narratives and the Eighteenth-Century Reader*.

**Kim Carpenter** received her PhD in German history from Georgetown University in 1998. She has taught at several institutions, including a recent adjunct position at the University of Akron in Ohio. Publications include '"Beggars Appear Everywhere!" New Approaches for Pauper and Migration Control in mid-Nineteenth-Century Munich', in *Migration Control in the North Atlantic World: The Evolution of State Practices in Europe and the United States from the French Revolution to the Inter-War Period* (Berghahn 2002) and '"For mothers only": mothers' convalescent homes and modernizing maternal ideology in 1950s West Germany', *Journal of Social History*, Summer, 2001.

**Alexander Cowan** is a Reader in History at Northumbria University in Newcastle. He is the author of *The Urban Patriciate: Lübeck and Venice, 1580–1700* (Böhlau 1986), *Urban Europe 1500–1700* (Arnold 1998) and the editor of *Mediterranean Urban Culture, 1400–1700* (University of Exeter Press 2000). He is currently completing a monograph on *Women, Marriage and Social Distinction in Early Modern Venice*.

**Hazel Hahn** is an Assistant Professor of History at Seattle University in Seattle, Washington. She is preparing a manuscript on advertising and commercial culture in Paris of the 1830–1914 period. She is also working on consumer culture of the French July Monarchy as well as on tourism and urban planning in French Indochina in the first half of the twentieth century.

**David Inglis** is a Senior Lecturer in Sociology at the University of Aberdeen. He writes in the areas of Social Theory and Sociology of Culture. He is the author (with John Hughson), of *A Sociological History of Excretory Experience: Defecatory Manners and Toiletry Technologies* (Mellen 2001), *Confronting Culture: Sociological Vistas* (Polity 2003), and is currently writing *Classical Sociological Theory: Roots and Branches* for Sage.

**Dorothy Rowe** is Senior Lecturer in Art History and Theory at Roehampton University. She is author of *Representing Berlin: Sexuality and the City in Imperial and Weimar Germany* (Ashgate 2003) and co-editor of *Europe and America, 1750–2000* in the 'Critical Anthologies in Art History' series (Blackwell 2005), as well as author of a number of articles on art, difference and the city.

**Jill Steward** teaches Cultural History at Northumbria University in Newcastle. She is the co-editor (with M. Gee and T. Kirk) of *The City in Central Europe. Culture and Society from 1800 to the Present* (Ashgate 1999) and is a member of the Research Group for European Urban Culture. Recent publications deal with the history of tourism in Italy and Central Europe and the growth of spa culture. She is currently working on the relationship between the travel press and the formation of social and cultural identities.

**Janet Stewart** is Lecturer in German at the University of Aberdeen, where she also teaches Cultural History and has recently established a taught postgraduate programme in Visual Culture. She is the author of *Fashioning Vienna: Adolf Loos's Cultural Criticism* (Routledge 2000), as well as numerous articles on Austrian and German cultural history. Her current research project focuses on public speaking and public space in Berlin and Vienna, 1890–1933.

**Ulf Strohmayer** is Professor of Geography at the National University of Ireland in Galway. He has published widely on urban geography, social theory and the history of geographic thought. Most recent publications include *Human Geography: A History for the 21st Century* (Arnold 2004) and *Space and Social Theory* (Blackwell 1997), both edited with Georges Benko.

**Rosemary Wakeman** is an Associate Professor in the History Department and Associate Director of the Urban Studies Program at Fordham University in New York. She is the author of *Modernizing the Provincial City: Toulouse, 1945–1975* (Harvard University Press 1997) and editor of *Themes in Modern European History Since 1945* (Routledge 2003). She is currently working on a study of the cultural politics of urban design in Paris during the 1940s and 1950s.

**Jo Wheeler** was awarded a PhD by the University of Warwick on the *sestiere* [district] of San Polo in the late fifteenth century. He has published on neighbourhood and local loyalties in Renaissance Venice, in A. Cowan (ed.), *Mediterranean Urban Culture 1400–1700* (University of Exeter Press 2000). Since 2001, he has been researching books of secrets and their relation to the print industry, charlatans and women healers in early modern Italy and has spoken on these topics at numerous international conferences. He is currently working on a book-length study.

**Laura Wright** is a Senior Lecturer in English Language at the University of Cambridge and a Fellow of Lucy Cavendish College. Recent books include *Sources of London English: Medieval Thames Vocabulary* (Oxford University Press 1996) and (as editor), *The Development of Standard English, 1300–1800: Theories, Descriptions, Conflicts* (Cambridge University Press 2000). She works on the history of the London dialect, and is currently editing a book on the language of early settlers on the London East India Company island of St Helena in the South Atlantic.

# Acknowledgments

The process of creating this book has been a collective exercise from the start. The idea arose from discussions among the members of the Research Group for European Urban Culture at Northumbria University in Newcastle upon Tyne. While the editing process has been the responsibility of the book's two editors alone, Malcolm Gee and Tim Kirk (now of the University of Newcastle) have been unstinting in their support and advice. Discussions at the session devoted to 'The City and the Senses' at the European Urban History conference in Venice, where some of the essays in this book received a first airing, also provided useful comparative contexts within which to develop this project. Finally, we would like to thank all the contributors to the book. In addition to the usual delays in bringing together a book of this kind, several of the contributors and the editors experienced major life-cycle events that touched us all. While we are sad at our bereavements, we celebrate the birth of three daughters among us. Editing is a process that requires a high patience threshold on the part of the editors. In this case, patience was more often the virtue required of its contributors. We would like to thank them for their forbearance.

*Alexander Cowan*
*Jill Steward*

# Historical Urban Studies
# General Editors' Preface

Density and proximity are two of the defining characteristics of the urban dimension. It is these that identify a place as uniquely urban, though the threshold for such pressure points varies from place to place. What is considered an important cluster in one context – may not be considered as urban elsewhere. A third defining characteristic is functionality – the commercial or strategic position of a town or city which conveys an advantage over other places. Over time, these functional advantages may diminish, or the balance of advantage may change within a hierarchy of towns. To understand how the relative importance of towns shifts over time and space is to grasp a set of relationships which is fundamental to the study of urban history.

Towns and cities are products of history, yet have themselves helped to shape history. As the proportion of urban dwellers has increased, so the urban dimension has proved a legitimate unit of analysis through which to understand the spectrum of human experience and to explore the cumulative memory of past generations. Though obscured by layers of economic, social and political change, the study of the urban milieu provides insights into the functioning of human relationships and, if urban historians themselves are not directly concerned with current policy studies, few contemporary concerns can be understood without reference to the historical development of towns and cities.

This longer historical perspective is essential to an understanding of social processes. Crime, housing conditions and property values, health and education, discrimination and deviance, and the formulation of regulations and social policies to deal with them were, and remain, amongst the perennial preoccupations of towns and cities – no historical period has a monopoly of these concerns. They recur in successive generations, albeit in varying mixtures and strengths; the details may differ.

The central forces of class, power and authority in the city remain. If this was the case for different periods, so it was for different geographical entities and cultures. Both scientific knowledge and technical information were available across Europe and showed little respect for frontiers. Yet despite common concerns and access to broadly similar knowledge, different solutions to urban problems were proposed and adopted by towns and cities in different parts of Europe. This comparative dimension informs urban historians as to which were systematic factors and which were of a purely local nature: general and particular forces can be distinguished.

These analytical and comparative frameworks inform this book. Indeed, thematic, comparative and analytical approaches to the historical study of towns and cities is the hallmark of the Historical Urban Studies series which now extends to over 30 titles, either already published or currently in production. European urban historiography has been extended and enriched as a result and this book makes another important addition to an intellectual mission to which we, as General Editors, remain firmly committed.

Richard Rodger                        *University of Leicester*
Jean-Luc Pinol                        *Université de Lyon II*

# Introduction

## Jill Steward and Alexander Cowan

The starting point of the *City and the Senses* is an historical interest in the sensory dimension of city life to which the five bodily senses, traditionally recognised in Western thought,[1] contribute. And although psychologists tell us that the bulk of the information that fuels the human perceptual system is provided by the visual sense, each of the other sensations, touch, taste, sound and smell, contribute to the processes that produce an individual's particular sensory world.[2] Cities conceived of as sensory environments and sites of habitation generate their own distinctive smells and sounds. They are full of visual and tactile stimuli, each with their own range of symbolic meanings for the sentient, perceiving subject. But, as Walter Benjamin noted of nineteenth-century Paris, 'All that remains of the increasingly swift dissipation of perceptual worlds is "nothing other than their names: *Passagen*".'[3]

The impact of the material and cultural environment of cities on the sensory lives of their inhabitants has, until recently, received relatively little attention from urban historians and yet changes in the nature of the sensory experiences offered by particular cities are just as much part of their history as economic, political and social change. In recent years theoretical interest in the embodied subject has begun to produce work that specifically locates the body in ways which remap and refigure both the body and the city that it inhabits.[4] Histories of noise, vision,

[1] C. Classen, *Worlds of Sense: Exploring the Senses in History and Across Cultures* (London, 1993), pp. 1–7.

[2] The French philosopher Maurice Merleau-Ponty wrote: 'Sense experience is that vital communication with the world, which makes it present as a familiar setting our life. It is to it that the perceived object and the perceiving subject owe their thickness. It is the intentional tissue which the effort to know will try to take apart': *The Phenomenology of Perception* (London, 1974), p. 53. New interest in phenomenology has contributed to the reactivating of the question of the nature of the relationship between the material body and the world, although the ontological and epistemological implications have more often been explored within the world of art rather than historical scholarship. See also J. Urry, 'City life and the senses', in G. Bridge and S. Watson, eds, *A Companion to the City* (Oxford, 2000), pp. 388–97.

[3] Cited in D. Gregory, *Geographical Imagination* (Oxford, 1994), p. 245.

[4] For example, N. Thrift, *Spatial Formations* (London, 1996); A. Vidler, *The Architectural Uncanny: Studies in the Modern Unhomely* (Cambridge, Mass.,

manners, tactility, sexuality, gustation and olfaction show that sensuous encounters between individuals and environments are produced and structured, not just by their material features, but also by the particular social and cultural contexts in which encounters take place. Changes in manufacturing, distribution and retailing systems, in the state and municipal institutions and the regulations relating to urban growth, development and in the state of technology and forms of commercial and leisure activity were all factors influencing the nature of the sensory environment. At the same time changes in the way that resultant sensations were marked, represented and evaluated within specific modes of discourse influenced the way that urban spaces were used and represented.

Some of these changes are noted in this collection, particularly the shift from the less regulated environments of the early modern period to the relatively heavily controlled one of the modern world. These essays, for the most part, focus on the history of particular sensations, but together they point to the importance of situating them in the context of a wider understanding of the relationship between the human body as *sensorium* and its urban environment. Moreover, they emphasise the way that, in any given era, the meaning and significance of particular sensory experiences are determined by the philosophical, linguistic and cultural systems through which they are produced and represented. It is not just aesthetic tastes and experiences that are the outcome of dispositions inculcated by particular cultural forms and ways of life,[5] for the same may be said of other forms of sensory experience that involve the ascription of meaning and value.

## Theoretical and methodological contexts

Theoretical interest in the sensory dimension of the urban environment is not new. The German sociologist Georg Simmel (1858–1918) regarded the metropolitan city of the early twentieth century as the site of a new kind of urban consciousness manifested in the emergence of a new rhythm of 'sensual–intellectual life'.[6] His discussion of social space

---

1992); R. Sennett, *Flesh and Stone. The Body and the City in Western Civilisation* (London, 1994).

[5] See P. Bourdieu, *Outline of a Theory of Practice* (Cambridge, 1987); for an assessment of the issues associated with Bourdieu's work see, for example, R. Jenkins, *Pierre Bourdieu* (London and New York, 1992).

[6] G. Korff and R. Rürup, eds, *Berlin, Berlin: die Austellung der Geschichte der Stadt*, Catalogue (Berlin, 1987). See D. Frisby, *Sociological Impressionism: a Reassessment of Georg Simmel's Social Theory* (London, 1981).

included an essay on the sociology of the senses in which he identified sight, hearing and smell as the basic elements of human interaction, as significant as any other forms of sociation within the larger social complexes of social class or the state.[7] In the *Philosophy of Money* (c.1900), a study of the exchange relationships generated by a money economy, Simmel also dealt with touch, both directly and indirectly, in an essay on prostitution,[8] while elsewhere he analysed the meal from a sociological point of view.[9] Recent interest in, and re-evaluation of, Simmel's work has focused attention on the way in which themes and concepts in his work established some of the distinctive tropes of modern urban culture, particularly those relating to the psychological effects of metropolitan cities on the consciousness of those who lived in them, as well as issues relating to control, particularly in the 'distancing' surveillance of individuals in large city crowds.[10] Subsequent investigations of the everyday life of the streets and the emergence of forms of modern visually oriented urban culture have also been stimulated by Walter Benjamin's influential discussions of the effects of the forces of capitalist modernity on nineteenth-century Paris.[11]

There are a number of ways in which it is possible to study the sensory environment of the city, one of which is through an examination of the direct testimony of people themselves. Much of the evidence relating to early modern cities has come from outsiders, sensitive to material and cultural differences and eager to make comparisons. The comments and recollections of urban visitors, noted in letters, diaries and travelogues, were always based on perceptions of difference, the unfamiliar often implicitly compared with the familiar, the foreign with the domestic

---

[7] G. Simmel, 'The sociology of space', in D. Frisby and M. Featherstone, eds, *Simmel on Culture. Selected Writings* (London, 1997), pp. 155–6 and D. Frisby, *Sociological Impressionism* (London, 1981).

[8] D. Rowe, *Representing Berlin: Sexuality and the City in Imperial and Weimar Germany* (Aldershot, 2003), p. 79, n. 24.

[9] G. Simmel (1997), 'The sociology of the meal', in Frisby and Featherstone, eds, *Simmel on Culture*, pp. 130–35.

[10] D. Frisby, *Fragments of Modernity. Theories of Modernity in the Work of Simmel, Kracauer and Benjamin* (Cambridge, 1985); D. Frisby, *Cityscapes of Modernity* (Cambridge, 2001).

[11] W. Benjamin, *Charles Baudelaire: A Lyric Poet in the Era of High Capitalism* (London, 1973). See also A. Latham, 'The power of distraction, tactility, and habit in the work of Walter Benjamin', *Environment and Planning* (1999). On visual culture, see for example, T.J. Clark, *The Painting of Modern Life: Paris in the Art of Manet and his Followers* (London, 1985); T. Mitchell, 'The world-as-exhibition', *Comparative Studies in Society and History*, 31 (1989), pp. 217–36; S. West, *The Visual Arts in Germany 1890–1937: Utopia and Despair* (Manchester, 2000), pp. 52–3; Rowe, *Representing Berlin*, pp. 62–3.

starting point of the journey.[12] Travellers commented above all on what was to be seen – fine buildings, the cleanliness or otherwise of the streets, the dress of men and women – but there were also frequent references to food and drink, to smells which were considered to be unusually strong and to the sounds of the place, whether out in the streets or inside religious buildings and places of entertainment. The English diarist John Evelyn visited Venice in 1641–42 and described a sensory encounter with the Merceria:

> one of the most delicious streets in the world, hung with cloths of gold, rich damasks and other silks, which the shops expose and hang before their houses from the first floor. Passing along the street lined with the shops of perfumers and apothecaries, and innumerable cages of nightingales which they keep, so as shutting your eyes you would imagine yourself in the country when indeed you are in the middle of the sea; besides, there being neither rattling of coaches nor trampling of horses, 'tis almost as silent as the field.[13]

For the modern city the sources of information are much more diverse, ranging from government and press reports to works of art and literature. The writer and journalist Charles Dickens drew on his familiarity with nineteenth-century London to give a particularly vivid account of the underbelly of that city as witnessed by the young Oliver Twist.

> A dirtier and more wretched place he had never seen. The street was very narrow and muddy, and the air was impregnated with filthy odours, there were a good many small shops; but the only stock in trade appeared to be heaps of children, who, even at that time of night, were crawling in and out at the doors, or screaming from the inside. The only public places that seemed to prosper amid the general blight of the place were the public houses.[14]

In these few sentences, Dickens invokes all five bodily senses to create the context for his novel. Moreover, his description reminds us that, for both inhabitants and visitors, cities were complex sensory environments that were frequently experienced and represented as assaults on the senses. For most of those who lived in cities, whether pre-modern, or modern, the majority of sensory experiences were so commonplace as to pass unrecorded, but from the perspective of the cultural historian, such records as exist represent a way of acceding to the complexity of urban

---

[12] See, for example, the writings of the English sixteenth-century gentleman Fynes Moryson, later published as *Shakespeare's Europe* (London, 1903) and *An Itinerary* (Glasgow, 1907) and J.G. Goethe's *Italienische Reise* (Munich, 1786–88).

[13] Cited in J.G. Links, *Travellers in Europe* (Oxford, 1980), p. 188.

[14] C. Dickens, *Oliver Twist* (London, 1985 [1837–39]), p. 103.

culture, for it was precisely these experiences, either singly or in conjunction with each other, which shaped everyday behaviour and the all-important relationships between individuals and between people and spaces.

However, any kind of personal testimony was itself strongly influenced by the social and cultural context, both the experience and the telling of the tale mediated by the social and cultural conventions of the day for, as the anthropologist Mary Douglas observed, the 'social body constrains the way the physical body is perceived. The physical experience of the body, always modified by the social categories through which it is known, sustains a particular view of society.'[15] Descriptions of sensory experience have therefore, to be supported by an exploration of the cultural constitution of Douglas's 'social body' and the manner in which its relationship with the environment is mapped out in the discursive formations of the period. Useful insights have come from recent historical investigations into the body; in particular, those dealing with issues of gender and health have examined the way in which specific senses have contributed to the organisation of knowledge and definitions of human subjectivity, with consequences for everyday urban life. Practices involving touch, vision and smell, such as medicine and midwifery, artistic production, domestic service, prostitution and commerce, were structured by the hierarchical and gendered ordering of the senses in ways that had an impact on the nature of interpersonal experience, social labelling and their representation in art and literature.[16]

Tropes in recent urban studies reveal a concern with spatiality.[17] This has been manifested in various ways, including explorations of the way that the cultural and spatial practices of mobile bodies have contributed to the production of urban spaces and the particular meanings associated with them.[18] Other lines of inquiry relate to the way

---

[15] M. Douglas, *Natural Symbols: Explorations in Cosmology* (London, 1973), p. 93. See also S. Stewart, 'Prologue: from the Museum of Touch', in M. Kwint, C. Breward and J. Aynsley, eds, *Material Memories, Design and Evocation* (Oxford and New York, 1999).

[16] For example, E. Keller, 'The subject of touch; medical authority in early modern midwifery', in E.D. Harvey, *Sensible Flesh On Touch in Early Modern Culture* (Philadephia, 2003), pp. 62–80.

[17] See H. Lefebvre's influential *The Production of Space* (Oxford, 1991); also the personal essay, 'Seen from the window', in E. Kofman and E. Lebas, eds, *Writings in Cities: Henri Lefebvre* (Oxford, 1996, trans E. Kofman and E. Lebas).

[18] M. de Certeau, *The Practice of Everyday Life* (Berkeley, 1984, trans. S.F. Rendall). See also M. Ogborn, *Spaces of Modernity: London's Geographies: 1680–1780* (New York, 1998); L. Nead, *Victorian Babylon; People, Street and Images in Nineteenth-Century London* (Cambridge, 2002).

in which information gleaned from the different senses has contributed to the formation of complex semiotic systems that have facilitated human navigation in time, space and the social world of the city.[19] The recent interest shown in materiality and visual culture by scholars in the field of early modern studies has opened up new avenues for exploration, particularly in relation to the significance of objects in everyday life, the tangibility of which introduced a tactile dimension to an urban life increasingly centred on their production, distribution and consumption.[20] The discovery of soundscapes has directed attention to the perceptual situatedness of people in particular environments.[21] As the anthropologist Steven Feld puts it, 'as place is sensed, senses are placed; as places make sense, senses make place',[22] while Alain Corbin's essay, 'A history and anthropology of the senses' points to the way that each of the five senses has played a part in the formation of the sensory, discursive, institutional and cultural regimes through which the urban environment is rendered intelligible, distinctive and controlled.[23]

The case studies in this volume demonstrate the range and heterogeneity characteristic of contemporary approaches to urban history.[24] They demonstrate the emergence of a number of useful models, which can be used to investigate the role of the senses in the production, regulation and contestation of particular city spaces and the cultural

---

[19] K. Lynch, *The Image of the City* (Cambridge, Mass., 1960) focused attention on the visible legibility of cities, on the interaction between environmental cues and spatial orientation, a subject developed in the concept of 'mental mapping' utilised by behavioural geographers in the 1970s and subsequently applied to the cultural interpretation of the use of space and the interpretation of the geographies of everyday life; see C.C. Pooley, 'Getting to know the city: the construction of spatial knowledge in London in the 1930s', *Urban History*, 3, 2 (2004), pp. 210–28.

[20] See R. Porter and C. Brewer, *Consumption and the World of Goods* (London, 1991). Recent studies include L. Cowen Orlin, *Material London, c.* 1600 (Philadephia, 2000); P. Fumerton and S. Hunt, eds, *Renaissance Culture and the Everyday* (Philadelphia, 1998); L. Gowing, *Common Bodies: Women, Touch and Power in Seventeenth-Century England* (New Haven, 2003).

[21] B.R. Smith, 'The soundscapes of early modern England: city, country, court', *The Acoustic World of Early Modern England: Attending to the O-Factor* (Chicago, 1999). See, for example, F. Kisby, ed., *Music and Urban History*, special issue of *Urban History*, 29, 1 (2002); see also F. Kisby, ed., *Music and Musicians in Renaissance Cities and Towns* (Cambridge, 2001).

[22] Cited in Smith, *The Acoustic World*, p. 47.

[23] A. Corbin, 'A history and anthropology of the senses', *Time, Desire and Horror: Towards a History of the Senses* (Cambridge, 1995, trans. J. Birrell). See also D. Lowe, *History of Bourgeois Perception* (Brighton, 1982).

[24] See M.M. Smith, 'Making sense of social history – new topics and historians', *Journal of Social History*, 37 (2003), pp. 165–86.

meanings associated with them.[25] One such, influenced to some extent by interest in visuality, is the conception of the city as a theatrical space, a setting for forms of spectacular culture and an arena for the symbolic representation of different forms of social and cultural space.[26] This metaphor is particularly adaptable since the theatre, like the city itself, has a history in which relations between audience and players, script and performance are mediated by historically and culturally grounded conventions that generate different forms of sensory experience.[27]

Interest in urban life as mode of performance and in cultures of display and representation, combined with the theoretical interest in modernity, has focused attention on the emergence of distinctively modern and visually oriented forms of culture.[28] The privileged status of vision is one of the dominant tropes in discussions about the discursive formations of urban modernity, a subject discussed by Ulf Strohmeyer and Dorothy Rowe in this volume.[29] This phenomenon is often treated as an effect of other forces and relations of power associated with the development of institutionalised and rationalising forms of control, but, as Jonathan Crary has pointed out, an emphasis on spectatorship and 'visuality' can easily generate 'a model of perception and subjectivity that is cut off from richer and more historically determined notions of "embodiment" in which an embodied subject is both the location of operations of power and the potential for resistance'.[30]

In this context, considerable attention has been given to the conception and representation of urban spaces by architects and planners and

---

[25] K. Hetherington, *The Badlands of Modernity* (London and New York, 1997), p. 21.

[26] For example, R. Sennett, *The Fall of Public Man* (Cambridge, 1973); C. Boyer, *The City of Collective Memory, its Historical Imagery and Architectural Entertainment* (Cambridge, Mass., 1994).

[27] D. Chaney, *Fictions of Collective Life: Public Drama in Late Modern Culture* (London and New York, 1993), pp. 45–80.

[28] For example, L. Charney and V. Schwartz, *Cinema and the Invention of Modern Life* (Berkeley, 1995).

[29] For the privileging of vision, see J. Crary, *Techniques of the Observer* (Cambridge, Mass., 1990); M. Jay, *Downcast Eyes, the Denigration of Vision in Twentieth-Century French Thought* (Berkeley, 1993). Feminist readings have pointed to the gendered aspects of modern spectacular culture, for example, J. Wolff, 'The invisible flâneuse: women and the literature of modernity', *Feminine Sentences: Essays on Women and Culture* (Oxford, 1999), pp. 34–50.

[30] J. Crary, *Suspensions of Perception: Attention, Spectacle, and Modern Culture*, Cambridge, Mass., 1999), p. 3. Moreover, in the nineteenth century the arrival of new additions to popular culture – the dance hall, music halls – and, in the next century, radio, the gramophone, the talkies, created new and more complex cultural forms. See, for example, A. Rifkin, *Street Noises: Parisian Pleasure 1900–40* (Manchester, 1993).

others involved in their production, whose visually oriented conceptions of the nature and function of urban spaces were often distanced from, and in conflict with, the actual practices of the people who used and inhabited them.[31] For, as Hazel Hahn shows in her essay, close encounters on the streets with traffic and sandwichmen, and other marginal figures of society such as the prostitutes and rag-pickers described by Walter Benjamin, could lead to a different kind of sensory experience than that envisaged by city planners like Baron Haussmann.[32] A related issue is that of power, for relationships of dominance and subordination are encoded in representations of space and place.[33] Those relationships are also expressed and performed through the production and maintenance of multiple and contested spatial relations, mediated by social class, gender and ethnicity.[34]

As Crary suggests, the non-visual senses contribute to that process of contestation, directly reminding us of the sensuous life of the body and its embeddedness in urban life. Together, the essays in this volume by Jo Wheeler, Alexander Cowan, Laura Wright, Ava Arndt, David Inglis, Kim Carpenter, Janet Stewart and Rosemary Wakeman demonstrate the way that affective and arousing experiences of smell, sound, touch and taste remain central to city life.[35] Patterns of speech and habits of eating and

---

[31] See, for example, D.L. Parsons, *Streetwalking the Metropolis: Women, the City and Modernity* (Oxford, 2000) where she discusses *flâneurie*, a subject that relates to both spatial practices and urban semiotics.

[32] See S. Buck-Morss, 'The flâneur, the sandwichman and the whore: the politics of loitering', *New German Critique*, Special Issue on Walter Benjamin, 39, Fall (1996), pp. 99–140.

[33] For example, F. Driver and D. Gilbert, *Imperial Cities: Landscape, Display and Identity*, Studies in Imperialism (Manchester, 1999).

[34] See Freud's account of his father being verbally assaulted with the cry, 'Jew! Get off the pavement!': S. Freud, *The Interpretation of Dreams* (London, 1976), p. 286. See also M.M. Roberts, 'Pleasures engendered by gender: homo-sociability and the club', in R. Porter and M.M. Roberts, eds, *Pleasure in the Eighteenth Century* (London, 1996), pp. 48–76. See J. Walkowicz, *City of Dreadful Delight, Narratives of Sexual Danger in Late-Victorian London* (London, 1992); S. Zimmermann, 'Making a living from disgrace: the politics of prostitution, female poverty and urban gender codes in Budapest and Vienna, 1860–1920', in M. Gee, T. Kirk and J. Steward, eds, *The City in Central Europe: Culture and Society from 1800 to the Present* (Aldershot, 1999).

[35] A point appreciated by members of the European avant-garde; for example, see Luigi Russolo, 'Let us cross a great modern capital with our ears more alert than our eyes, and we will get enjoyment from distinguishing the eddying of water, air and gas in metal pipes, the grumbling of noises that breathe and pulse with indisputable animality, the palpitation of values, the coming and going of pistons, the howl of mechanical saws, the jolting of a tram on its rails, the cracking of whips, the flapping of curtains and flags. We enjoy creating mental orchestrations of the crashing down of metal shop blinds, slamming doors, the

drinking are shown by Wright, Carpenter and Stewart to be constitutive
features of the identities of peoples and places. The symbolic significance
of touch in commercial and interpersonal relationships is demonstrated
in essays by Cowan and Arndt while the importance of olfactory and
auditory sensations in everyday life is evidenced by the persistence of
attempts of the kind described by Wheeler, Inglis and Wakeman, to
suppress and control features of the sensory environment perceived as
distasteful, disruptive, subversive and oppositional.

### The urban context from pre-modern to modern

The case studies chosen for this volume represent particular types of
sensory environments exemplified by a limited number of cities that
share important characteristics. Of these Venice, Paris and London are
taken as exemplifying important features of the early modern city,
although Paris and London, together with Vienna, Munich and Berlin,
also demonstrate features characteristic of the modern, metropolitan
city. In order to highlight the themes discussed below, and to emphasise
the changes that differentiate the particular sensory environment
characteristic of the early modern period from the modern world, the
book has been organised in three chronological parts. 'An environment
of all the senses' focuses on smell, sound and vision in early modern
Venice, London and Paris. 'The culture of consumption' deals with
touch, smell, taste and vision in London, Munich and Paris from the late
seventeenth to the late nineteeth century. Finally, 'Cultural control and
cultural subversion' focuses on Vienna, Berlin and Paris from the late
nineteenth century to the post-war period.

Each of the cities covered in these studies was a capital city, a function
that injected into the commercial activity common to all cities a strong
administrative element as well as all the richness and theatre of public
rituals. This often influenced the production and representation of the
built environment in cities as chronologically apart in time as early
modern Paris and metropolitan Berlin, described by Strohmayer and
Rowe, respectively. Capital cities therefore often possessed a sense of
dynamism and forms of spectacular culture often absent in other urban
centres lower down the urban hierarchy, which, in the seventeenth and
eighteenth centuries in particular, experienced widespread economic and

---

hubbub and shuffling of crowds, the variety of din from stations, railways, iron
foundries, spinning mills, printing works, electric power stations, and
underground railways.' Cited in C. Tisdall and A. Bozzoli, eds, *Futurism*
(London, 1977), p. 114.

social stagnation. Capital cities also attracted a higher level of immigration than other cities, fuelling social and cultural inequalities and differences expressed within their geographical and social spaces. Over the centuries growth led to important shifts in the nature of particular urban environments as, in both early modern and modern cities, demographic and geographical expansion produced various kinds of strains affecting sensory experience. As Wheeler and Inglis demonstrate, pressures on space resulting from the growth of industrial activity led to increasingly densely populated locales, intensifying certain kinds of olfactory sensations, to the extent that city authorities were obliged to intervene to control unpleasant smells and deal with faecal wastes.

In cities such as Vienna and Munich, discussed by Carpenter and Stewart, that were characterised by the diversity of their social, ethnic or confessional communities, interpersonal experiences contributed to the production of the stereotypical images through which social and cultural differences between localities and communities were registered. As Wright demonstrates in the case of London, immigrants from elsewhere formed diverse speech communities and soundscapes, producing diverse forms of language that reflected distinctions between communities of long-term residents and newcomers as well as patterns of speech that were specific to given communities. The relationship between the hierarchy of the senses and the 'social body' was evident in notions of touch, which influenced social relationships and patterns of interaction in ways described by Cowan. Nineteenth-century tropes of 'contagion' and 'contamination' applied to the way in which the middle classes viewed city life as they tried to avoid other potentially dangerous elements within the city.[36] In the seventeenth- and eighteenth-century city the building of new roads and bridges such as the Pont Neuf discussed by Strohmayer, facilitated the circulation of people and goods and the increased availability and speed in circulation of goods and money generated a new commercialised 'culture of tactility' that required new imagery of the kind that appeared in fictitious accounts of London, described by Arndt, to make sense of it.

The size of nineteenth-century cities like Paris, Vienna and Berlin dwarfed that of early modern cities, but common features persisted, including practical and cultural responses to the problems created by rapid population growth and an expanding market for consumer products. With growth came changes in scale as populations expanded

---

[36] P. Stallybrass and A. White, 'The city, the sewer, the gaze and the contaminating touch', *The Politics and Poetics of Transgression* (Ithaca, 1986), pp. 125–48.

and their activities diversified, putting pressure on geographical boundaries. New and spacious quarters were constructed for the wealthy and new zones developed to accommodate industrial activity. Consequently there was an expansion in the numbers of objects and bodies circulating through the streets with increasing rapidity, leading to the redefinition of existing spaces and changes in their use. Cities became arenas for the competitive display and promotion of goods, exemplified in the Parisian advertising strategies described by Hahn. As she demonstrates, the streets remained the locus of much human activity, becoming even more crowded as they accommodated more diverse activities than before for longer periods of the day following the introduction of gas lighting and then electricity. Overcrowding reinforced the importance of the sites of sociability and consumption that contributed to the formation of social and cultural identities, symbolised for example by the Viennese dumplings and coffee houses discussed by Stewart; the latter representing a specifically urban tradition of conviviality, as do the beer gardens in Munich described by Carpenter, who looks at the effect of the production and consumption of beer on the peripheral and social spaces of the city.

City authorities responded to these changes and problems by introducing further controls on activities likely to prevent easy circulation on the streets and olfactory, auditory and visual pollutants such as street musicians, sewage, beggars and prostitutes. Anxieties about civility were often expressed in ways relating to the body. [37] The new urban middle classes, for example, self-consciously distinguished themselves from others by their emphasis on cleanliness, decorum, positive smells, restrained and quieter speech and the development of the home as a private and controlled space for leisure activities from which the sounds, sights and smells of the street were to be excluded. By contrast, in the modern *Größtadte* of the late nineteenth and twentieth century discussed by Stewart and Rowe, public spaces are always potentially multivalent and contested, an unstable situation that, as Wakeman shows, makes possible the tactical and subversive deployment of sensory weapons such as the noise and sounds of Liberation Paris.

In both early modern and modern cities therefore, the history of the senses was bound up with their material and cultural development, contributing to the way that the urban environment was experienced, understood and represented by those who inhabited it.

---

[37] The starting point for any discussion of the culture of civility remains the work of Norbert Elias, *The Civilising Process* (Oxford, 1978). See also R. Muchembled, *Société et mentalités dans la France moderne XVIᵉ–XVIIIᵉ siècles* (Paris, 1990).

## Sensory contexts

### *Touch*

In the everyday life of early modern cities touch was one of the most important forms of sensory experience, despite its established position as the lowest of the senses in the philosophical hierarchy. For conceptions of touch, and practices of touching, influenced the symbolic expression and representation of relationships between individuals and groups across all areas of life. Prostitution, for example, was a constant feature of urban life even though its physical location within each city shifted over time as the general uses of space changed. Much business continued to take place in sites of relaxation and entertainment during hours prolonged by the introduction of artificial light. An important criterion for the drawing of distinctions within the urban social hierarchy remained that of the manual work in which the majority of the urban popular were engaged, whether as domestic servants, artisans or unskilled workers, even though different levels of skill created a spectrum of social status.[38] For those who dealt professionally with the human body, the stigma which once placed surgeons and bone-setters beyond the pale of social respectability was gradually removed and replaced by the higher social value associated with professionals with university educations.[39]

Tactility was embedded in the commercialised culture of the eighteenth century, the expansion of which created new and ephemeral ways of touching. As Arndt shows, coins passed rapidly from hand to hand and increased prosperity for a wider cross-section of urban society led to a changed perception of money. People still touched goods for sale, but the multiplication of available goods and new ways of marketing them opened up to the general public new forms of visual pleasure of the kind described by Hahn. In the nineteenth century, environmental changes had an impact on bodily sensation, most noticeably as people moved through the city. Until the twentieth century, most people still walked, but over the street surfaces that had evolved from smelly mud or dust to routes paved with stones.[40] Pedestrians became separated from

---

[38] For gender issues, see L. Gowing, *Women, Touch and Power in Seventeenth-Century England* (New Haven, 2003). For a more comparative perspective, see G. Crossick, ed., *The Artisan and the European Town 1500–1900* (Aldershot, 1997), and G. Crossick and H-G. Haupt, *The Petite Bourgeoisie in Europe 1780–1914* (London, 1995).

[39] I. Loudon, *Medical Care and the General Practitioner: 1750–1850* (Oxford, 1986).

[40] P.J. Corfield, 'Walking the city streets: the urban odyssey in eighteenth-century England', *Urban History*, 16, 2 (1990), pp. 132–74.

wheeled traffic by pavements constructed along thoroughfares wide enough to accommodate both, making it easier for long-skirted women to venture out in bad weather. At the end of the century, urban trains, trams and omnibuses sheltered people from the dirt and smell of the streets, but increased their proximity to others.

Economic, social and cultural changes created a culture that was less tactile in many respects, particularly for the middle classes, a group whose practices influenced the 'respectable' poor. Social distinctions were maintained by the introduction of a series of 'distancing' activities such as the practice of using eating utensils, particularly the fork, into the capitals of the later seventeenth century, reducing direct contact with food and drink. New rules of hygiene and cleanliness altered eating habits, while greeting behaviour and the sealing of business bargains became more restrained. Early modern forms of behaviour, such as spitting in the palm of one's hand before slapping it against the other party to an agreement, were relegated to the market place in favour of a notarised contract. It became the custom to announce one's presence to other members of the middle or upper classes by leaving a calling card.[41] As people travelled or migrated further away from home and new technologies were developed, much direct human contact was replaced by other means of communication – letters, postcards and telegrams.

## Sound

Interest in the study of auditory landscapes and their social and cultural context began with Corbin's study of village bells.[42] Sound plays a crucial role in the perceptual and cognitive processes that determine the way that geographical and social spaces are mapped out and negotiated by individuals.[43] Mobile audiences were alerted to changes in locality as they noted changes in the texture of the urban soundscape, in its rhythms and volume, in modulations in the distinctive combinations of patterned sounds and the random and chaotic 'noise' emanating from speech,

---

[41] L. Davidoff (1974), *The Best Circles: Society, Etiquette and the Season* (London, 1974).

[42] A. Corbin, *Village Bells. Sound and Meaning in the Nineteenth-Century French Countryside* (New York, 1998), trans. M. Thom, and *The Foul and the Fragrant: Odour and the Social Imagination* (Leamington Spa, 1986).

[43] K. Lynch, *The Image of the City* (Cambridge, Mass., 1960) focused attention on the interaction between environmental cues and spatial orientation, a subject developed in the concept of 'mental mapping' utilised by behavioural geographers in the 1970s and subsequently applied to the cultural interpretation of the use of space and the interpretation of the geographies of everyday life; see C.C. Pooley, 'Getting to know the city: the construction of spatial knowledge in London in the 1930s', *Urban History*, 3, 2 (2004), pp. 210–28.

traffic, song, industry, church bells and street cries.[44] Specific localities were identified by the distinctive sounds associated with their industrial activities as much as the smells that went with them. As Wheeler comments, Dante noted the noise emanating from the Venetian Arsenal in his *Inferno*. In the pre-modern city, sound was an important and practical aid to vision in judging distance at night and, until the late nineteenth-century improvements in street lighting,[45] acuteness of hearing was an essential weapon in avoiding danger after dark. Seasons and times of the year were marked by particular types of sounds, such as those of carnival, while diurnal rhythms were registered through the sound of church bells and clocks, the night watchman's cries or the rumble of the night soil cart. Auditory experiences were directly influenced by nature of the material environment. Gas lighting generated its own distinctive sound while changes in the pattern of sounds generated by urban traffic were mediated by the appearance of new types of vehicle and the laying of cobbles, pavements and asphalt. The sound of trains, trams and the motor car gradually began to drown out the clatter and rumbles of horse-drawn vehicles while the expansion and growth of cities was invariably accompanied by the noise of construction.

In both pre-modern and modern cities, different kinds of sounds carried social and symbolic meanings and as such marked out the boundaries and limits of social interaction. As Wright demonstrates, demographic, social and educational changes were mapped out in the variety of speech patterns, dialects and accents audible on the streets. Like smells, particular sounds were associated with the behaviours of the different social orders as well as with gender and ethnicity, and classified accordingly. Such perceptions depended upon the social and cultural position of the audience. Changes in conceptions of what constituted 'noise' led to shifts in the way that particular types of sound were evaluated and registered as dissonant, disordered and impolite. Chaotic noise was traditionally perceived as typically urban, while relative levels of noise or quietness differentiated types of locality. From the fifteenth century onwards fireworks were used for celebrations and, until the 1830s, appreciated more for sound than for visual effects. The 1749 firework display in London's Green Park was accompanied by music composed by Handel. In nineteenth-century Paris, as Hahn shows, mobile forms of advertising led to a commensurate increase in the

---

[44] J. Attali, *Noise: The Political Economy of Music* (Minneapolis, 1985), trans. B. Massumi. See D. Garrioch, 'Sounds of the city: the soundscape of early modern European towns', *Urban History*, 30, 1 (2003), p. 6.

[45] W. Schievelbusch, *Disenchanted Night: the Industrialisation of the Light in the Nineteenth Century* (Oxford, 1988), trans. A. Davies.

volume of street noise, represented by sensitive souls as an attack on the senses. Control of noise, such as that made by drunken revellers or street hawkers, was one of a number of ways in which attempts were made to regulate and discipline the urban environment. In Victorian London, middle-class campaigns against noise were associated with the emergence of new forms of sensibility that served as markers of social distinction.[46]

More musical features of the auditory landscape were the sounds produced by the aural traditions and practices of city life ranging from the collective singing traditions of popular culture and the festivities and celebrations of religious and civic life to commercial entertainments such as pleasure gardens and the Victorian music hall and the rituals and protests of political organisation and protest.[47] The fight against street music represented a struggle for control over urban territory against, not just the lower orders, but also foreign influences. Conversely the production of noise was a favoured tactic of popular protest. Wakeman's essay demonstrates the way that the noisy reoccupation of public spaces and outpourings of celebratory music that accompanied the 1945 Liberation of Paris were rooted in the indigenous music and song of Parisian working-class life and the 'distinctively rebellious, disputatious patterns' of civic life with which it was associated.

*Smell*

If the embodied self used ears to navigate the city streets, it also used its nose. In the early modern city smell was an important indicator of locality, since the residential areas of particular social groups were differentiated by their smells. Tanners and dyers, for example, used strong-smelling by-products as part of the production process. In the case of dyers before the introduction of chemical dyes in the nineteenth century, this was human urine. Prevailing winds could extend the zones of impact considerably, filling the air with the not unpleasant odours of brewing or cooking on the one hand, and the stench of concentrations of coal smoke on the other. Abattoirs, commonly located on the edge of cities where the animals could be driven in from the countryside on foot, combined the smells of slaughter and of live herds of farm animals.[48]

---

[46] J.M. Picker, 'The sound-proof study: Victorian professionals, work, space and urban noise', *Victorian Studies*, 42, 2 (1999–2000), pp. 427–53.

[47] P. Bailey, *Popular Culture and Performance in the Victorian City* (Cambridge, 1998).

[48] On attempts to control abattoirs in London, see C. Otter, 'Cleansing and clarifying: technology and perception in nineteenth-century London', *Journal of British Studies*, 43, Jan. (2004), pp. 44–53.

Even in the pre-modern city attempts were made to control the olfactory environment.[49] The subjectivity that informs the categorisation of smells is evident in Jo Wheeler's study of stench in early modern Venice in which he draws a distinction between 'the gut-wrenching odours of festering rubbish and excrement, discarded entrails, putrid meat and fish', and the by-products of shipbuilding at the Arsenal, located on the edge of the city and associated with the positive qualities of official ships built to increase the well-being of the Venetian Republic.

If the case can be made for a lessening of the tactile nature of urban culture between the sixteenth and twentieth centuries, it is even stronger for reductions in the level of smells and their symbolic meaning in the face of the sanitising and suppressive regimes of the modern era.[50] What constituted acceptable smells? The answer is only to be found by elimination. Odours that were imbued with characteristics neither positive nor negative were so integrated into daily urban experience that they were rarely remarked upon except by visitors from the countryside, whose olfactory ranges were substantially different from those of city dwellers. 'Acceptability' is a value-loaded way to describe them for many were tolerated out of a sense that they could not be eliminated. The smell of poverty, which exercised the ruling classes from the Middle Ages onwards, was one from which it was impossible to escape and created the desire to keep away from others whose odour was too strong.

Many odours acceptable to pre-modern townspeople ceased to be so under the influence of new scientific thinking about the nature of disease and the composition of the air, as Inglis demonstrates in his essay on sewers and sensibilities. In the nineteenth century, the introduction of factories and gaslight added a new series of smells to the city.[51] The smell of the gas used in street lighting was indicative of technological progress, but also revealed its limitations since many regarded it as a threat to health.[52] Changes in the quality of soap and detergents changed the odours given off by clothing and skin. The constant emphasis on the

---

[49] This point was well made in Lynda Nead's discussion of the blind man in a metropolitan world in which experience was increasingly described in visual terms: *Victorian Babylon: People, Streets and Images in Nineteenth-Century London* (New Haven, 2002), pp. 61–2.

[50] For an overview of dominant attitudes to smell, see Corbin, *The Foul and the Fragrant*; C. Classen, D. Howes and A. Synnott, *Aroma. The Cultural History of Smell* (London, 1994).

[51] E. Baret-Bourgoin, 'Sensibilités publiques et privées aux nuisances indus-trielles: l'exemple du travail des peaux à Grenoble au XIX$^e$', *Cahiers d'Histoire*, 4, 1 (1999), pp. 127–50.

[52] A. Beltan and J-Pierre Williot, 'Lights and modernity in nineteenth-century European cities', draft paper presented at the Seventh International Conference of the European Association of Urban Historians, Athens, 29 October 2004.

smell of the poor in writings on health issues also reflected the extent to which smell functioned as a social marker for individuals as well as amorphous social groups. A merchant or lawyer and their wives in the eighteenth century may have perfumed themselves in certain ways in order to signal to their peers that they belonged to the same social group with the same cultural insistence on covering bodily odours with pleasant smells, but they also did so in order to distinguish themselves from artisans and shopkeepers, whose work-related odours impregnated their clothes wherever they went. Similarly, the newly emergent 'respectable urban poor' in the later nineteenth century placed a heavy insistence on the cleanliness of their homes both inside and out to distinguish themselves from those nearby. Odours were associated with those identified as 'outsiders' or 'other' such as ethnic minorities, and given positive or negative values by those of the host community around them.[53]

*Taste*

Smells associated with the production and consumption of food and drink were a major feature of city life, and both played an important role in the creation of particular types of urban space.[54] Travellers, ancient and modern, were invariably quick to identify places by the gustatory and olfactory experiences they offered and to recall impressions of taste and smell. What, where and how people ate and drank was a function of social class and gender, ethnic and religious affiliation, climate and local tradition.[55] As cities grew they were dependent on an increasingly complicated infrastructure for the production, distribution and retailing

---

[53] B. Beer, 'Geruch und Differenz: Körpergeruch als kennzeichen konstruierter "rassicher" Grenzen', *Paideuma*, 46 (2000), pp. 207–30.

[54] W. Smith, *Consumption and the Making of Respectability, 1600–1800* (New York, 2003). For histories of eating and drinking, see S. Mennell, *All Manners of Food: Eating and Taste in England and France from the Middle Ages to the Present* (Oxford, 1985); P. Clark, *The English Alehouse: a Social History* (London, 1983); T. Brennan, *Public Drinking and Popular Culture in Eighteenth-Century Paris* (Princeton, 1988); G. Hirschfelder, *Alkoholkonsum am Beginn des Industriezeitalters (1700–1815) Vergleichende Studien zum gesellschtlichen und kulturellen Wandel. No. 1. Die Region Manchester* (Vienna, 2003); G. Hirschfelder, 'Das Wassertrinken: Prolegomena zu einer Kulturgeschichte', *Archiv für Kulturgeschichte*, 80, 2 (1998), pp. 325–50.

[55] A Spanish picaresque novel of the sixteenth century set in Rome associates taste in food with cultural identity. When the heroine, Lozana, is told of another woman cooking meat with quinces, she replies, 'I'm not surprised; she's Valencian.' Quoted in J. Edwards, 'The culture of the street. The Calle de la Feria in Cordoba, 1470–1520', in A. Cowan, ed., *Mediterranean Urban Culture 1400–1700* (Exeter, 2000), p. 77.

of foodstuffs. In the nineteenth century, one of the signs of modernity was the appearance of advertisements for industrially processed foods. Modern means of preparation also changed patterns and levels of consumption. As Carpenter shows, new technologies influenced beer production, as well as the availability of bottled water, while dried food in packets was later followed by frozen food. In the nineteenth century, middle-class access to a wider range of foodstuffs and the influence of cookery books and magazines on styles of presentation led to increases in the quality of food, as well as raising health issues. Middle-class women were encouraged to eat less and less while working-class consumption was based on a limited diet of copious quantities.

Designated retailing spaces such as markets and shops were also coterminus with social spaces in that they were regulated by cultural conventions as well as economic codes, as were those in occupations associated with them, such as merchants, traders and street vendors. In the pre-modern period, inns and cook shops, alehouses and taverns not only provided food and drink, but also performed a number of different functions and were important public arenas for the circulation and dissemination of information and ideas.[56] At the same time, as potential centres of dissent and disorder, they were regulated by various kinds of ordinances relating to public order and to the establishment of gender and group identities expressed in particular attitudes to drunkenness, gambling and brawling. A recent study of biconfessional Augsburg argues that the rules that governed the use of alcohol in the early modern period reflect the rules within a city at large.[57]

As a greater variety of foodstuffs became available patterns, types of foodstuffs and modes of consumption became even more important markers of social and cultural distinction and, as Stewart shows in her essay on Vienna, 'signifiers of urban modernity'.[58] Over time items originally associated with particular social groups became adopted by others, generating new forms of exclusiveness. From the seventeenth century, coffeehouses and cafes were important popular meeting places in most European cities. Eighteenth-century London coffeehouses

---

[56] B. Kuemin and B.A. Tlusty, eds, *The World of the Tavern: Public Houses in Early Modern Europe* (Aldershot, 2002); G. Hirschfelder, *Europäische Esskultur; eine Geschichte der Ernährung von der Steinzeit bis heute* (Frankfurt and New York, 2001); J. Burnett, *Liquid Pleasures. A Social History of Drinks in Modern Britain* (London and New York, 1999).

[57] B.A. Tlusty (2004*), Bacchus and Civic Order: the Culture of Drink in Early Modern Germany,* Studies in Early Modern German History (Charlottesville and London, 2004).

[58] See, for example, N. Elias, *The Civilising Process*; J. Goody (1982), *Cooking, Cuisine and Class* (Cambridge, 1982).

constituted important forms of semi-public space for commercial intelligence and political intrigue, where information and ideas circulated, supporting a culture increasingly oriented towards consumption.[59] At the same time, they were venues for the performance of masculinity, as were Parisian restaurants until the end of the nineteenth century, unlike tearooms that were patronised primarily by women.[60] In Vienna, as Stewart notes, the coffeehouses became 'a ubiquitous culinary signifier' of the city.

In nineteenth-century Paris, the growth of restaurants and cafés encouraged the habit of eating out and a discourse centred on gastronomy.[61] These establishments were also locations from which the spectacle of urban life described by Hahn could be watched in comfort. Working-class Parisian cafés have been identified as interstitial 'transitional spaces' between the public world of early modern France and the private worlds of the late twentieth century, particularly for nineteenth-century women.[62] Carpenter shows how, in Munich, the consumption of beer played a central role in its evolution from small provincial capital into a modern city, marking its difference from wine-drinking localities. Breweries and taverns allowed the lower classes to establish a new sort of semi-public urban life as the consumption of beer played a central role in the production of lower-class identity and patterns of sociability, while the city's beer culture became a permanent feature of its urban life and tourist place-image, persisting into the present day. As cities became more homogenous in terms of the facilities

---

[59] H. Berry (2003), *Gender, Society and Print Culture in Late-Stuart England: The Cultural World of the* Athenian Mercury (Basingstoke, 2003). See also I. Khmelnitskaia, 'Restaurant life of St-Petersburg and Moscow in late imperial Russia', paper presented at the Seventh International Conference of the European Association of Urban Historians Association, Athens, 29 October 2004.

[60] B. Cowan, 'Feature: public faces and public spaces. What was masculine about the public sphere? Gender and the coffeehouse milieu in Post-Restoration England', *History Workshop Journal*, 51 (2001), pp. 127–57; R. Spang (2001), *The Invention of the Restaurant: Paris and Modern Gastronomic Culture* (Cambridge and London, 2001); K. Becker, 'The French novel and luxury eating in the nineteenth century', in M. Jacobs and P. Scholler, eds, *Eating Out in Europe: Picnics, Gourmet Dining and Snacks since the late Eighteenth Century* (Oxford and New York, 2003), pp. 209–10.

[61] M-F. Boyer, *The French Cafe* (London, 1994); S. Mennell, 'Eating in the public sphere in the nineteenth and twentieth centuries', in Jacobs and Scholler, eds, *Eating Out in Europe*, pp. 245–52.

[62] See W.S. Haine, *The World of the Paris Café: Sociability among the French Working Class: 1789–1914* (Baltimore, 1999); J. Burnett, *England Eats Out* (London, 2004); K. Allen, *Hungrige Metropole. Essen, Wohlfahrt und Kommerz in Berlin* (Hamburg, 2002).

they offered, it was often the distinctive nature of the food and drink associated with them and the places where it was consumed that constituted one of their distinguishing features.[63] Cafés offering different types of coffee accompanied by apple strudel, *Sachertorte* and whipped cream became as much part of tourist images of twentieth-century Vienna as its wine taverns (*Heuriger*) and Strauss waltzes, an image, according to Stewart, the critic Adolf Loos condemned as belonging to a bygone era.

*Vision*

If touch was generally ranked as the lowest of the senses then the highest position was accorded to vision, over the last few centuries,[64] particularly after the invention of the printing press enhanced the power of the written word and the maps and images discussed by Strohmayer. Urban life and visual spectacle have long been bound up together. Carnival, religious events and the urban promenade were all visually important features of pre-industrial society, while architectural monuments and city planning from the Renaissance onwards constituted the city itself as a visual spectacle, in theory, if not in practice. In his essay on the innovatory conception, construction, usage and representational after-life of the Pont-Neuf in Paris, Strohmayer focuses on the aesthetic vision represented by the building of the bridge and its visual representations. He characterises the Pont-Neuf as a space of reduced functionalities intended to ease the flow of goods to sites elsewhere, an example of a material change of the kind that makes for epochal changes which can be regarded as 'openings to modernity'.

Two centuries later, nationalist and imperialist ideologies influenced the development and reconstructions of the urban environment, producing vistas and settings that emphasised the power of the state, while the controlling and distancing effects of the visualising process signified the 'separation' of the visual sense, particularly from touch and hearing.[65] In central Paris, however, despite Hausmannisation, it was the old multifunctional Grands Boulevards that became the centre of the new spectacular culture and where, as Hahn argues, the city's modern commercial economy was most visibly linked to a visually-oriented culture of consumption. At the same time the noisy and disruptive

---

[63] See B.M. Gordon, 'Going abroad to taste: North America, France and the continental tour from the late nineteenth century to the present', *Proceedings of the Annual Meeting of the Western Society for French History*, 25 (1998), pp. 156–70.

[64] Classen, *Worlds of Sense*, pp. 3–4.

[65] See Urry, 'City Life and the Senses'; also Driver and Gilbert, *Imperial Cities*.

advertising on the Grands Boulevards led the city authorities to try and maintain the public spaces of the streets as controlled and orderly sites in which a well-behaved public could experience the spectacle of the city. This anticipates Wakeman's account of the way that the efflorescence of the dynamic and popular public life of the post-Liberation period was gradually replaced by staged performances and facile spectacles that confined the people to the role of spectators rather than participants in a manner that anticipated modern mass entertainments.

These particular examples support the argument that the pre-eminent position ascribed to vision in nineteenth-century discourse about urban modernity was inherently unstable in the twentieth century as the modern metropolis became a key site in a struggle for control in which cultural discourse played an important part. Rowe, for example, demonstrates that, in Berlin at least, the hegemony of vision characteristic of earlier decades was no longer so significant, in that, as Crary argues, it constituted only one layer of a body that could be captured, shaped or controlled by a range of external critiques.[66] Rowe considers the way that the changes accompanying the transformation of Berlin into a *Weltstadt* generated conflicting discourses. She places this in the context of a discussion of the celebratory and aestheticising images of a narrow range of sites in central Berlin by the painter Lesser Ury articulated within visual codes that function as dominant signs of cultural stability. Spatial tropes linking visuality and modernity have been applied to the construction of the self in Western societies. While Strohmayer focuses on citizenship, both Hahn and Rowe comment on the gendering of the visual: Rowe argues that the discourses supporting Ury's work are structured by masculinist tropes that prepare the way for a visual culture of urban modernity. What these essays make clear is that, despite the theoretical prominence given to the visual sense in the modern period, the other non-visual senses continued to play an important part in the experience and representation of city life. For, as Rowe points out, in the struggle for political and social control, the deployment of sensory tropes can operate as a key strategic element in that struggle.

## Ways forward

These detailed studies demonstrate the complexity of urban society and the multiplicity of ways in which interaction took place between the embodied self and the spaces of habitation, and between one individual

---

[66] Crary, *Suspensions of Perception,* 3.

and others through the medium of the senses. These elemental sensuous experiences were also infinitely complex.

In a book of this size, we have only been able to discuss certain aspects of each of the five senses, but, as they are discussed and illustrated here, we believe these essays make a contribution to a broader discussion about ways in which it might be possible to develop a multisensory historical investigation into the study of urban culture. There are many areas for further exploration. The capital cities discussed in this collection need to be placed in a broader comparative context to establish how far they were typical of other large urban centres in Western and Central Europe. There is no doubt that some of the characteristics of the capitals in question were also present in other, smaller or less highly developed centres, but on a smaller scale and in many cases at a later date. This volume has also emphasised the centres of cities, rather than peripheral areas, the built environment rather than the green spaces which did exist in a number of cities and the nineteenth-century suburbs, as well as leaving underexplored much of the cultural liminality of these key areas that so often linked the urban and the rural, the recent arrival and the established inhabitant, the outcast and the socially acceptable. While some of our studies have referred to the cultural dimension of the physical relations between the sexes, gendered cultures and the significance of physical relationships in the city, amply explored from other historical perspectives, remain a fruitful field for research in the history of urban culture.

# PART ONE

# AN ENVIRONMENT OF ALL THE SENSES

# CHAPTER ONE

# Stench in sixteenth-century Venice

## *Jo Wheeler*

An analysis of contemporary perceptions of stench is essential to understanding the increasing regulation of the urban experience in the sixteenth century. In the medical theory and natural philosophies of the time, stench was equated with disease. To look at practical measures to fight stench is therefore to examine the ability of urban authorities to cope with formidable problems of disease, sanitation, rising poverty, overcrowding and crisis migration. Anxieties ran highest in the face of the age's great killers, infectious diseases, above all, plague. Responses were shaped as much by the increasing experience of pestilence and typhus in a milder endemic form as by the horror of devastating epidemics in Italy, Spain, Germany and the Netherlands in the first half of the sixteenth century. Venice makes a particularly important case study, since it was this city that 'adopted the most stringent health regulations anywhere in early modern Europe'.[1] Arguably, the Republic also established the most active and effective permanent machinery to monitor and combat stench in this period.[2] Despite all this, in 1575–77, the city was stricken by a plague outbreak so terrible that over a quarter of the population perished. The Venetian example also reveals much about the limits of intervention in urban health in this period and the extent to which the threat of stench was employed to extend social controls.[3]

In the now vast literature on understandings of epidemic disease and

---

[1] J. Hale, *Renaissance Europe 1480–1520* (London, 1971), p. 23.

[2] This machinery is also exceptionally well documented. For instance, Ernst Rodenwaldt's study is an extended commentary on a massive compilation of official decrees between autumn 1575 and summer 1577 by the *scrivan* of the Health Board, Cornelio Morello; E. Rodenwaldt, *Pest in Venedig, 1575–15: ein Beitrag zur Frage der Infektkette bei den Pestepidemien West-Europa* (Heidelberg, 1953).

[3] This attempt at a synthesis examines the period up to 1575, and is greatly indebted to the innovative studies of Carlo Cipolla and Piero Camporesi, the exhibition catalogue, *Venezia e la peste* and the researches of Richard Palmer, Brian Pullan, Paolo Preto and Rodenwaldt on plague and poor relief in Venice. I would also like to thank Renato Sansa for supplying his important unpublished paper on the management of environmental problems in Italian cities in the early modern period.

fevers from the Black Death to the late seventeenth century, one constant is the perceived threat of foul vapours released from decaying matter and from stagnant water. These stenches were thought to corrupt and putrefy the surrounding air, producing poisonous and pestilential miasmas.[4] Breathing in this venomous air caused the humours to putrefy and generate plague in those most vulnerable to infection. The air literally reeked of death. Notions of infection and contagion were also imagined very differently. No real distinction was made between airborne spread and contact, as both terms referred to the passing of a poison or taint and both were used interchangeably.[5] Miasma was thought to lurk and be transported in victims' clothes, in their baggage or to be spread through their foul breath. As stenches were thought to cling to and impregnate fabrics in the same manner as perfumes, they could remain dangerous for weeks.[6] The impact of new contagious diseases such as the pox served to accentuate these understandings of how stench was transmitted from person to person.

Ground-breaking studies of miasma in early modern Tuscany and France have documented these attitudes in stunning detail and how this thinking was shaped by Hippocratic and Galenic theories in which illness was thought to originate in the environment.[7] Galen, for instance, in *On the Difference of Fevers*, singles out putrefaction arising from corrupt air as the manifest cause of plague, which struck certain individuals when foul air was accompanied by predisposing factors such as an imbalance in the humours.

---

[4] See C. Cipolla, *Miasmas and Disease: Public Health and the Environment in the Pre-industrial Age* (New Haven, 1992), for the fullest exploration of these theories. Also A. Pastore, 'Culture mediche e politiche sanitarie', Review Essay, *Studi Storici*, 38, 2 (1997), pp. 579–88; and W. Eamon, 'Plagues, healers and patients in early modern Europe', Review Essay, *Renaissance Quarterly*, 52, 2 (1999), pp. 474–86, for an introduction to recent literature.

[5] I take this point from J. Arrizabalaga, J. Henderson and R. French, *The Great Pox: the French Disease in Renaissance Europe* (New Haven and London, 1996), p. 248. See also V. Nutton, 'The seeds of disease: an explanation of contagion and infection from the Greeks to the Renaissance', *Medical History*, 27 (1983), pp. 1–34.

[6] However, in Renaissance Venice I have not found any evidence to support Cipolla's argument that miasmas were perceived in terms of exceptionally 'sticky' atoms (which may be a seventeenth-century development).

[7] See especially the studies of Cipolla, *Miasmas and disease*; J. Henderson, 'Epidemics in Renaissance Florence: medical theory and government response', in N. Bulst and R. Delort, eds, *Maladies et société, XIIe–XVIIIe siècles: actes du colloque de Bielefeld, novembre 1986* (Paris, 1989), pp. 165–86; G. Calvi, *Histories of a Plague Year: the Social and the Imaginary in Baroque Florence* (Berkeley, 1989); and A. Corbin, *The Foul and the Fragrant. Odour and the Social Imagination* (Leamington Spa, 1996).

Contemporaries also had a shrewd grasp of the connections between dangerous environments and diseases: brackish marshes were especially feared since they were ridden with fever. The seasonal rhythms of disease served to confirm these understandings: the hot months when stenches were most offensive coincided with fresh outbreaks of epidemics.[8] Cities became graveyards of fever. Plague which had only temporarily subsided during the winter returned. Only typhus abated.[9]

In Venice, the Health Commissioners took the threat of stench so seriously that they asserted in 1501, 'Knowing that of all the measures that can and must be taken to keep this city healthy, the principal one is to remove all the causes giving off fetor and stenches.'[10] Rotten meat could 'infect this city with pestilential disease'. In what follows, surviving records provide a rich mine of material for exploring what was defined as stench in Venice and how the cultural meanings of stench took on distinctive form here because of the city's unique location. It is possible to reconstruct rival theories of foul air connected to key political debates and to analyse closely when and why policy changed. Medical treatises, printed orders and legislation all provide a wealth of detail about counter-measures against stench, above all the use of specific odours and perfumes to rectify the air and protect from disease.

Perceptions of stench in sixteenth-century Venice have to be carefully unpacked. In the context of eighteenth-century France, Alain Corbin argues that 'what was intolerable was the odour of putrefaction, not combustion'.[11] The Venetian evidence lends some qualified support to this position. The gut-wrenching odours of festering rubbish and excrement, discarded entrails, putrid meat and fish were all identified as

---

[8] F. Braudel, *The Mediterranean and the Mediterranean World in the Age of Philip II* (London, 1975), trans. S. Reynolds, vol. 1, p. 258.

[9] What contemporaries labelled as 'plague' may also have been 'mixed mortality crises'. See, for example, J. Henderson, '"La schifezza, madre della corruzione": peste e società nella Firenze della prima età moderna 1630–31', *Medicina e Storia: rivista di storia della medicina*, 1, 2 (2001), pp. 23–56, on Florence in 1630–31.

[10] Archivio di Stato di Venezia (ASV), Provveditori della Sanita, Notatorio, R.725, c.63v, 5.1.1500 more veneto (=1501). My translation differs from that of Richard Palmer in his 'In bad odour: smell and its significance in medicine from antiquity to the seventeenth century', in W.F. Bynum and R. Porter, eds, *Medicine and the Five Senses* (Cambridge, 1993), p. 66. For expressions of almost identical anxieties (and use of similar language), see R. Palmer, 'The control of plague in Venice and Northern Italy 1348–1600', University of Kent PhD thesis, 1978, p. 127, and *Venezia e la peste*, scheda 85, a decree by the Health Commissioners of 30 June 1502 on rubbish dumped outside stores.

[11] Corbin, *The Foul and the Fragrant*, 66.

stench by the *Provveditori della Sanità*,[12] the Health Commissioners, and all were targets of a barrage of ordinances. Similarly, here, as throughout Europe, smoke did not evoke feelings of disgust but was instead perceived as a counter-measure against stench. Every expert knew, through Galen, that Hippocrates himself had ordered bonfires lit in the streets against plague. 'Experience tells us,' wrote the irregular practitioner and surgeon, Leonardo Fioravanti, 'that during the 1556 plague, Murano did not suffer any corruption and this by virtue of the glass furnaces.' Similarly the physician Andrea Marini (d.1571), in his *Discourse on the Air of Venice*, identified Murano and the parish of San Barnabà as the healthiest parts of the city because 'the furnaces of glass makers and potters there continually cleansed the air of its gross humid vapours'.[13]

The same logic that linked stench and putrefaction explains the association of certain trades in Venice with stench and filth, and why the Health Board made them their targets to the exclusion of others. Tomaso Garzoni, in his *Piazza universale di tutte le professioni del mondo* (Venice, 1585), branded tanners 'an exceedingly dirty, fetid and stinking trade. In time of pestilence they are the first to be expelled.'[14] Furriers too were prime suspects: the nauseating smells of skins left for months smeared with millet flour and oil to absorb the putrefying particles must have been unbearable in the heat.[15] Dyers who used ox blood as an auxiliary product to produce the intense red known as *rosso turco* were banished, from 1413 onwards, every March to the 'margins and extremities' of the city.[16] This may also have been motivated by the fact that workers in this craft trod cloths up to their knees in vats of fermented urine, used both as a detergent and to aid the absorption of dyes.[17] Such measures did often provoke successful resistance by these guilds, in the form of petitions.

Surprisingly, the thirty or so trades massed in the Arsenal, the dockyards and the largest industrial complex in Europe at the time were

---

[12] For example, ASV, Provveditori della Sanità, Notatorio, b.725, f.11r, 6.9.1493, Notatorio, b.727, f, 85v, 12.10.1530. See especially Palmer, 'The control of plague', 66–9.

[13] The same point is also made by the physician Tommaso Rangone in his *Consiglio come i Venetiani possono vivere sempre sani* (Venice, 1565).

[14] M. Berengo, *L'Europa delle città* (Turin, 1999), p. 469.

[15] See R. Delort, *Le commerce des fourrures en Occident à la fin du Moyen Age (vers 1300–vers 1450)* (Rome, 1978), vol. 1, pp. 716–17.

[16] ASV, MC, Leona, f.227r. 21.9.1413, quoted in full in *Venezia e la peste*, Appendix of Documents, 364.

[17] See P. Camporesi, *La miniera del mondo. Artieri, inventori, impostori* (Milan, 1990), p. 62.

not associated with stench (despite Dante's description of the heat and noise there in the *Inferno*). This silence is difficult to explain, but it seems highly significant that the Arsenal was located outside the 'guts' [*viscere*] of the city.[18]

Thresholds of tolerance of stench, though, were lowered by concerns of 'decorum' which focused particularly on the city's commercial and political centres, St Mark's Square and the Rialto. Both were invested with a slew of symbolic meanings, and representations of the city interpreted them as symmetrical, as the two '*piazze*' around which the 'body' and 'bowels' of the city were organised. Here concerns about stench were inextricably linked to controversial concerns to exclude the poor and humble trades from these public spaces.

Jacopo Sansovino, elected *proto* [superintendent of works] at San Marco in 1529, famously swept away a series of hostelries and stalls of butchers and cheese sellers in renovating the area around St Mark's Square (1536–37).[19] If we can trust Vasari, he also removed latrines around the columns at the same time, 'something foul and shameful for the dignity of the palace and the public square, as well as for foreigners, who coming to Venice by way of San Giorgio saw all that filthiness first'.[20] These measures must be seen in the context of a contentious programme of radical renewal undertaken by a group around Doge Gritti, one strand of which was an unrealised project for a magistracy to embellish the city, removing 'ugly' sites that 'denigrate its splendour' (1535).[21] Yet, seven years later, the fetid smoke spewing out of the Mint at St Mark's Square was considered so unwholesome in so important a place that the furnaces were pushed out to a peripheral parish, San Gerolamo.[22] And, after more than three centuries on the

---

[18] For this concept, see E. Concina, *Venezia nell'età moderna. Struttura e funzioni* (Venice, 1989), pp. 35–52.

[19] D. Howard, *Jacopo Sansovino: Architecture and Patronage in Renaissance Venice* (New Haven and London, 1975), p. 41; M. Morresi, *Piazza San Marco. Istituzioni, poteri ed architettura a Venezia nel primo Cinquecento* (Milan, 1999), p. 59, nn. 47, 55; also D. Howard, 'Studies in Jacopo Sansovino's Venetian architecture', Courtauld Institute, University of London PhD thesis, 1973, p. 97.

[20] P. Barocchi, ed., *Giorgio Vasari, Le vite* (Pisa, 1994), p. 501.

[21] M. Tafuri, *Venice and the Renaissance* (Cambridge, Mass., 1989), pp. 108–12; and M. Tafuri, ed., *'Renovatio urbis': Venezia nell'età di Andrea Gritti, 1523–1538* (Rome, 1984).

[22] Two years later, a latrine next to the entrance to the Ducal Palace was also removed: Morresi, *Piazza San Marco*, p. 47, n. 59. On the smoke from the Mint, see G. Cozzi, M. Knapton and G. Scarabello, *La Repubblica di Venezia nell'età moderna. Dal 1517 alla fine della Repubblica*, Storia d'Italia XII, vol. 2 (Turin, 1992), pp. 281–2. The original documents are transcribed in G. Bonfiglio Dosio, ed., *Il 'Capitolar dalle broche' della zecca di Venezia (1358–1556* (Padua, 1984).

*piazzetta*, by 1556 the meat market was considered a 'polluting' presence by Sansovino, a proposal that encountered stiff opposition. The situation was only resolved in 1580, when the *Beccheria* was transferred from next to the Mint to Santa Maria in Broglio (at the far end of the Piazza), an area ironically occupied by a rubbish tip.

Notions of stench were shaped as much by moral and social prejudices as by observation.[23] Diseases such as typhus and plague hit the poor hardest, encouraging magistrates to portray their suffering as divine punishment inflicted on them for their filthy and corrupt habits. The danger of contagion created opportunities for social control. In 1521, destitute victims of the pox 'loitering' and begging on the streets were accused of 'emitting a great stench and infecting their neighbours' which could 'breed infection and diverse illnesses', justifying the establishment of the *Incurabili* hospital.[24] As early as 1506, brutal distinctions were made between the deserving long-term resident poor and outsiders, stigmatised as dangerous or fraudulent vagabonds, an infestation to be expelled from the city.[25] The disastrous sequence of famine, hunger, typhus and pestilence in 1527–29, when masses of starving peasants, who literally embodied stench and disease, crowded the streets, provoked crisis measures. An emergency poor law was passed, assisting the local poor and authorising expulsion and forced labour for foreign and 'fraudulent' beggars.[26]

More efficient and repressive measures against the stench of the poor were stimulated more by recurrent famine than by epidemics, since their incidence decreased. In 1539, the Health Commissioners drove out 'four or five thousand persons, beggars and others, who had recently come to this city', sentencing many to galley service against the Turks. Chronicles in fact describe a flood of male migrants who arrived by boat with their wives and children, who took up residence under the city's bridges, dying of hunger.[27] It was only in another famine year, 1545, that the poor law was systematically applied, when some six thousand 'beggars' poured into Venice. Suspicion spread to refugee populations: if it was the Albanians and Slavs in the mid-fifteenth century, a century later it was

---

[23] See especially P. Slack, 'Responses to plague in early modern Europe: the implications of public health', *Social Research*, 55, 3 (1988), pp. 433–53.

[24] Arrizabalaga, Henderson, French, *The Great Pox*, p. 166.

[25] B. Pullan, *Rich and Poor in Renaissance Venice* (Oxford, 1971), p. 221.

[26] B. Pullan, 'The famine in Venice and the new poor law', *Studi Veneziani*, 5–6 (1963–64), pp. 141–94; and D.S. Chambers and B.S. Pullan, with J. Fletcher, eds, *Venice. A Documentary History 1450–1630* (Oxford and Cambridge, Mass, 1992), pp. 303–6.

[27] Pullan, *Rich and Poor*, p. 296; Braudel, *The Mediterranean*, vol. 2, p. 743.

the Marranos, Portuguese New Christians.[28] Their expulsion in 1550 was justified by fears of infection because of their squalid and overcrowded living conditions.

As during the Florentine epidemic of 1630–31, the routine behaviour of the poor was transformed into symptoms of lethal diffusion.[29] The attack on stench was highly discriminatory, and it did meet resistance. For example, we find cases of artisans prosecuted for hiding infected goods, women for ignoring the ban on selling secondhand clothes. Those who enforced these measures, *netizini* [cleaners/fumigators] were so despised that only convicts could be forcibly recruited for the task.

The attitudes to stench outlined so far were not unique to Venice: they are strikingly similar to those documented in contemporary cities in central and northern Italy. What then was distinctive about perceptions of stench here? For some answers we can turn to a cluster of medical treatises in the mid-sixteenth century, which underline the disagreements and confusions over the many causes of foul air. The first is the *Discourse on the Air of Venice*, by Andrea Marini (d.1570), composed some time between 1559 and 1566.[30] What Marini provides is a stark diagnosis of the deteriorating state of the lagoon, drawing heavily on the authority of the Hippocratic *Airs, Waters and Places*. In the past, he says, the excessive humidity of Venice's air had been corrected by three factors: the vigorous ebb and flow of the tides, the saltiness of the lagoon (which dried gross vapours out) and the prevailing winds. Not only had they agitated, thinned and purged the air of 'any strange qualities', but they also counteracted each other: the west wind, the *maestrale*, corrected the defects of its adversary, the *sirocco*, whilst the north wind, the *tramontana*, offset the *ostro*. But not now.

Only the frequent and continual fires in the city now protected Venice, cleansing the air of its malign vapours. Marini points to one cause, and one cause only, for the city's declining health: the state of the lagoon. As it silted up, the lagoon had shrunk, causing tidal flows to weaken. At the same time, the southerly winds became increasingly dangerous because they now carried the 'grossness of marshes and the stench of stagnant waters'. Four recent and massive floods,[31] unknown when the lagoon was much larger, had done 'incomparable damage': turning the air stale and putrid in now dank basement rooms. Since the course of Venice's

---

[28] B. Pullan, 'Plague and perceptions of the poor in early modern Italy', in T. Ranger and P. Slack, eds, *Epidemics and Ideas. Essays on the Historical Perception of Pestilence* (Cambridge, 1992), p. 113.

[29] Calvi, *Histories of a Plague Year*, pp. 5–6.

[30] Andrea Marini, *Discorso sopra l'aere di Venezia*.

[31] In 1535, 1542, 1549 and 1559.

canals was now so sluggish, they 'remained very often at low tide without or with little water', filling the air with an 'intolerable' and 'pestiferous stench'.

As we read into this text, we see its highly political character. Marini, who had now lived in the city for seven years, was adding his voice to the heated debate over the problem of preserving the lagoon and land reclamation.[32] His comments echo the position staked out by Cristoforo Sabbadino, the hydraulic engineer employed by the *Savi alle Acque*, who launched a scathing attack against the daring project of Alvise Cornaro, a former patrician struck off the list of nobles, to enclose the lagoon inside a continuous embankment and drain off the 'high marshes'. In total contrast, Sabbadino called for 'restoration on a grand scale' of the 'original' conditions of the lagoon; it had to be 'made larger and greater than its present state', and any obstacle removed that blocked the purifying action of the tides. 'In order for this body to stay alive, beautiful, healthy and hardy,' he wrote, 'it must be conserved in its entirety . . . its food must be saltwater, which it receives every six hours and throws back after six hours.' Marini's arguments are clearly derived from this reasoning. To recapitulate: combining an understanding of locales taken from *Airs, Waters and Places* with Sabbadino's views, Marini worked out a relationship between Venice's unique setting and stench, a link which had long been recognised.

Anxieties about the lagoon as a dangerous source of stench surface, for example, in Gerolamo Priuli's *Diaries* in 1509. The fresh water disgorged at Lizzafusina from the Brenta River had contaminated the salt waters of the lagoon: once 'fresh water mixed with salt, the air was contaminated, inducing pestilence or fever'.[33] The mixture of fresh with salt water and advancing reed beds were also blamed for the malaria (understood as bad air) responsible for the abandonment of the port of San Nicolò. This distinctively Venetian concept of stench later evolved into a fear of stench produced by salt and fresh water mixed in wells (1575).

Such a direct link between Venice's site and stench is missing in three other medical texts printed in 1555–56 and 1565. This reticence and ambivalence is understandable, for to perceive the lagoon as dangerous territory was tantamount to perceiving Venice itself as unhealthy, and risked associating the character of its inhabitants with moral decay and

---

[32] On the debate, see S. Escobar, 'Il controllo delle acque: problemi tecnici e interessi economici', in *Annali della Storia d'Italia*, 3 (Turin, 1980), 117ff; also L. Puppi, ed., *Architettura e utopi nella Venezia del Cinquecento* (Milan, 1980), pp. 130–43.

[33] R. Cessi, ed., G. Priuli, *I Diarii*, vol. IV (Bologna, 1938), 21 (c.8v).

grossness. So the anatomist Nicolo Massa (d.1569), writing as plague flared in 1555, put the blame on freak weather conditions.[34] Unseasonably humid and hot weather had turned the air pestilential, putrefying the humours of those susceptible because of their wretched diet. At the same time, though, he recognised the appalling housing conditions of the poor lay at the root of the problem and he urged a thorough cleansing of those areas, filthy and cramped alleyways. Yet, less than a year later, he ascribed the 1556 epidemic to infected goods and contagion, arguing, though, it was not 'true plague'. The Bolognese empiric, Leonardo Fioravanti, who practised in Venice from 1558 to 1571, put forward three very different causes for plague in his tract: foremost, divine fury, or depopulation, or the 'corruption of the elements, which corrupt the air and corrupt our bodies (1565)'.[35] We see this, he says, when fog or smoke and other 'bad' [tristi] vapours fill the air.

Two main points can be made about these texts. First, they reflect and restate distinctive anxieties about stench that repeatedly surfaced in legislation whenever epidemics threatened. Secondly, they should be read against a sort of official discourse about the incredible quality of the city's air. This was ingrained in city descriptions, whose prime purpose, of course, was to publicise the glories of Venice. These descriptions ignored any flaws, and idealised Venice's site. The city's rarefied atmosphere reflected the purity of its customs and inhabitants, its moral superiority. As in *Airs, Waters and Places*, climate determined character. The writer and publisher, Francesco Sansovino, son of the architect, in his many city descriptions (1556 onwards) repeated the claim made in Marc'Antonio Sabellico's *De Situ Urbis Venetae* (1493).[36] Venice's air was so wonderful that nowhere else could you find such a large number of people surviving into old age in robust health. Nowhere was this myth more potent than amongst those drawn to Venice: for instance, Fioravanti recycles the topos in his last semi-autobiographical work. He wrote, 'You will not find a city in the whole of Europe where people live longer and are more healthy.' Venice's temperate air was so benign that

---

[34] N. Massa, *Ragionamento sopra le infermità che vengono dall'aere pestilentiale del presente anno MDLV*, Venice Giovanni Griffio for Giordano Ziletti (1556), f.4v. On this text, see Palmer, 'The control of plague', p. 113, and *Venezia e la peste*, scheda 26, p. 58.

[35] On Fioravanti, see P. Camporesi, *Camminare il mondo. Vita e avventure di Leonardo Fioravanti medico del Cinquecento* (Milan, 1997); W. Eamon, *Science and the Secrets of Nature. Books of Secrets in Medieval and Early Modern Culture* (Princeton, 1994), pp. 168–93.

[36] See Anselmo Guisconi: *Tutte le cose notabili* (Sansovino's pseudonym) and the many editions of his *Delle cose notabili della città di Venetia*. On Sansovino, see E. Bonora, *Ricerche su Francesco Sansovino : imprenditore librario e letterato* (Venice, 1994).

head wounds quickly healed, as did leg pains, whilst greens and spinach grew faster than elsewhere. These platitudes were picked up by impressionable travellers, such as the Englishman Fynes Moryson. In 1594, he reported, 'though the floud or ebbe of the salt water be small, yet with that motion it carrieth away the filth of the city, besides that, by the multitude of fiers, and the situation open to all windes, the ayr is made very wholesome, whereof the Venetians bragge, that it agrees with all strangers complexions by a secret vertue'.[37] Unlike today, travellers' accounts did not generally associate Venice with stench. Montaigne is the exception to the rule. He called attention to Venice's 'filthy, foggy, ill-savouring and unwholesome airs', which yielded 'muddy, sharp and offending savors' due to its 'fennie and marish situation' (Florio's translation).[38]

The anxieties suppressed by this official discourse are most evident, as I have argued, in the surviving records of Venetian magistracies. I want now to use those same records, which trace, in great detail, an uninterrupted sequence of decrees in which the sources of miasma were regulated, to explore the practical measures taken to combat stench. Rather than describe health controls that have already been thoroughly studied, such as the regulation of the meat and fish markets, the movement of people and the isolation of the sick, I want to focus on two less familiar areas. The first is the use of odours to counteract stench (and how this relates to medical advice and popular practices). The second is the cleansing of the city and the problem of household waste.

The recommended government advice in 1576 to render houses 'safe' and 'clean' was to burn perfumes of pitch, turpentine, incense, storax and myrrh over red-hot coals for twenty-four hours with all the windows shut. Infected houses were fumigated with a similar and incredibly pungent combination of sulphur, pitch and myrrh. The only novel aspect of this method of neutralising stench is the use of acrid odours. Since antiquity, medical theory had recognised that 'pungent aromas and perfumes were powerful, therapeutic, restorative and stimulating medicaments . . . which were particularly effective in combating illness due to poisoning' (Piero Camporesi).[39] And, like a diseased body, the air

---

[37] F. Moryson [1617], *An Itinerary Containing his Ten Yeeres Travell: Through the Twelve Dominions of Germany, Bohmerland, Sweitzerland, Netherland, Denmarke, Poland, Italy, Turkey, France, England, Scotland & Ireland* (Glasgow, 1907–1908), p. 164.

[38] M. de Montaigne, 'On Smells', in *The Complete Essays* (London, 1991), trans. M.A. Screech, book 1, pp. 55, 354.

[39] P. Camporesi [1983], *The Incorruptible Flesh: Bodily Mutation and Mortification in Religion and Folklore* (Cambridge, 1988), p. 179. See also Corbin, *The Foul and the Fragrant*, pp. 61–6.

could be purged, altered and corrected.[40] Resting on these assumptions, Nicolò Massa, for instance, advocated burning juniper, cypress, laurel and larch against stench (1555).[41] Dousing walls with vinegar also fought the heat and humidity of corrupt air with smell, and its cooling and drying properties. Orthodox theory advised different combinations of aromatics according to the prevailing season.

For personal protection against stench (and as preventive medicine), a battery of aromatic counter-measures was available. The most basic, suitable only for the poor, were to carry around sponges imbued with vinegar or the herbs rue and southernwood (significantly both reputedly effective against spells and demons). Chewing lemon or citron seeds, garden sorrel and thistleroot ground to a powder, drunk in aromatic wine, also kept contagion at bay.[42] Those with means were instead directed towards elaborate compound remedies, amalgams of dissonant and conflicting odours, based on exotic and costly ingredients. These ranged from theriac,[43] the poison 'antidote of antidotes', first described by Galen, to those described in books of 'secrets', compilations of cures and recipes. Fioravanti, for example, touted a 'miraculous' pomander, whose ingredients included benzoin, storax, cloves, mace, aloeswood and zedoary – 'all of which conserved against putrefaction'.[44] The self-styled Reverend Master Alexis of Piedmont (1555) alias the *poligrafo* Gerolamo Ruscelli (d.1566) prescribed this 'very good perfume' to ward off plague: 'mastic, incense, cypress, mace, wormwood, lignum aloe, musk, ambergris, nutmeg, myrtle, bay, rosemary, sage, elder, rasis, ginger

---

[40] See A. Wear, *Knowledge and Practice in English Medicine* (Cambridge, 2000), p. 320.

[41] This was not novel. In 1384, for example, Giovanni Dondi dall'Orologio recommended burning dry aromatic woods such as rosemary, juniper, laurel and ash.

[42] N. Massa, *Ragionamento [...] sopra le infermità, che vengono dall'aere pestilentiale del presente anno MDLV* (Venice, 1556), f.24v, f.26v.

[43] On theriac there is large literature: see especially P. Findlen, *Possessing Nature* (Berkeley, 1994), pp. 241–87, esp. 242. 'Theriac was reputed to cure plague, syphilis, epilepsy, apoplexy, asthma, catarrh, and a variety of everyday ills that preyed upon the human body: see Girolamo Donzellini, *De natura, causis, et legitima curatione febris pestilentis* (Venice, 1570), c.14v'. See also Girolamo Ruscelli, *De' secreti*, part 1, p.49v.

[44] L. Fioravanti [1565], *Il reggimento della peste. Nel quale si tratta che cosa sia la peste, & da che procede, & quello che doveriano fare i prencipi per conservar' i suoi popoli da essa; & ultimamente, se mostrano mirabili secreti da curarla . . . / nuovamente ristampato, ricorretto et ampliato di diversi bellissimi secreti et di 77 dottissimi afforismi, ne' quali . . . s'insegna a conoscer' et curare tutte le sorti et qualità di mali*, (Venice, 1571), ch. 9, pp. 49–51; P. Preto, *Peste e società a Venezia nel 1576* (Vicenza, 1978), pp. 197–200, transcribes a selection of Fioravanti's plague remedies.

and pitch all pounded together and set upon the coles' (English translation, 1562).[45]

In contrast, a more aggressive form of social intervention is evident in measures to combat filth and refuse. The task of cleaning the city was contracted out to teams of *nettadori/scovadori*, who toured each *sestiere* [district] in their barges, sounding their horns and carting away the filthy sludge which encrusted the banks of canals and emptying the '*chasse*' for ordure/rubbish [*scovaze*].[46] The Health Commissioners imposed their own regulator on them in 1499.[47] The system was backed up by one of draconian fines: anyone found guilty of throwing rubbish or rubble into canals had to pay five ducats or be publicly flogged. Its principles were rooted in a long tradition of devolving responsibility to householders. By 1536, this system was obviously unsuited to a rapidly expanding city and was evidently failing. A tougher form of local self-regulation was instituted: to stop the widespread dumping of waste into the canals, the *Collegio delle Acque* elected a captain in each parish with powers to fine and arrest offenders. What marks Venice out is that the authorities were most concerned with stench from the canals, not stench in the streets. The fine was five times higher for throwing rubbish into a canal.[48]

Just a few months earlier, alarming silting had provoked an order for the dredging of the entire Grand Canal, a project still continuing in 1542. Stench was used to fight stench, because the sludge was reused to reinforce the dikes that protected the lagoon from equally dangerous fresh water. These dredging operations were on an immense scale: 467 barge loads a week it was calculated in 1556.[49] Nine years later, over three thousand men were brought from the mainland to dig out mud banks.[50]

---

[45] G. Ruscelli, *The secretes of the reverend Maister Alexis*, f.36r. On Ruscelli, see Eamon, *Science and the Secrets of Nature*, 139–51 (my own forthcoming work on books of secrets modifies this picture).

[46] ASV, *Senato, Terra*, 5, c.2v–3r reproduced in G. Pavanallo, ed., *Antichi scrittori d'idraulica veneta*, vol. 1 (Venice, 1919), p. 153.

[47] ASV, Provveditori alla Sanità, Notatorio, reg.725, f.51v, 3.8.1499.

[48] ASV, Savi ed Esecutori alle Acque, reg.334, 68r–69v, 17.2.1535 more veneto (=1536). On street cleaning in sixteenth-century Venice, see I. Cacciavillani, *Le leggi ecologiche veneziane* (Padua, 1990), pp. 39–68; N. Vanzan Marchini (1985), *Venezia. Da laguna a città* (Venice, 1985), pp. 68–73; Palmer, 'The control of plague', p. 127.

[49] R. Berveglieri, *Le vie di Venezia. Canali lagunari e rii a Venezia: Inventori, brevetti, tecnologia e legislazione nei secoli XIII–XVII* (Sommacampagna, 1999), 292, document n.136, 9.8.1565, ASV, Savi ed Esecutori alle Acque, reg.338, cc.68v–69r.

[50] ASV. Savi ed Esecutori alle Acque, reg.345, c.50r, 13.6.1565. See also Palmer, 'The control of plague', who notes 'almost every decision of note relating

However, the records of action taken by the Health Commissioners against those who emptied *scoaze* [excrement/refuse] and other *immonditie* from balconies onto streets or in courtyards from 1530 to 1537 make it clear that the scale of the problem of stench in the city itself was as great.[51] Dozens of parishes and courtyards were blighted. An extraordinary document suggests that the problem had worsened by the cut-off point of this study, the devastating plague of 1575. Imprisoned for insolvency, the known Sienese heretic Cornelio Sozzini, in desperation, presented a new solution for cleaning the city, offering his services for 2000 *scudi* a year (later dropped to 900 ducats, the annual sum spent by the government). His proposal was dismissed out of hand, but his petition emphasises the filthiness of Venice's streets: a great source of 'annoyance' and 'irritation'; only one-third were passable, all clothes had to be hitched up.[52]

His comments are corroborated by a scathing report compiled by Dolfin Valier, *Savio alle Acque* for his colleagues in March 1568. He decried the 'total lack of respect' for laws: not only were many edicts a dead letter, but, worse still, the very officials appointed to crack down on these abuses [*pallatieri, soprastanti*] were actively tolerating these practices, fuelling '*disobedience and insolence*'. Valier's frustrations reveal an important conclusion about the Venetian evidence of stench, namely the very real limits and inefficiencies of early modern health controls and urban government. However, the depth of resistance he stresses suggests another conclusion. The highly discriminatory nature of the fight against stench was so controversial since ingrained habits, the normal processes of certain trades and the routine actions of the poor were all criminalised.[53] The evidence here is consistent with the

to the lagoon was justified, in least in part, by the need to protect the city's air', p. 128.

[51] ASV, Provveditori della Sanità, Notatorio, reg. 727, f.107r, 29.11.1530, f.116r, 13.1.1530mv(=1531), f.278r, 8.10.1533, f.239r, 28.11.1533, f.291r–293r, 13.11.1534, 2.12.1534, 4.12.1534, 8.1.1534mv(=1535), 15.2.1534mv(=1535), 31.3.1535, f.315r–v, 24.3.1536, 3.5.1536., f.316v–317r, 3.6.1536, 21.6.1536, f.322v, 2.8.1536, f.325r, 30.8.1526, f.329v, 10.1.1536 (=1537), f.336v, 23.5.1537, f.342v, 17.7.1537, f.355r–v, 5.3.1534(=1535), 9.4.1535.

[52] A. Stella, *Dall'anabattismo al socinianesimo nel Cinquecento veneto : Ricerche storiche* (Padua, 1967), p. 151; and ASV, Savi ed Esecutori alle Acque, reg.270, f.11v–12v.

[53] A. Cowan, *Urban Europe 1500–1700* (London and New York, 1998), p. 188, notes 'many of the restrictions [introduced because of plague] conflicted with customs at the heart of popular culture', citing examples from both London and France. The stresses caused by health controls are documented by P. Slack, *The Impact of Plague in Tudor and Stuart England* (London, 1985); Calvi,

documented resentment amongst the populace towards controls such as the burning of clothes and bedding in cities such as Florence,[54] Bologna and London. In these respects, Venice does not appear an exceptional case. Yet, at the same time, we also must recognise the distinctive nature of definitions of stench in this unique city.

## Further reading

P. Camporesi, 'Odori e sapori', introduction to A. Corbin, *Storia sociale degli odori. XVIII e XIX secolo* (Milan, 1983).

C.M. Cipolla, *Miasmas and Disease: Public Health and the Environment in the Preindustrial Age* (New Haven, 1992), trans. E. Potter.

A. Corbin, *The Foul and the Fragrant: Odour and the French Social Imagination* (London, 1996).

J. Henderson, '"La schifezza, madre della corruzione": peste e società nella Firenze della prima età moderna 1630–1632', *Medicina & Storia: rivista di storia della medicina e della sanità*, 1, 2 (2001), pp. 23–56.

R. Palmer, 'The control of plague in Venice and Northern Italy, 1348–1600', University of Kent PhD thesis, 1978.

F. Sansovino, *Venetia città nobilissima* (Bergamo, 2002).

S. Schama, *Rembrandt's Eyes* (London, 2000), pp. 311–13.

K. Thomas (1994), 'Cleanliness and godliness in early modern England', in A. Fletcher and P. Roberts, eds, *Religion, Culture, and Society in Early Modern Britain: Essays in Honour of Patrick Collinson* (Cambridge, 1994), pp. 56–83.

*Venezia e la peste: 1348–1797* (Venice, 1979).

---

*Histories of a Plague Year*; C. Cipolla, *Public Health and the Medical Profession in the Renaissance* (Cambridge, 1976); Henderson, '"La schifezza, madre della corruzione"'.

[54] Henderson '"La schifezza, madre della corruzione"', 39.

# CHAPTER TWO

# 'Not carrying out the vile and mechanical arts': touch as a measure of social distinction in early modern Venice

*Alexander Cowan*

This essay is a discussion of social boundaries within the early modern city, how they were defined, and the extent to which these definitions were blurred by social realities. As an exercise in social space, it demonstrates that, rather than being characterised by distinctive groupings, the upper levels of Venetian society in the sixteenth and seventeenth centuries represented overlapping spaces, where what was shared, be it lifestyle or membership of kinship networks, was more important than what was not, such as the monopoly of political power in the hands of the hereditary patriciate.[1] Contrary to what was believed by Venetians themselves, and by those of their contemporaries else- where in Europe who were influenced by the myth of the Most Serene Republic's political stability and longevity, Venetian society was organised on far more complex lines than a tripartite division into a ruling caste of patricians [*nobeli*], a semi-privileged group of citizens [*cittadini*], and ordinary people without any civic rights [*popolani*].[2]

---

[1] G. Simmel, 'Spatial and urban culture', in D. Frisby and M. Featherstone, eds, *Simmel on Culture. Selected Writings* (London, 1997), pp. 137–85; see also K. Ross, *The Emergence of Social Space. Rimbaud and the Paris Commune* (Minneapolis, 1988).

[2] For an example of a contemporary view of the tripartite divison of Venetian society, see Giannotti's comments in his *Della Repubblica de' Veneziani*, cited in G. Trebbi, 'I diritti di cittadinanza nelle repubbliche italiane dalla prima età moderna: gli esempi di Venezia e di Firenze', in G.M. Favaretto, ed., *Cittadinanze* (Trieste, 2001), p. 159. There is some debate over whether or not *civiltà* extended beyond the secondary Venetian order of *cittadini*. See A. Bellavitis, *Identité, mariage, mobilité sociale. Citoyennes et citoyens à Venise au xvi*e *siècle* (Rome, 2001); A. Zannini, *Burocrazia e burocrati in Venezia in età moderna: i cittadini originari (sec. XVI–XVIII)* (Venice, 1993); J. Grubb, 'Elite citizens', in J. Martin and D. Romano, eds, *Venice Reconsidered. The History and Civilisation of an Italian City State, 1297–1797* (Baltimore, 2000), pp. 339–64.

While there was no competition with the pre-eminent position of patricians at the head of Venetian society, two parallel developments called into question the social boundaries between patricians and non-patricians. On the one hand, as the work of Stanley Chojnacki has shown, the definition of a patrician had been refined by legislation on a number of occasions since the first closing [*Serrata*] of the city's ruling Council at the end of the thirteenth century.[3] By the late sixteenth century, the only people with access to membership of the Great Council and the right to be elected to political office were the legitimate sons of other patricians. A complicated series of checks had developed which required careful registration at birth, marriage and first admission to the Great Council.

On the other hand, while there was a strong element of endogamy within the patriciate, some patricians had always found wives from outside their immediate circles. Their reasons varied. The majority sought to make use of the capital represented by dowries from outsider brides to revive their family patrimonies.[4] Some brides came from the ruling families of the subject cities or from the feudal aristocracy of the Venetian Empire. Other wives were drawn from the women with whom patricians associated in the localities of Venice where they lived (there was no 'patrician' zone),[5] on their estates on the Italian mainland, or on the islands of the Eastern Mediterranean, where a Venetian colonial and naval presence was being increasingly contested by the Ottoman Empire.

The practice of marrying wives from outside the Venetian patriciate created yet one further difficulty over the definition of the men with the right to sit in the Great Council. From the early fifteenth century, legislation was introduced to establish criteria for the social acceptability of patrician wives.[6] This was an exclusively secular matter. The Church had a monopoly over the choice of couples to marry.[7] All children born

---

[3] S. Chojnacki, *Women and Men in Renaissance Venice. Twelve Essays on Patrician Society* (Baltimore, 2000); S. Chojnacki, 'Identity and ideology in Renaissance Venice. The third Serrata', in Martin and Romano, eds, *Venice Reconsidered*, pp. 263–94.

[4] A classic example of patrician motivation was that of Giacomo Pisani, to whom Giacomo Galli offered his niece Maria as a bride: 'And I knowing my straitened circumstances and that the girl was honourable, accepted the arrangement' (Archivio di Stato, Venice (ASV), Avogaria di Comun (AdC) p. 319).

[5] L. Megna, 'Comportamenti abitativi del patriziato veneziano (1582–1740)', *Studi Veneziani*, 22 (1991), pp. 253–324.

[6] S. Chojnacki, 'Nobility, women and the state: marriage regulation in Venice, 1420–1535', in T. Dean and K.J.P. Lowe, eds, *Marriage in Italy 1300–1650* (Cambridge, 1998), pp. 128–51.

[7] D. Lombardi, 'Fidanzamenti e matrimonio dal concilio di Trento alle riforme settecentesche', in M. de Giorgio and C. Klapisch-Zuber, eds, *Storia del*

of couples married according to canon law were deemed to be legitimate. Social legitimation, on the other hand, was central to the purity and the continuity of the patriciate. A process developed according to which only certain women were deemed to be socially acceptable and whose sons could therefore take their place as full members of the patriciate.[8]

This essay focuses on an important element of these criteria of social acceptability, the place of touch in defining the social status of a woman according to the activities carried out by her father and paternal and maternal grandfathers, best seen in the terms of the distinction between those activities which were *civile,* and those which were associated with *arte meccanica et manuale* – the vile and mechanical arts. As Tomaso Garzoni, one of the most widely read of social commentators on the sixteenth century, wrote:

> My discourse will clarify the positions of many of today's mechanicals who, because they have four pennies in their purse, and wear a fine cap, really like to be called *signori.* They openly behave as nobles, while all that the city has to say about them is that their grandfathers were porters, their fathers, water-carriers, their brothers, night-watchmen, their sisters prostitutes, their mothers bawds, and all their forebears smeared with lard, soaked with oil . . . and reeking of Greek fish. I say that matters will be clarified because one will see the nature of true nobility . . . and they will be obliged to confess that they are plebeians, and do not possess any noble status.[9]

The qualities underpinning *civiltà*, an abstract concept with important social connotations which were defined by contemporary commentators in the equally abstract terms of honour and good reputation, or were related to easily recognised dress codes and lifestyles, were widely understood both across a broad range of Venetian society and in Italian

---

*Matrimonio* (Rome and Bari, 1996), pp. 215–50; G. Cozzi, 'Padri, figli e matrimoni clandestini (metà secolo XVI – metà secolo XVIII)', *La Cultura,* 14 (1976), pp. 169–213.

[8] This study arises from a large-scale research project into women, marriage and social distinction in early modern Venice, funded by grants from the Arts and Humanities Research Board, the British Academy and the Gladys Krieble Delmas Foundation.

[9] T. Garzoni, *La Piazza Universale di Tutti le Professioni del mondo* (Florence, 1996), ed. G.B. Bronzini. The text was first published in Venice in 1585 and republished in many editions and translations, and became the most widespread, if not the most conventional, analysis of social distinction. This quotation (my translation) is on 223. On Garzoni's ideas, see U. Tucci, 'I mestieri nella *Piazza Universale* del Garzoni', in *Studi in onore di Luigi dal Pane* (Bologna, 1982), pp. 319–20; J. Martin, 'The Imaginary Piazza: Tomaso Garzoni and the late Italian Renaissance', in S.K. Cohn and S.A. Epstein, eds, *Portraits of Medieval and Renaissance Living* (Ann Arbor, 1996), pp. 439–54.

cities in general.[10] The meaning of *arte meccanica* was less clear, not least because, for the purposes of social distinction, it was defined more in terms of what it was not [*civiltà*] than what it was. We may read into this the simple division into society between those who worked with their brains, following a period of intellectual study, and those who worked with their hands. It was understandable in the terms of contemporary writing about gentility and nobility that, coming into direct contact with the earth through agriculture, with raw materials as an artisan, or with the human body as a bath attendant or barber invalidated a man's right to take his place alongside men dedicated to service to the state.[11] In many parts of Italy, including the subject cities of the Venetian Terraferma such as Brescia, Padua and Verona, trade of all kinds was included as *arte meccanica*.[12]

Venice stood apart from its neighbours on several counts. Trade, particularly long-distance trade, was not counted as *arte meccanica*. This can be explained by the importance of long-distance trade as the source of Venetian power during the city's political and commercial ascent during the Middle Ages. Equally important, however, was the close association between long-distance trade and high social status in Venice. Although most patrician patrimonies comprised investments in land and real estate by the end of the sixteenth century, this was a recent development. Long-distance trade by patricians had a long and honourable tradition.[13] Venice also stands out in terms of the richness and range of its archival sources, which allow the historian to explore the everyday assumptions and prejudices of Venetians from different levels of society.

---

[10] R. Corbellini, 'Modelli di aggregazione: tradizione urbana, tradizione communitaria, tradizione cetuale', in M. Bellabarba and R. Stauber, eds, *Identità territoriale e cultura politica nella prima età moderna* (Bologna, 1999), pp. 239–54; J-C. Margolin, 'La civilité nouvelle de la notion de civilité à sa pratique et aux traités de civilité', in A. Montandon, ed., *Pour une histoire des traités de savoir-vivre en Europe* (Clermont–Ferrand, 1994), pp. 151–77; M. Aymard, 'Pour une histoire des élites dans l'Italie moderne', in *La famiglia e la vita quotidiana in Europa del '400 al '600* (Rome, 1986), pp. 207–19.

[11] C. Donati, *L'idea di nobiltà in Italia. Secoli xiv–xviii* (Rome, 1988), pp. 93–150.

[12] A. Ventura, *Nobiltà e popolo nella società veneta del '400 e '500* (Bari, 1964), pp. 306–309; J. Ferraro, *Family and Public Life in Brescia, 1580–1650* (Cambridge, 1993), pp. 61–5; Tucci, 'I mestieri nella *Piazza Universale*'.

[13] U. Tucci, 'The psychology of the Venetian merchant in the sixteenth century', in J.R. Hale, ed., *Renaissance Venice* (London, 1973), pp. 346–78; A. Cowan, *The Urban Patriciate: Lübeck and Venice, 1580–1700* (Cologne and Vienna, 1986), pp. 195–203. Some patricians were too poor to be actively involved in any kind of investment strategy: L. Megna, 'Nobiltà e povertà. Il problema del patriziato povero nella Venezia del "700"', *Atti dell'Istituto Veneto di Scienze, Lettere ed Arti*, 139 (1981–82), pp. 319–40.

These were expressed in the testimony of witnesses called before the magistracy of the *Avogaria di Comun* to test the cases, known as *prove di nobiltà*, put forward on behalf of women who wished to marry into the Venetian patriciate, and in the comments and decisions of the *Avogadori* [the magistrates] who heard each case.[14] A second group of *prove di nobiltà* contained applications for patrician status by the sons of the marriages between patrician fathers and non-patrician mothers that had not been registered by the Venetian authorities. The same principles of social distinction were generally in play.[15] Finally, this analysis of the *prove di nobiltà* also brings out the perplexity with which contemporaries considered the dividing line between *arte meccanica* and 'civic' occupations as a means of establishing questions of high social status. This uncertainty arose from grey areas of definition. Other criteria, such as the large size of dowries offered by non-patrician families, and the political influence of the patrician families with whom they wished to be associated may also have played a part in establishing whether or not a woman's family was socially acceptable.

Explicit concerns about *arte meccanica* among the Venetian patriciate were well established by the beginning of the seventeenth century. Anxieties about the number and social background of non-patrician women who married patricians dated back as far as the early fifteenth century, but the earliest regulatory legislation, a law of 1422, only deprived men of patrician status whose mothers were slaves, servants and other women of low status.[16] The first reference to *arte meccanica et manuale* only appeared in legislation governing membership of the Great Council in 1589. Now, in addition to those listed in earlier laws, women were excluded from marrying patricians if their fathers or grandfathers had carried out *arte meccanica et manuale* or 'were of a similar status'.[17]

---

[14] Technically, the *Avogadori* did not take the final decision. Their task was to correlate the written and spoken evidence placed before them, and to place each case before the *Collegio*, who took the final decision, sometimes after multiple votes: P. del Negro, 'Forme e istituzioni del discorso politico veneziano', in *Storia della cultura veneta*, vol. 4/II. *Il Seicento* (Vicenza, 1984), p. 428.

[15] In the case of the *prove* of men wishing to join the Great Council, the *Avogadori* needed to satisfy themselves that the men were of legitimate birth and required witnesses of their parents' weddings and of their baptisms. This did not exclude investigations into the social status of their maternal grandfathers and great-grandfathers.

[16] S. Chojnacki, 'Marriage legislation and patrician society in fifteenth-century Venice', in B.S. Bachrach and D. Nicholas, eds, *Law, Customs and Social Fabric in Medieval Europe* (Kalamazoo, 1990), pp. 167–8.

[17] AdC 108. Because of its importance, this law was given a wide circulation in manuscript form. A second copy may be consulted at the Biblioteca Marciana, Venice, It. VII 196 (8178), fol. 29v.

The inclusion of these groups in the 1589 legislation was partly a reflection of a substantial growth in the numbers of patricians who married women from artisan backgrounds, but it also articulated the broader Italian concern to protect noble status from contamination by outsiders by means of drawing increasingly rigid distinctions between noble and non-noble.[18] The three-generation rule emphasised the part played in a man's status by his ancestry.[19] The legislation of 1589 also established a new procedure, the *prova*, by which applications on behalf of potential non-patrician brides were to be presented and evaluated. An applicant had to meet a range of criteria. She was to be born of legitimate marriage. Her father and grandfathers should not have carried out *arte meccanica*, nor be known for infamy (guilty of major crimes). She and her mother should always have lived modestly and without a stain on their virtue.[20]

The formal procedure to examine the backgrounds and reputation of women wishing to marry into the patriciate remained largely unchanged until the end of the Republic in 1797. It enabled the *Avogadori* to examine written submissions and supporting documentation. Oral testimony by witnesses chosen by the applicants was complemented by testimony from other witnesses by the *Avogadori* to test the veracity of applicants' claims. Between them, the noble magistrates who posed the questions and evaluated the evidence, the nobles of the *Collegio* who took the final decision about social status, and the colourful dramatis personae of witnesses, wet-nurses, clergy, boatmen, merchants, artisans, lawyers, patricians and servants, offer detailed but sometimes confusing testimony over the dividing lines in early modern Venetian society and the part played in this by touch.[21]

How clear-cut were the criteria used to reject women wishing to marry patricians and to become the mothers of future members of the Great Council? The cases of Paulina Aivoldi Marcellini and Andrianna Ponte demonstrate that the *Avogadori* were faced with finding a balance

---

[18] Ventura, *Nobiltà e popolo*, pp. 301–3; Tucci, 'I mestieri nella *Piazza Universale*', pp. 319–20; L. Ferrante, 'Differenze sociali e differenze sessuale nella questione d'onore (Bologna sec. xvii)', in G. Fiume, ed., *Onore e storia nelle società mediterranee* (Palermo, 1989), pp. 106–10.

[19] Applicants in Venice for the status of *cittadino originario* also had to demonstrate three generations of freedom from *arte meccanica*: Zannini, *Burocrazia e burocrati*, 70.

[20] AdC 109, f.34.

[21] A. Zannini, 'Il "pregiudizio meccanico" a Venezia in età moderna. Significato e trasformazioni di una frontiera sociale', in M. Meriggi and A. Pastore, eds, *Le Regole dei mestieri e delle professioni. Secoli XV–XIX* (Milan, 2000), pp. 36–51, considers these issues in a longer-term perspective, based on the author's work on the *cittadini originari*.

between different criteria, often from different generations. Paulina Aivoldi Marcellini, a forty-three-year-old widow, applied in 1684. Andrianna Ponte applied eleven years later. Paulina's petition appeared to have a high probability of success. She was the daughter of one wholesale merchant and the widow of another. She had been educated at the convent of San Iseppo, in common with other women of status. Her mother had brought a substantial dowry into the marriage. There were even family links to a high-ranking churchman, the Papal Nuncio, Aivoldi Marcellini, who had died recently in Milan.[22] The magistrates who examined Paulina's case stated their reasons for rejection quite explicitly. They had severe doubts about the *civiltà* of her father because of the way in which he conducted his business and because of the occupations carried out by his relatives. Not only had he been seen selling goods directly to important customers, which involved touching these commodities, but his wife's sister, who lived in Malamocco, at the extremity of the littoral of the Lido, had married a baker.[23] Andrianna Ponte's application was turned down on the grounds that her grandfather had been a silk-spinner, an artisan, in spite of the fact that both her father and grandfather met most of the criteria of social status.[24] The *Avogadori*'s summary of the case concluded that 'there was universal agreement that both lived *civilmente*'. Silvestro Ponte, the grandfather, was described by witnesses as 'a very wealthy merchant' who, 'having lived with great *civiltà*, left many riches'. While the *Avogadori* might have discounted all this evidence because it was presented by witnesses nominated by the Ponte family to substantiate their claims, they did not do so. Although their own selection of witnesses was directed at the one area of doubt, whether or not Silvestro and Giovanni Antonio Ponte were engaged in unacceptable occupations at any time, some of the latter also corroborated this sense of a *civile* life style. A tailor who lived in the same parish of Santa Maria Nova as Silvestro Ponte remembered that he had many houses in the parish.[25]

It should have been much easier than this to identify artisans with manual work. Once again, it was not. We have already established that the authors of contemporary treatises on nobility excluded artisans from *vita civile* on the grounds that their manual work placed them beyond the pale. Tomaso Garzoni specified that it was not so much the work itself, but the nature of the raw material which was used, that designated an occupation as base and low in status. Castrators dealt with testicles.

---

[22] AdC 232, f.11.
[23] AdC 232, f.11.
[24] AdC 238, f.2.
[25] AdC 238, f.2.

Bowyers and catapult makers, whose occupations had been known since antiquity, used timber and animal intestines. Pork butchers were greasy. Dyers' faces were stained.[26] The problem arose from the distribution of work carried out by artisans. In common with most other European cities of the time, the Venetian manufacturing sector was hopelessly entangled with the process of selling what had been made. While there could be a lengthy chain linking the producers to the long-distance merchants who organised large-scale overseas exports, most master craftsmen were directly engaged in the retail trade. A minority were also wholesale merchants. Herein lay the problems facing the *Avogadori di Comun*. If wholesale merchants were believed to possess the virtues of *civiltà*, and many of the most prestigious had both successfully applied for the status of *cittadino de intus et extra* and achieved approval for their daughters to marry patricians, where was the line to be drawn? The question was not theirs alone. Families aspiring to upward social mobility of the kind who promoted their daughters and sisters as the potential wives of patricians also wished to place clear water between themselves and those engaged in *arte meccanica*.

There was a growing sense of self-esteem among the men who perceived themselves to be in some way beyond the world of the artisan. Evidence for this lies in the way in which the sons of men engaged in the world of production moved on to become lawyers and encouraged their sisters to marry into legal circles. This construction may also be placed on the evidence placed by the Weaver's Guild in the case of Cattarina Pirocco in 1695. Cattarina, the daughter of Marco Pirocco, and her patrician husband, Giacomo Antonio Marcello, had applied for their sons to be accepted as members of the Great Council. Their marriage had not been registered by the authorities. Indeed, it was one of the *Matrimoni Segreti*, legitimately administered by the Venetian Church, but recorded in registers stored far from the public gaze in the Palazzo Patriarcale.[27] The major potential stumbling block to the boys' eventual successful admission to the Great Council after six ballots in the *Collegio* in 1703 was Marco Pirocco's membership of the Weaver's Guild, the *Scola di tesseri*, as a master craftsman. The Weaver's Guild stated:

---

[26] Tucci, 'I mestieri nella *Piazza Universale*', pp. 328–9; Martin, 'The Imaginary Piazza', p. 445. Attitudes such as these were reinforced in the case of certain activities that were so 'dirty' that their practitioners were even excluded from artisan society. See K. Stuart, *Defiled Trades and Social Outcasts: Honor and Ritual Pollution in Early Modern Germany* (Cambridge, 1999); A. Blok, *Honoured Violence* (Cambridge, 2001), pp. 44–68.

[27] On the *Matrimoni Segreti*, see A. Cowan, 'Patricians and partners in early modern Venice', in E.E. Kittell and T.F. Madden, eds, *Medieval and Renaissance Venice* (Chicago, 1999), p. 27.

All weavers who wish to work or who do work at this occupation must be members *per maestri*. If they are not described as masters, they are not allowed to organise production. It is the practice that the sons of master craftsmen may be registered as masters, without having been *garzoni* [apprentices] or *lavoranti* [journeymen], and without having submitted a masterpiece. When they are masters, they make others work for them, even though they do not work. Those who are not the sons of masters, however, cannot become masters without apprenticeship or ten years as journeymen.[28]

This statement was followed by another, that, following a diligent search of the records of masters who had been trained as apprentices and served their time as apprentices, the names of Piero, Anzolo and Marco Pirocco had not been found.[29] The weaver's guild shared a growing tendency across Western Europe for guild masters to promote the interests of their sons above other candidates for the status of master by manipulating the rules in their favour.[30] While their statement in the Pirocco case may have been designed to present Marco Pirocco in the best possible light as a man who organised production without ever having engaged in the manual aspects of production, it also reflected a wish on the part of the dominant group of masters in the guild to project a higher social status.

Equally ambiguous evidence of status arose in the cases of Appolonia Bianchi, the non-patrician wife of the patrician, Piero Michiel di Antonio, and of Laura Petrobelli, the concubine and later the wife of the patrician, Carlo Corner di Hierolamo, whose sons applied for patrician status in 1678 and 1644, respectively. There is no record that either application was successful, and although Laura's earlier position as a patrician concubine may well have played a part in the negative decision, it is clear from the line of questioning by the *Avogadori* that it was her grandfather's occupation which concerned them most.[31] Valerio Bianchi, the father of Appolonia, was recorded in her baptismal entry as a *muschier*, a glover. He had a shop at the sign of the Lion di Francia. Because his name also appeared among the members of the mercer's guild, he therefore straddled the dividing line between producers and

---

[28] AdC 238, f.11.

[29] AdC 238, f.11.

[30] See for example, S. Cerutti, 'Group strategies and trade strategies: the Turin tailors guild and the late seventeenth and eighteenth centuries', in S.J. Woolf, ed., *Domestic Strategies. Work and Family in France and Italy, 1600–1800* (Cambridge and Paris, 1991), 102–47; J.A. Farr, *Hands of Honor: Artisans and their World in Early Modern France* (Ithaca, 1988); H. Kellenbenz, 'Zur Sozialstruktur der Rheinischen Bischofsstädte in der Frühen Neuzeit', in F. Petri, ed., *Bischofs und Kathedralstädte des Mittelalters und der Frühen Neuzeit* (Cologne and Vienna, 1976), pp. 118–45.

[31] AdC 231, f.94; 209, f.24.

retailers.[32] On the other hand, glovers were engaged in small-scale production. Their shops sold items in small quantities. They were associated with other socially doubtful activities whose business would have been well known to patrician customers, such as the perfumers who made their products smell sweeter.[33] Bianchi was known to several witnesses as a *cittadino*. Although he seems to have given up his shop and to have lived from an indirect income,[34] it was not enough to guarantee the future of his grandsons.

The case of Santo Petrobelli was in many ways analogous to that of Bianchi. He also was a shopkeeper who sold high-quality products manufactured under his direction. Petrobelli manifested signs of considerable social esteem. His shop was in one of the two arcades bordering on the Piazza San Marco, a high-rent prestigious location.[35] He followed the dress code of a man of *civiltà*. 'He dressed in silk, with a coat of damask or similar material which reached below his knees, and a silken *ferariol*', a garment worn by *cittadini*, but not by patricians.[36] He was the *gastaldo* [treasurer] of the confraternity of the Santissimi Sacramenti in the parish Church of San Maurizio. His portrait was displayed 'close to the high altar'.[37] Suspicions about his status arose because of two independent elements in his business which, when combined, potentially placed him among a group of men whose activities were entirely beyond the social pale, the charlatans, or quack doctors.[38] On the one hand, he sold oils and other distillations for medicinal purposes. On the other, in common with many other shopkeepers in the arcades along the Piazza San Marco, he placed a bench in the square, from which his products were also sold.[39]

---

[32] AdC 231, f.94, Tucci, 'I mestieri nella *Piazza Universale*', p. 325; for the wide-ranging activities of the mercers and their attempts to achieve a more enhanced social status in the later sixteenth century, see R. Mackenney, *Tradesmen and Traders. The World of the Guilds in Venice and Europe, c.1250–c.1650* (London, 1987), pp. 90–97.

[33] Garzoni, *La Piazza Universale*, p. 795. For the cultural significance of positive odours, see C. Classen, D. Howes and A. Synnott, *Aroma. The Cultural History of Smell* (London, 1994), pp. 51–92.

[34] AdC 231, f.94

[35] AdC 209, f.24.

[36] *Vestiva in sette et una vesteria sotto il ginocchio di Damaschino, o cose simili, et anco il ferariol le portiva di sette.* AdC 209, 24. For the ferariol, see G. Boerio, *Dizionario del Dialetto Veneziano* (Venice, 1856), p. 728.

[37] AdC 209, f.24. Testimony of Bortolo dei Bianch di Francesco, *pisier*.

[38] D. Gentilcore, '"Charlatans, mountebanks and other similar people": the regulations and role of itinerant practitioners in early modern Italy', *Social History*, 20, 3 (1995), pp. 297–314; D. Gentilcore, *Healers and Healing in Early Modern Italy* (Manchester, 1998), pp. 115–17.

[39] AdC 209, f.24.

The link with the behaviour of charlatans was only hinted at by the line of questioning directed at witnesses, but in 1649, a year after Carlo Corner's death, his widow Laura sent the *Avogadori* a strongly worded objection to the evidence which had been submitted: 'Those with evil intent have led the authorities to believe that Santo Petrobelli, my grandfather, was called the man of oils, owned shops and carried out the occupation of a charlatan.' She argued that this could not have been possible, both because her husband would never have considered marrying a woman of this social background – a point which lay at the heart of the debates about the social background of women worthy of marrying patricians – and because Santo's activities were entirely honourable. His was the thought behind the creation of the oils. Others manufactured and sold them. She presented the *Avogadori* with a new set of witnesses who confirmed that Santo never sold his goods from the bench in the Piazza.[40] Petrobelli could not have been a charlatan because one of the characteristics of this activity was its itinerant nature. He was well established in the city and had a shop in a select position. On the other hand, even the slightest association with such activity could be damaging and may well have been used to undermine the application on behalf of Carlo and Laura Corner's sons.[41] In a surprising admission, one of Corner's former servants testified that his master had told him that Laura was of low social status. A member of her family, either her father or grandfather, had sold oils in the piazza, and for that reason there could be some difficulties in demonstrating the boys' right to sit in the Great Council.[42]

Laura Trevisan, the wife of the patrician, Girolamo Barozzi di Antonio was described as a *persona ordinaria* by the patrician-born Capuchin friar, Father Marin. When pressed by the *Avogadori*, he replied that he had meant that she was neither noble, nor *cittadina* nor a person of status from the Terraferma.[43] Subsequent witnesses built up the detail to such an extent that Laura's sons were rejected in their search for patrician status. Laura and Barozzi had met in Istria (a Venetian territory now in present-day Slovenia), whence she had accompanied her father. Marco Trevisan was an iron merchant from the minor lagoon island of Burano, whose internal trade within the Venetian territories and the

---

[40] AdC 209, f.24.

[41] Attempts to blacken the social reputation of boys' families in these circumstances were not unknown. See A. Cowan, 'Innuendo and inheritance: strategies of scurrility in medieval and Renaissance Venice', in D. Cavanagh and T. Kirk, eds, *Subversion and Scurrility. Popular Discourse in Europe from 1500 to the Present* (Aldershot, 2000), pp. 125–37.

[42] AdC 209, f.24.

[43] AdC 238, f.18.

nature of the commodity traded placed him immediately at a level below the international merchants operating from Venice. Burano society offered fewer opportunities for social distinction based on occupation. Marco worked in the shop associated with this business. His son, Rocco, was a blacksmith: the iron trade could be seen as an adjunct to this occupation. Rocco testified that several of his sisters married artisans, fishermen and boatmen, although he himself succeeded in marrying into patrician circles. After going into business with Nobil Huomo Marco Barbaro, importing grain, he had married his niece, Chiaretta. Nothing more is known about her background. The information may only have reinforced the disquiet experienced by the patricians evaluating the status of the Barozzi sons.[44]

Men associated with the medical profession generally enjoyed high status as physicians or surgeons. In the case of the latter, however, there was always an element of doubt. This represented a major concern in the case of Laura Castello in 1607. Her father, Alessandro Castello, had been a member of the Venetian College of Surgeons since 1593. He worked for many convents and monasteries. His father was also known as a surgeon. They both dressed *a manega comedo*. Laura's mother was a patrician, admittedly only a member of the Candian (Cretan) branch of the Ruzzini family, but a patrician even so. It finally emerged that both Alessandro and his father Francesco had been barber-surgeons. At least, they had a barber's shop in the *sestiere* of Castello, conditions in which it was common for minor injuries to be treated. In the words of a man who had worked in the barber's shop in his youth, 'afterwards [Francesco] turned to treating people through surgery, and I believe that from the time of the plague [*contaggio*] he began to dress *a manega comedo* and to work as a surgeon'.[45] Opinions of barber-surgeons varied. Garzoni observed that their art was 'clean and neat, having as its end goal the cleanliness of the body'. He excluded them from his list of 'vile' occupations. On the other hand, Tiraguera stated that surgery was *mecchanica et illiterates*.[46] The Venetian College of Surgeons was always careful to distinguish itself from the guild of barbers, although contemporaries elsewhere were often less concerned about this distinction. In the absence of a qualified surgeon, the Terraferma city of Feltre petitioned for permission in 1580 to employ a barber-surgeon who had

---

[44] AdC 238, f.18.

[45] '*Et dopo si messe a medicar da cerusia, et credo dal contaggio in se vestisse a manega e comedo et si dottori in chirurgia*' (Leonardo Barbitonio di Domenico). AdC 109, f.30.

[46] Tucci, 'I mestieri nella *Piazza Universale*', p. 445; Donati, *L'idea di nobiltà*, p. 117.

been trained by one of the previous incumbents.[47] A list of Tuscan surgeons drawn up in the plague year of 1630 also included a number of barber-surgeons.[48] Surgery was itself regarded as a manual occupation, but one that counted among the liberal professions. It required its practitioners to come into direct contact with the human body and its effluvia.[49] On the other hand, the requirement for surgeons to study at university raised the occupation to a level almost equivalent to that of the physician.

The considerable care with which the *Avogadori* examined questions of social status related to a man's occupation may be illustrated by the case of Elisabetta Righetti, whose application to marry a patrician was submitted in 1689, but only approved by the *Colleggio* in 1705. There were considerable difficulties over her grandfather, the wine merchant, Lodovico Righetti, who was listed in 1630 as *vende vin alle Volpe*.[50] The ownership of a shop with a sign, in this case the sign of the wolf, placed him closer to merchants with shops, but also raised the possibility that he was primarily engaged in the retail trade. Merchants of food and drink rarely proposed their daughters as wives of patricians. Buying wine over the counter was less likely to be within the direct experience of the *Avogadori*. It would have meant mixing with artisans and others of even lower status. The wine trade had also been the subject of regulatory legislation earlier in the seventeenth century. Following a pause in the investigation, it was decided to examine the organisation of the wine trade in order to base the *Avogadori*'s decision on detailed information. A retired merchant in his mid-eighties who had specialised in importing Greek wines told them that there used to be fifty-four wine shops with signs between San Marco and the Rialto. These were *Magazeni*, where wine was sold both wholesale and retail. All had been closed down at a single stroke [*tutti in una volta*] by the *Senato* during the 1670s. The merchant was not asked to explain this, but it would appear that this

---

[47] R. Palmer, 'Physicians and surgeons in sixteenth-century Venice', *Medical History*, 23 (1979), pp. 451–60, esp. pp. 453, 455–6.

[48] C.M. Cipolla, 'The medical profession in Galileo's Tuscany', in C.M. Cipolla, *Public Health and the Medical Profession in the Renaissance* (Cambridge, 1976), pp. 77, 85.

[49] A Venetian physician, Gian Giacomo Strata, who had originally trained as a surgeon, was said to have combined *l'arte physical* with *l'operation manual, cioè la chierusia*: Palmer, 'Physicians and surgeons', p. 458. The choice of two contrasting terms, *arte* (for a profession based on lengthy study) and *operation*, for the manual activity of the surgeon is significant, placing the latter in the world of artisans and merchants. Surgeons were excluded from the Council in sixteenth-century Padua: Ventura, *Nobiltà e popolo*, p. 326.

[50] AdC 236, f.77.

action was taken to remove illegal wine shops that had not registered in the hope of avoiding taxes.[51]

Wine was also officially sold retail in *bastioni* and *osterie*. Other witnesses narrowed down the location of most of these *magazzeni* to the parish of San Luca in the Calle de Carbon, with a scattering in San Marco and San Zaccaria. Wholesale wine merchants, on the other hand, had their guild on the opposite side of the Grand Canal, in the parish of San Silvestro. Members comprised both merchants and *bastioneri*. It became clear that there was considerable confusion over the regulation of the wine trade in Venice. The *bastioneri* were regulated by the *Sette Savii della Mercanzia*, but this was so recent that few records existed, and certainly none which might have recorded whether or not Piero Righetti, Elisabetta's father, was among them. The clerks of several government offices were called before the *Avogadori*, but none was able to provide any definitive information. Eventually, one of the wholesale wine merchants explained that owners of wine shops in his experience did sell wine in the shops, but only wholesale. This information, together with confirmation that the shop at the sign of the wolf was a *maggazeno*, was enough to arouse considerable doubts about Righetti's *civiltà*.[52]

The *Avogadori*'s question in the Righetti case about the exact nature of the work carried out by the owners of shops was central to the consideration of the social status of the majority of men considered in this uncertain area. Merchants who did not own shops were above suspicion. Carlo Bottoni was described by a fellow merchant in 1621 as a merchant 'who was honoured in this city, trading particularly with Puglia, wealthy, but who never had a shop, nor carried out any vile or mechanical art'.[53] Domenico Cabrini was 'a wholesale merchant trading in all things. He did not have a shop'.[54] Owning a shop could have a variety of implications. It might mean an investment, similar to the ownership of land or real estate, in which the owner rarely participated at all in the day-to-day activities of the shop. It might also have been one of a series of enterprises, in which case he would not have spent much time physically in any one of them. Several men under investigation were reported as owning a number of shops at the same time, often drawing income from additional sources. Giulio Cesare Aivoldi Marcellini, the

---

[51] AdC 236, f.77; U. Tucci, 'Commerci e costumi del vino a Venezia in età moderna', *Quaderni della Rivista di Storia dell'Agricoltura*, 1 (1989), pp. 191–5.

[52] In this case, however, these doubts were not enough to convince the *Colleggio*, who voted in favour of Elisabetta's *prova*. AdC 236, f.77.

[53] AdC 109, f.34.

[54] AdC 214, f.26.

spicer, had three or four shops but also received an income from land near Lake Como that he had inherited from his father.[55] Others owned shops as an extension of manufacturing carried out in their own houses, or as outlets for goods imported wholesale from elsewhere.

Ownership of a single shop could also have been a full-time supervisory function. In every case, witnesses emphasised the division of labour between the shop owners and their subordinates, the *fattori* and *garzoni*, who carried out the manual labour of moving goods around, selecting it, wrapping it up and handing it to customers. Giovanni Girolamo Vento had a shop on the Rialto, trading in velvet, damask and say. His factor, Zuanne, did the selling, while Giovanni Girolamo spoke about his goods.[56] According to the barber who went to shave Giovanni Giacomo Bosello, the latter 'never worked manually in his shop, but had his *fattori* and many workers who worked for him'.[57] Giovanni Cossali 'bought and sold merchandise. For manual and inferior operations he had apprentices and other workers who packed the goods, and others who did what was needed for the shop'.[58]

The distinction between the supervisory role undertaken by merchants and other shop owners and *fattori* may have played a part in the rejection of Andrianna Ponte by the *Avogadori* in 1695. Her case was one of the few for which an official summary survives, listing the evidence and explaining the negative conclusions of the investigation. The conclusion that her grandfather, Silvestro, was a silk-spinner before he became a silk merchant has already been discussed. Doubts about the family's social status were compounded by the information that her father, Giovanni Antonio, had served as a *fattor* of the Badoer [patrician] and Gozzi [merchant] families. While one witness had explained that he was *Fattor General* for the Gozzi, 'in charge of all the business, and to whom all the other *fattori* were responsible', others had described Giovanni Antonio as working as an ordinary *fattor* beforehand, an experience which was not unusual for a young man training to become a merchant on his own account one day.[59] The activities which he carried out were largely administrative and secretarial. Ultimately, this was enough for the *Avogadori* to conclude that they were doubtful if the

---

[55] AdC 232, f.11.

[56] AdC 206, (cases not numbered). Case of Cristina Vento, 1639.

[57] AdC 222, f.48. Case of Cesare Basadonna, 1666.

[58] AdC 221, f.22, *Egli operava a vender e comprar mercantia, per le operationi poi manuali et inferiori havessi giovini et altri operaii, che si essertivano a far bolle, et alter, che recovero per esercitio della bottega.*

[59] See the case of the mercer, Bartolomio Bontempelli: G. Corazzol, 'Varietà notarile: scorsi di vita economic e sociale', in G. Benzoni and G. Cozzi, eds, *Storia di Venezia* VI. *Economia e Finanza* (Rome, 1996), pp. 780–83.

work of *fattor* should exclude Giovanni Antonio from association by marriage with the patriciate.[60]

This distinction between shop owners in a supervisory capacity and *fattori* and others who did the manual work becomes clearer following an examination of the detailed behaviour of merchants described by witnesses in these cases. One key distinction was the location in which merchants worked. They were not necessarily inside their shops. It was their task to stand outside and discuss business. They also devoted time to travelling between their homes, shops, warehouses and suppliers. Giovanni Giacomo Bosello manufactured woollen cloth in his house for sale in his shop and storage in his 'vaults' on the Rialto. 'He came into the shop from time to time but did not carry out any work there *because he was a merchant*'[61] (my emphasis). The description of a man as 'a merchant on the Piazza' was both value-based and literal. Merchants devoted much of their time to walking around either the Rialto or the Piazza San Marco, exchanging news, doing business and making their presence felt.[62] The concept of 'selling' clearly also had more than one meaning. Giulio Cesare Aivoldi Marcellini was described as selling his goods in the shop, but the witness immediately qualified this to give the conventional picture that he did not work or sell in the shop, only his young men. The latter sold goods manually by selecting them, wrapping them up, carrying them to the customer and handing them over.[63] Selling involved talking up one's merchandise. Santo Petrobelli 'sat in a chair and discoursed on the quality of his goods to those who came to buy . . . He showed them the certificates from the Health Office so that they would believe that his goods were perfect, wholesome, unique and rare.'[64]

Much of the merchant's work was administrative. Aivoldi Marcellini answered letters, came to his two shops in the evening, and sent money to the bank.[65] Zuanne Cosalli traded, sold and kept his accounts. On the other hand, before he took over the shop at the sign of the Unicorn from his relatives, the Morana, he had worked there as an employee, 'selling and buying merchandise, but leaving manual work to the young men and other workers'.[66] This suggests that there was a very thin dividing line

---

[60] AdC 238, f.2.

[61] *El capitava qualche volte in bottega, ma non operava niente perche era mercante.* AdC 222, f.48.

[62] Domenico Cabrini was described as *honoratissimo et delli principali della Piazza.* AdC 214, f.26. Bartolomio Vaura was *mercante principalissimo della piazza.* AdC 220, f.37.

[63] AdC 232, f.11.

[64] AdC 209, f.24.

[65] AdC 232, f.11.

[66] AdC 221, f.22.

between merchants who owned shops, and shop managers, in terms of the non-manual work that was carried out.

Once again, these clear distinctions were blurred by the realities of the working day. According to a dyer, Giovanni Giacomo Bosello di Marc'Antonio, a wool merchant, sometimes weighed out his merchandise. While most of his activity was involved in taking payment and selling his goods, he also touched it. The witness felt obliged to explain to the *Avogadori* that, while it was the task of the merchant's employees to weigh the wool, on occasion the master would also do so.[67] Giulio Cesare Aivoldi Marcellini sometimes also worked manually: 'Sometimes he sold and had many apprentices and *fattori*, sometimes he worked, but only a little, for he was only in the shop for short periods.'[68] Luca Pesenti and his father 'worked, sold and measured their goods; I believe that they also engaged in trade'.[69]

The mixed responses by the *Avogadori* and members of the *Collegio* towards these families who were in some way close enough to *arte meccanica* to be of uncertain social status were replicated in two analogous contexts, the assessment of *Cittadini Originari* (the highest in status of the Venetian *cittadini*, who were allowed to take on privileged positions in the chancellory and to trade freely abroad), and the judgments on and subjective responses to the social background of the men who successfully purchased patrician status for 100 000 ducats from the middle of the seventeenth century, when financial difficulties forced the Republic to break with tradition.[70]

Comparisons with Zannini's study of applications for *cittadino* status, which were examined in the same magistracy as the *prove di nobiltà* by *cittadino* notaries rather than patrician magistrates, leave the clear impression that the Venetian government not only used the same criteria for *civiltà* when granting *cittadino* status (absence of links with *arte meccanica*, and the retail trade, legitimate birth, appropriate dress *a manega e comedo*), but also manifested the same uncertainties over how to evaluate the evidence. One typically thorny case was that of the spicer,

---

[67] AdC 109, f.32.

[68] AdC 232, f.11. Testimony of Francesco Alcido di Cesare.

[69] AdC 233, f.25, *s'impiegavano, vendevano, misuravano, e credo facessero anco a lui negocii.*

[70] For applicants to the status of *cittadini originari*, see Zannini, *Burocrazia e burocrati*, pp. 69–76. Responses to newly aggregated families believed to be of low status are discussed in R. Sabbadini, *L'acquisto della tradizione. Tradizione aristocratica e nuova nobiltà a Venezia* (Udine, 1995), pp. 33–55; D. Raines, 'Pouvoir ou privilèges nobiliaires: le dilemme du patriciat vénitien face aux agrégations du xvii^e siècle', *Annales: économies, sociétés, civilisations*, 46 (1991), pp. 827–47; Cowan, *The Urban Patriciate*, pp. 84–6.

Zuan Bernardo Franceschi, whose three grandsons applied to become *cittadini* in 1577. Bernardo sold medicines and wax in his shop, where the goods were sometimes weighed out by the proprietor, and sometimes by his assistants. Their application was only approved at the third vote.[71]

Suspicion of the social status of new families who applied to purchase patrician status was reflected in the votes on each application in the Great Council. While it was common for votes opposing an application to be in the seventies or the eighties, families such as the Zolio, who received 709 votes in favour, 344 votes against and 34 abstentions, or the Minelli, who received 548 votes in favour, 346 against and 40 abstentions, were far from popular.[72] Both sold olive oil and salted fish.[73] An anonymous patrician commentator wrote of the new families, after they had been admitted to the patriciate, 'the great part of them were artisans, shopkeepers, oil-suppliers and small-scale merchants. I fear that their baseness has defiled the nobility more than noble status has refined their manners'.[74] His tone was substantially less virulent than some of the other contemporary comments on their lack of gentility.

The admission of new families into the patriciate placed a new focus on the two separate issues judged in the *prove di nobiltà*: what were the criteria according to which a women could be permitted to marry a patrician so that in due course their sons could sit in the Great Council, and what were the criteria for admitting men to the Great Council whose mothers were neither patricians nor had been married to patricians with the approval of the Republic? The evidence for the criteria governing social distinction in this discussion has drawn on both kinds of *prova*. The lines of the investigation and the decisions taken were often entirely consistent with each other, but there is some suggestion that the sons of unofficial mixed marriages were treated according to a harsher interpretation of the criteria than the women applying to marry patricians. The case of Andrea Pisani in 1654 is a good example. Pisani's parents, Lucietta Damiani and the patrician, Piero Pisani di Marin, married in the church of Sant'Elena in 1620. They did not apply to the government for permission to marry, and it was therefore necessary for both Andrea and his sister Chiara to apply for a *prova* once they had grown up so that he

---

[71] Zannini, *Burocrazia e burocrati*, pp. 69–76. See also A. Zannini, 'La presenza borghese', in G. Benzoni and G. Cozzi, eds, *Storia di Venezia*, vol. 7, *La Venezia Barocca* (Rome, 1997), pp. 225–72.

[72] Cowan, *The Urban Patriciate*, p. 85.

[73] Biblioteca Civico Correr, Venice, P. D. 613. C/IV. See also Sabbadini, *L'acquisto della tradizione*, pp. 43–4.

[74] G. Bacco, ed., *Relazione sulla organizzazzone politica della Repubblica di Venezia al cader del secolo decimo settimo* (Vicenza, 1846), p. 41; Cowan, *The Urban Patriciate*, pp. 85–6.

could sit in the Great Council and she could marry a patrician. Chiara Pisani's application was accepted *nem con*. Very little attention was paid to her. Her father was a patrician and her maternal grandfather a silk merchant.[75] The file on her brother was much thicker. Quite early in the investigation, one of the *Avogadori*, Zuanne Dandolo, intervened to say that no marriage certificate had been presented with the written evidence from the family, nor any documents attesting to the condition of Domenico Damiani, Andrea's maternal grandfather. His patrician uncle also opposed the application, arguing that Damiani was a silk-weaver, and the case went against Andrea.[76] Personal circumstances may have entered into this opposition, but the Pisani cases suggest that, while a girl with a patrician father had an advantage when applying to marry another patrician, to the extent that negative evidence about her grand-father could be conveniently ignored,[77] the road was much less easy for the sons of patricians wishing to enter the Great Council. Defending the purity of the membership of the Great Council was a subject of considerable discussion, but the potential benefits to members underlay many of the concerns raised in individual cases such as that of Andrea Pisani. The growing tendency on the part of patricians to disinherit heirs in their testaments if they were not 'members of the Great Council' was both an indication of an awareness that this was a distinct possibility as a result of the rise in mixed marriages, and an incentive on the part of the sons of patricians to ensure that they were allowed to become members.[78]

The Venetian legislation of 1589 to regulate the entry of non-patrician women to patrician circles through marriage established clear criteria for *civiltà*. By permitting women to enter the patriciate whose families had been free from the taint of *arte meccanica* for three generations, it was anticipated that, in future, patricians would only be borne by women of high status and good breeding. They also believed that this legislation would reinforce the barriers between patricians and those below them in Venetian society by preventing men who lacked *civiltà* from drawing on the positive benefits of kinship links with patricians. On the basis of the cases analysed in this essay, this legislation was only a partial success. It broke down for two main reasons. One was the sheer complexity of Venetian society and its economic organisation. Any attempt to identify occupations of great merit, such as long-distance wholesale merchants, doctors or even government officials, broke down in the face of the

---

[75] AdC 217, f.102.

[76] AdC 217, f.106.

[77] A. Cowan, 'Mogli non ufficiali e figlie illegittime a Venezia nella prima età moderna', *Quaderni Storici*, 114, 3 (2003), pp. 849–65.

[78] Cowan, 'Innuendo and inheritance', pp. 133–4.

ambiguities of what individuals did in order to earn a living, and how far different facets of their activities transcended straightforward divisions between making and selling, or between working in a shop and engaging in the abstract business of trade. This was compounded by the social ambition of those whose economic success had provided them with the wealth and means to adopt a lifestyle closer to patricians' than artisans'.

The second factor was the uncertain attitudes of the patricians themselves towards the criteria for *civiltà*. For the most part, the views of the *Avogadori* may only be seen through the prism of questions to witnesses. These were consistent with the laws setting out the basis for the *prove di nobiltà*. If there was any hint of *arte meccanica*, witnesses were pressed to give details. Even if the answers were a categorical denial of any association with *arte meccanica*, the question was frequently restated, but in greater detail, in case the witnesses had not understood the implications of the first question. From this, one might conclude that touch was the central indicator of the dividing line between manual and other work. On the other hand, in those cases where the judgments of the *Avogadori* are recorded, they frequently established that evidence suggesting *arte meccanica* was not valid. Giovanni Antonio Ponte was judged to be *civile*, in spite of the evidence that he had worked as a *fattor* in a merchant company. The frequent use of *dubbio* (doubt) in the wording of their judgments reinforces the view that not only were difficult investigations carried out with great care but also that the men entrusted with establishing clear social dividing lines were not entirely certain themselves.

Finally, there remains that puzzling evidence that, in several disputable cases of touch-related work, even though the *Avogadori* considered them to be beyond the social pale, subsequent voting in the *Colleggio* led to the woman's approval. While the length of time between the initial application and the final vote must be emphasised, much more needs to be known about the process of voting in the *Colleggio* in individual cases before we can deduce clear social attitudes from these approvals. These votes were no different from others in the various organs of Venetian government. In other words, they were highly political and susceptible to outside pressure from the parties involved.[79] In every case of a woman wishing to marry into the patriciate, there was a patrician family waiting to benefit from the projected marriage. In every case of a young man under consideration as a future member of the Great Council, he had a patrician father, who was determined to ensure the legitimate continuation of his family's status.

[79] D. Raines, 'Office-seeking, *Broglio* and the pocket political guidebooks in Cinquecento and Seicento Venice', *Studi Veneziani*, 22 (1991), pp. 137–94.

One recent study of the analogous investigations into men applying for *cittadino* status concluded that 'One has the impression of being present at a kind of *commedia* whose plot was known to both witnesses and interrogators.'[80] If this were entirely the case, then all participants would have known their lines and there would be little to learn. This analysis suggests that it was precisely because no one was quite sure of their lines the play has much to tell us.

## Further reading

A. Bellavitis, *Identité, mariage, mobilité sociale. Citoyennes et citoyens à Venise au xv^ie siècle* (Rome, 2001).

S. Chojnacki, *Women and Men in Renaissance Venice. Twelve Essays on Patrician Society* (Baltimore, 2000).

A. Cowan, *The Urban Patriciate: Lübeck and Venice, 1580–1700* (Cologne and Vienna, 1986).

E.E. Kittell and T.F. Madden, eds, *Medieval and Renaissance Venice* (Urbana, 1999).

R. Mackenney, *Tradesmen and Traders. The World of the Guilds in Venice and Europe, c.1250–c.1650* (London, 1987).

J. Martin and D. Romano, eds, *Venice Reconsidered. The History and Civilisation of an Italian City-State, 1297–1797* (Baltimore, 2000).

R. Sabbadini, *L'acquisto della tradizione. Tradizione aristocratica e nuova nobiltà a Venezia* (Udine, 1995).

G. Simmel (1997), 'The sociology of space', in D. Frisby and M. Featherstone, eds, *Simmel on Culture* (London, 1997), pp. 137–70.

A. Zannini (1993), *Burocrazia e burocrati in Venezia in età moderna: i cittadini originari (sec. XVI–XVIII)* (Venice, 1993).

---

[80] Zannini, *Burocrazia e burocrati*, p. 74.

# CHAPTER THREE

# Speaking and listening in early modern London

*Laura Wright*

This essay discusses the coexistence of the two dialects of English available to early modern London speakers, London English and the newly-emerging dialect of Standard English. It outlines how recent work in the field of historical sociolinguistics approaches the topic of social rank and social geography encoded in speech, using social network theory. One function of language is to exchange information, so that speakers and listeners can navigate their way around their world. This is the usual reason why adult speakers try to learn foreign languages. However, another primary function of language is to transmit socially salient features, so that a listener who is experienced in listening to a particular dialect and accent can infer social information about the speaker regardless of what that speaker is saying.

Typically, native speakers of London English today have (at least) their sex, age and social class encoded in their voices. Experienced listeners may even be able to make an educated guess about such personal matters as a speaker's political or sexual orientation, and whereabouts a working-class London speaker comes from, either East End or non-East End. This set of socially salient features varies from speech community to speech community. In present-day British English, social class is encoded in the voice because, historically, rank has been important in British society. Speakers with regional accents are marked for middle class if slight and for working class if broad. Speakers without regional accents, who use the Standard English dialect and the supraregional Received Pronunciation accent (sometimes known as 'BBC English' or 'the Queen's English'), are marked for middle class and above. This does not apply in other English-speaking communities. For example, in the United States, race is as socially salient as class, to the extent that listeners can often infer from a stranger's voice on the telephone whether that speaker is black or not. In Tristan da Cunha English, neither race nor class is socially salient, and neither is encoded in the islanders' voices. This is because the South Atlantic island of Tristan da Cunha has a small native population (265 in 2004), all of whom are mixed-race. The main socially salient divide in this speech community is whether an islander has spent time away from the island or not, and so it is this feature which is apparent to islanders listening to other islanders.

Listeners in early modern London would have heard various other languages spoken, as well as English. The seventeenth- and eighteenth-century *Proceedings of the Old Bailey*[1] mention people on trial in London from France, Italy, Spain, Portugal, Germany, Holland, Poland and Russia, amongst other places:

> An Indictment was likewise brought against a French woman, formerly a Servant to a person of quality for taking away a parcel of Jewels, Rings, and other Rich commodities, (formerly mentioned in the Gazett) of several hundred pounds value, being an Alien, she had the priviledge to have a mixt Jury de medie at Lingue, of French and English; she understood English pretty well, but could not speak it.[2]

> Michael Levi was indicted for stealing four pieces of velvet, being part of a man's coat, value 14s. six pieces of flowered silk, being part of a woman's gown, value 10s. the property of Lazarus Barnard, March 15. Lazarus Barnard, being a Polish Jew, and speaking the Hebrew language, Samuel Jacobs was sworn interpreter.[3]

The speech patterns of such foreigners were sometimes mimicked in the *Proceedings*:

> Edward Taylor, John Smithson, alias Smitton, and Joseph Phillis, were indicted for assaulting John Violone on the Highway, putting him in Fear, and taking from him a Hat, value 6s. April 3.
> John Violone. I ave noting to say to de Preesonars, but von day lass mont, I tink it vas de tree day of *April*, I vas to go home to mine house by St. *Ann Shurch*. It vas vary dark in de night, and dare vas von or two men, and so soon as I go cross de street, von take old of mine hat and pull me down, and den von nock me down upon de arm vid a great stick, and I taut mine arm vas broke, da take ava mine hat, but da do noting else, for so soon as I cry murder, de people put de candale in de street, and de teef run ava, and no body cash 'em till two week; and den de Coonstauble come and fesh me to de Shustice, and dare da tell ame I muss prosecute. I no tink of such a ting as prosecute, but da put it in mine head. Vell, I say, I vas rob, I lose mine hat, sis hour, sis time, but it vas dark night, and I no see oo take it avay, dat vas all I can tell.[4]

---

[1] T. Hitchcock and R. Shoemaker, eds, *The Proceedings of the Old Bailey* (http://www.oldbaileyonline.org) [22 October 2004]. There are some examples of cases involving speakers from Italy (T16840903-8), Spain (T17851019-56), Portugal (T16950508-16), Germany (T16900903-23), Holland (T16750707-5), Poland (T17510911-3) and Russia (T17730707-3).

[2] 7 July 1675, *The Proceedings of the Old Bailey*, Ref: t16750707=3.

[3] 2 May 1764, *The Proceedings of the Old Bailey*, Ref: t17640502-44.

[4] 10 May 1733, *The Proceedings of the Old Bailey*, Ref: t17330510-28.

George Wells, of Clerkenwell, was indicted for stealing a Hen, value
1s. 6d. the Goods of John Bishop, the 4th of November last.
John Bishop. Dare vas de Hen in my Yard, and it vas Dead, but
vader it dye or vas kill, me no can tell dat. And dare vas a leetell Boy
in de Yard, and he take a de Hen up, and say, *I vill have dis Hen.*
And dare vas anoder Boy, and dat vas de Preesoner at de Bar, and he
say to de leetell Boy, *No, you shant have a dis Hen, for I vill have it
for my Dog.* And so he take a de Hen avay from de leetell Boy, and
dat is all as I cant tell of de Mater.[5]

The Jury acquitted the prisoner, and the court granted him a copy of his
indictment. Both Violone and Bishop are represented as being unable to
pronounce the voiced and voiceless dental fricative in *the, there, month*
and so on, which is marked on the page as *d* and *t*. Their bilabial voiced
fricatives in *was, one, whether*, are represented on the page as *v*. This
kind of visual mimicry provides us with information about the informal
London speech of the day: for example, we can deduce that the word *one*
was no longer pronounced with a word-initial vowel in the 1730s but
had already developed the backglide with which it commences today,
and that the word *whether* had already lost its voiceless *wh* element in
London by the 1730s, which can still be heard in some present-day
Scottish and American accents.

From the late sixteenth- and seventeenth-century Bridewell Court
Records we know of dealings between London prostitutes and
Hanseatic traders from the countries around the Baltic who lodged in the
Steelyard:

Also she saieth that she wente with one Jane Revell to ratliffe at a
newe Inne, beinge the signe of the Lyon, within this vij Daies, and
there was two straungers of the stylliarde beinge britheren, one of
them dwelleth with the dowche poste in lumberstrete & thother
thereby with a merchante, and there they dyned and supped, and
from thence they came to the saide Janes Lodginge within Algate,
And there the eldest of the straungers had the vse of the bodie of
Jane Revell, and the saide Thomasen willed hir to come to the bell
in S$^t$ Jonestrete./ Also she saieth that she hathe bene kepte moste by
one Jon Above a stylliarde man at M$^{rs}$ Esgriges aboute a quarter of
ayere a goe, and there had the vse of hir bodie manie tymes, and he
gave hir iiij or v*li*.[6]

The same records tell of dealings between London prostitutes and
members of the Portuguese and French ambassadors' households:

Also she saieth that M$^{rs}$ Goldinge hath a Daughter which hath bene
dyvers tymes at the portingale ymbassatores house And had lx

---

[5]  8 December 1731, *The Proceedings of the Old Bailey*, Ref: T17311208-82.
[6]  Minutes of the Court of Governors of Bridewell and Bethlem, 2 June 1576,
fol. 13v.

crownes at tymes as *willia*m Mekyns saieth w*hi*ch M^{rs} Goldinge dwelleth nigh the stronde And is prevy to her daughters doeing*es*.[7]

> She sayeth the firste that had thuse of her body was a straunger and he Dwelte in Tower streate and he was the ffrenche Inbassators man he had thuse of her body iij or iiij tymes & gave her monye & ffullers wyef had thone halfe She sayeth the ffrenche Imbassadors Steward had thuse of her body aboute a yere past one tyme & gave her money.[8]

The Bridewell Court Records also provide evidence of London prostitutes visited by Spaniards and Italians, amongst other non-English speakers:

> He saieth also that one Peter the spanyorde at Anthony Goras whoe is nowe in spayne And wilbe here w*i*thin a moneth he hath a flat nose he is a noble whoremaster And he will haue eu*ery* Day a harlott/ And the said Peter lay w*i*th Jane Trosse and she picked then vj duble pistelott*es* out of his pokett/ He saieth that Thomas ffortene hath a garden by the spittell And thether come to him fyne wemen every weke ij or iij tymes He saieth also that w*illia*m Brownynge in Holbo*ur*ne vseth lewde delynge And many harlott*es* resorte to his house viz M^{rs} Breme Megge Goldsmyth M^{rs} Gomas He saieth also that M^{rs} whalley in Bisshopsgate strete is kept by one Pollyto a stranger at his garden at tower hill And she is also kept by Lusty M^r Carowe she is a noble fyne whore He saieth also that Acerbo velutelly is a notorious whoremonger.[9]

These various sources indicate that English as a second language was spoken in the capital, and that continental languages and continental accents were heard daily. Within Britain, the indigenous Celtic languages were more widely spoken during the early modern period than nowadays. As well as Scottish Gaelic, Irish Gaelic and Welsh, Cornish and Manx were still living languages, and visitors to the capital from those parts would have brought their speech to London with them.

Further, it is likely that creole languages were spoken in London. Creoles are language systems built out of two or more existing languages and, as a generalisation, would have been spoken by immigrant, poorer, city dwellers, the servants and slaves. The *Proceedings of the Old Bailey* extract of John Bishop's speech of 8 December 1731 given above shows some features typical of English-based creoles (for example, the *me no*

---

[7] Minutes of the Court of Governors of Bridewell and Bethlem, 26 June 1576, fol. 22v.

[8] Minutes of the Court of Governors of Bridewell and Bethlem, 15 December 1576, fol.100.

[9] Minutes of the Court of Governors of Bridewell and Bethlem, 28 June 1576, fol. 29, 30.

construction in *me no can tell dat*), although it also shows other non-creole features such as the modal auxiliary verbs *can* and *vill* ('will'), and is presumably a representation of English spoken with some substrate interference. The *Proceedings of the Old Bailey* do not provide verbatim early modern London creole data, because they are filtered through the court recorder's own English language system, and perhaps further filtered by an editor looking to entertain the reading public, but they do indicate that creole language systems were part of the soundscape.

As well as hearing foreign languages spoken by others, Londoners would have routinely incorporated words of foreign origin into their English, without necessarily knowing that they were of non-English etymology. Numerous words denoting foreign-produced everyday commodities had been borrowed into English in previous centuries, such as *raclefish*, 'type of stockfish', probably a strip of halibut, salted and dried, or *palingman*, a seller of a type of eel which was bought and eaten by Londoners, both words borrowed from Middle Dutch.[10] But despite the multiple language systems voiced aloud in early modern London, this essay will be confined to a consideration of just a few of the speech sounds of two of the English language dialects that early modern London listeners would have regularly heard. This is because sounds foreign to the speech patterns of native Londoners have been heard every day in the city for hundreds of years, whereas what is peculiar to the early modern period is the emergence of a supraregional dialect.

Early modern London English speakers, unlike those of previous centuries, had access to two 'native' dialects, although they would not have been as distinct from each other as they are nowadays because Standard English was only just coming into existence during the period. Citizens of London could speak in the London English dialect, or they could avoid specifically London features that were becoming stigmatised as vulgar.

Natural language is constantly subject to change. This is partly because people move, and so listeners are continually experiencing accents and dialects that are new to them; and partly because the next generation never quite replicates the speech of the previous one. All language is in a constant state of flux, and Standard English, being no exception, is a process rather than a fixed event. Before about 1400, speakers' voices were encoded for regionality; that is, speakers from different regions used different Middle English dialects, spoken with regional accents, with little if any implication for social rank. There was

---

[10] Mentioned in the fifteenth-century Custumals of the City of London. See L. Wright, *Sources of London English: Medieval Thames Vocabulary* (Oxford, 1996), pp. 10–45, 210.

as yet no such thing as a supraregional standard variety of English. The main supraregional varieties up to the late 1400s were Medieval Latin and Anglo-Norman, especially the kind of commercial written mixed Latin/Anglo-Norman/English business-type that was used by merchants, traders, estate managers and others engaged in business, although there is no particular evidence that this was ever a spoken variety.

In the late 1400s, this written trading language system became superseded by the new written dialect of English, which is now called Standard English, although it was not at the time, and which contained features from several regional dialects. Standard English is not just a mutation of London English or, as is sometimes claimed, London English informed by court speech and that of the universities of Oxford and Cambridge. It contains words that originated far from London or the South. For example, non-southernisms in Standard English are the *they/them/their* set (southern Old English had *he/hem/here*; the *th* is probably from Old Norse); or the plural present tense *are* form of the verb *to be* (southern Old English used *be* forms throughout the present tense paradigm). These forms show the influence of Old Norse-speaking settlers from the Danelaw area. The Standard dialect marking of the third person singular present tense verb paradigm with –*s* (that is, *I/you/we/they walk*, but *he/she/it walks*) is unlike other dialects, most of which level to –*s* throughout (that is, *I/you/he/she/it/we/they walks*), and some of which level to zero in all persons (that is, *I/you/he/she/it/we/they walk*). The many provincial visitors into the capital brought their regional Englishes with them, and Standard English has ended up as something of a haphazard repository of such visits, informed by many regional dialects but identical to none. Standard English did not begin as a top-down phenomenon imposed by those on high, be it a social or an educated elite.

This kind of claim has often been made, especially by eighteenth-century orthoepists, but Rissanen has shown how such claims usually postdate the acceptance of the feature under discussion into Standard English.[11] Rather, Standard English is an amalgamation of the language choices made by centuries of educated speakers and writers all over the country, writing for serious purposes such as religion, business, medicine, the law, journalism, literature, accounts, recipes, inventories, commonplace books and so on: all the reasons why one might write for posterity,

---

[11] M. Rissanen, 'Standardisation and the language of early statutes', in L. Wright, ed., *The Development of Standard English, 1300–1800. Theories, Descriptions, Conflict* (Cambridge, 2000). See also, in particular, with reference to multiple negation, still stigmatised in Standard English to this day, although present in all other Englishes.

as opposed to informal letters, diaries, shopping lists, ditties, and so on, written as ephemera. Standard English is not simply middle-class London English, as educated writing for serious purposes could be written anywhere in the country by writers born and raised in each and every province. It involved elements of levelling (that is, the removal of regional features that are very marked because they occur in only a few dialects) and avoidance of features that had become stigmatised because they were used by the masses, that is, uneducated and lower-rank speakers.

The process of stigmatisation is as yet poorly understood. For example, *ain't* remains stigmatised in Standard English, yet *aren't* is now acceptable, although it was not acceptable for some speakers as late as the early twentieth century.[12] Standard English has ended up with parts of systems. For example, as well as the third person singular present tense indicative –s, and *ain't* mentioned above, multiple negation is acceptable in every non-standard dialect, and was acceptable in all pre-standard English, but is not so in the Standard dialect. The tense now known as the 'historic present' or 'storytelling present' became stigmatised in written Standard English, although there is nothing obviously vulgar about it other, perhaps, than the fact that it is mostly used for relating anecdotes. An example comes from the Bridewell Court Records:

> my M$^{rs}$ wolde vse to go a night*es* (when M$^r$ ffarmo$^r$ was abedd) w$^{th}$ hir gowne & hir Pettie cote vnlaced as the mayde did saie to scratch his hedd, for I haue harde him Diu*ers* tymes call hir, & so one tyme it was my fortune to come out of the shoppe before my fellowes, M$^r$ ffarmors men beinge newe gon to bedd, I did see my M$^{rs}$ make hir selfe vnredie standinge in the chamber windowe nexte to M$^r$ ffarmo$^{rs}$ chamber, & when she was all vnlaced she **goeth** into M$^r$ ffarmo$^{rs}$ chamber, & I did steale vppe the stayres, to se what she wolde do there goinge in that order, & so I **see** hir come to the hether side of M$^r$ ffarmo$^{rs}$ bedd, & after she had stayed there a while, she wente to the further syde of of [*sic*] the bedd & there stayed also a good while, & so I colde see hir no long*er* at that tyme, but I colde not Judge whether she was afterwardes by the bedd, in the bedd or vppon the bedd, but after a while I harde M$^r$ ffarmo$^r$ give agreate puffe, & w*i*th the same the bedd gave agreate cracke, fie saieth she how you sweate, marrie saieth he I alwaies Do so, when I ame in the Countrie.[13]

Such usage of the present tense to relate past events is marked for orality, and if used nowadays in a written context (other than that of literature),

---

[12]  See A. Grove, *The Social Fetich* (London, 1907).
[13]  Minutes of the Court of Governors of Bridewell and Bethlem, 21 December 1575, fol. 220v.

would be regarded as uneducated. Yet it is glimpses such as this which allow us to see past the filter of the professional court recorder, and to listen to the speech of the day.[14] Another oral feature that is only represented in some written text types (such as court testimonies, drama, personal letters) is the pragmatic marker. Early modern London examples included *fie* and *marrie* in the extract above, and *what then*, and *whie* from further on in the same case: '. . . And ther they had one Christian Grene a fensers sister of whitefriers and they supped ther together One of the yonge men lacketh one eye another is a fat fellowe & not hyghe.'[15]

> then I tolde him, that there was suche tales broughte vppe on me, & the mayde that there sholde be some love betwene vs, w^ch was not so, & that those that broughte vppe suche talke wolde be beleved, when that we sholde not, & mighte wolde ou*er* come righte, what then, saieth he, lett them seeke their proofes that will do, not you saieth he to me, whie saied I what wolde yo^u haue me Do, then he saide to me abide the brunte to beare it of w^th hedd & sholders, & not to seeke for proofes.[16]

Pragmatic markers rarely carry any semantic meaning as such, but indicate the emotional temperature of the discourse. They can indicate topic changes, or give attitudinal information on the part of the speaker. As such, they tend not to proliferate in formal texts written for a wide audience, or for posterity, but cluster in everyday spoken discourse. So-called 'private' verbs are another feature of oral language rather than writing. These are verbs which express non-observable intellectual acts, such as the verb *to judge* in the extract from folio 220v, 'I colde not Judge whether she was afterwardes by the bedd'. Only the speaker could be aware of whether he could pass judgment or not; an onlooker could not know this. Another feature typical of speech-based texts is the use of *deictic* terms; that is, words which change their referent each time they are used. In the extract from folio 220v, the writer uses the proximal marker *hither* ('the hether side of M^r ffarmo^rs bedd') and the distal marker *further* ('the further syde of the bedd'). *Hither* and *further* only carry any meaning in relation to the speaker's own position, closer to or away from the speaker's point of perception. The text from which these

---

[14] For further discussion of this court case, see L. Wright, 'On the construction of some early modern English courtroom narratives', in G. di Martino and M. Lima, eds, *English Diachronic Pragmatics* (Naples, 2000), pp. 79–102.

[15] Minutes of the Court of Governors of Bridewell and Bethlem, 26 June 1576, fol. 22v.

[16] Minutes of the Court of Governors of Bridewell and Bethlem, 21 December 1575, fol. 220v.6.

extracts are taken is a personal written statement, ostensibly by one person, although it has been copied down by the court recorder. Whether that recorder has changed anything we cannot know, but when features co-occur that are not usually represented in high ratios in written Standard English, but which are commonplace in spoken English, then it is reasonable to assume that the written text contains features from someone's spoken usage. In general, as well as the people immediately present in the court, and the future readers of the court minutes, the society and culture to which speakers belong are also part of the audience and constrain the writer, whether consciously or unconsciously.

Today, speakers in London use either the Standard English dialect with a Received Pronunciation accent, or, London English with a London English accent (which differs from East London to West London), and the two systems simply coexist side by side. Social class determines which variety a speaker uses, and by and large speakers do not shift; they are either London English speakers or Standard English speakers. At the start of the early modern period, speakers' level of education and social rank were just becoming encoded in their voices, and historical sociolinguists attempt to track this development. The seeming paradox facing historical linguists is that dialects show stasis on the one hand, whereby regional features are transmitted from generation to generation and perdure for hundreds of years; and change on the other, whereby every visitor from elsewhere potentially donates some of their language to the locals.

For historical sociolinguists, a popular current methodology, not limited to language study, is that of social networks. Pathologists, for example, use it to examine how viruses spread throughout a population. In the field of linguistics, it was first tailored for use by James and Lesley Milroy. The Milroys pioneered the application of social network theory to dialect change by surveying separate speech communities within the city of Belfast in Northern Ireland. They posited certain opposing forces which determine whether elements of a speaker's language system stay the same or whether they change. Change may be due either to outside influence or to internal systemic pressure, as language changes slightly from generation to generation, and the interaction between the two. The Milroys are particularly interested in the effects of language contact causing change, and so they looked at the ways in which speakers come into contact with speakers from outside their local area, and how language is transmitted from speaker to speaker. Social network theory is based on working out patterns of human interaction. With regard to language, the Milroys have shown how some speakers live in strong-tie, multiplex, dense networks. This means, essentially, that such speakers do not know very many people, and that they speak to the same people over and over again. Not much influence from elsewhere comes their way. Secondly, they studied speakers who live in weak-tie, loose social networks. These are people who come into contact with strangers on a regular basis. For example, they may travel away from home to work. They become conduits of language change, as they are constantly hearing forms that are foreign to their own language system, which they then adopt into their own speech, and pass on, in turn, to their interlocutors.

How might this have worked in early modern London? We can begin by assuming numerous small-scale London communities containing dense, multiplex networks of lower-rank speakers. For example, it is interesting to plot the (temporary, multiple) residences of prostitutes as they came before the Bridewell Court in the late sixteenth century. Although these women moved about the City and the West End, we hear of specific areas where they were wont to work, such as the Whitefriars.

> She saieth that one John Shawe and his wiffe dwellinge late in white friers and nowe by S^t laurens churche are bothe bawdes and wold haue had her to lye in ther house Also Elizabeth Joynour lay in his house a longe tyme And many prentises resorted thether then/ She saieth that Thomas wysse and his wiffe in the white friers are bawdes And he is a whoremonger And kepeth Elizabeth Cowper and others . . .

> . . . And he brought iiij merchantes seruauntes as she thought them to westminster to M^rs Bremes lodgeinge And from thense they went to one Stalles house at wolstabel hall And ther M^rs Stalle beinge full of the poxe and a naughty pack And ther they had one Christian Grene a fensers sister of whitefriers and they supped ther together One of the yonge men lacketh one eye another is a fat fellowe & not hyghe . . .[17]

In dense networks, speakers know each other in more than one social capacity. For example, as well as being neighbours, they may also be co-workers at the same enterprise, or perhaps be relatives. They regularly have the same daily routines, such as drawing water, washing clothes, visiting shops, or church, or drinking places. Alternatively, we could track the daily routine of a high-ranking citizen, visiting certain coffeehouses, shops in the Royal Exchange, offices and dining at friends' houses (an instance might be Samuel Pepys, with his visits to the Navy Office and the court).[18] This too would constitute a dense, strong-tie

---

[17] Minutes of the Court of Governors of Bridewell and Bethlem, 26 June 1576, fol. 22v.

[18] To pick a day at random from Pepys's diary, on 17 February 1663, Pepys went to his office in the morning, then dined with Mr Pett. He then went to the

network, in that the geographical area covered might be quite wide, but such a citizen would have met and revisited the same people repeatedly, and would have dealt frequently with citizens from within the same social class. Their paths would have crossed frequently and they would have interacted regularly and repeatedly.

In opposition to this, we can posit the larger-scale community of the entire city, made up of numerous weak-tie networks, containing both the mainstream native community and the various incomer groups, be they from elsewhere in Britain speaking in regional dialects, from elsewhere in Britain speaking another language, or from abroad, speaking other languages. The prostitutes of the Whitefriars would have come under weak-tie conditions each time they interacted verbally with a client from outside their own dense network, as would the socially active Pepys, every time he interacted with a stranger. Under weak-tie conditions, speakers may interact on one occasion only, or in one direction, such as from mistress to kitchen-maid, where the speaking rights are non-reciprocal.[19] The fascinating yet commonplace occurrence of long-term dwellers under the same roof having different dialects and accents can be accounted for by the fact that such speech interaction is not really a dialogue. The master or mistress issues orders, but the slave or servant cannot talk back as an equal, saying what they want when they want. Nevalainen and Raumolin-Brunberg posit these two levels of abstraction with regard to the city speech community.[20] The abstraction is useful

---

Temple to discourse with Mr William Montague about borrowing money, and then went to Westminster to Sir W. Wheeler to talk about the same subject. Then he went to my Lord of Sandwich's to report on his progress in borrowing money on his behalf. Pepys then went home to his wife and sister-in-law, where they played upon their musical instruments. On the way, he gave Mr Pickering a lift in his coach. He then went back to his office for a while, and then home and to bed: R. Latham and W. Matthews, eds, *The Diary of Samuel Pepys: a New and Complete Transcription* (London, 1971), vol. 4, pp. 45–9.

[19] B. Capp, *When Gossips Meet. Women, Family and Neighbourhood in Early Modern England* (Oxford, 2003), pp. 127–84.

[20] For more information about social networks, see, for example, L. Milroy (2001), 'Social networks', in J. Chambers, P. Trudgill and N. Schilling-Estes, eds, *Handbook of Variation and Change* (Oxford, 2001), pp. 549–72; J. Milroy and L. Milroy, 'Exploring the social constraints on language change', in S. Eliasson and E. Hakon Jahr, eds, *Language and its Ecology: Essays in Memory of Einar Haugen* (New York, 1997), pp. 75–104; L. Milroy, 'Social network analysis and language change: introduction', in I. Tieken-Boon van Ostade, T. Nevalainen and L. Caon, eds, *Social Networks and the History of English, European Journal of English Studies* (special issue), 4, 3 (2000), pp. 217–23; J. Milroy and L Milroy, 'Mechanisms of change in urban dialects: the role of class, social network and gender', *International Journal of Applied Linguistics*, 3, 1 (1993), pp. 57–78; L. Milroy and J. Milroy, 'Social network and social class: towards an integrated

because dialectal features can be envisaged as starting life under the intense speech conditions of the small-scale localities populated by dense, multiplex, strong-tie speech communities, and then diffusing out to the larger community as a whole. Thus cities can be both home to speakers of each and every language and dialect on earth, and yet still develop their own unique dialects and accents.

Nevalainen and Raumolin-Brunberg have pioneered study of the effects of social rank on the speech patterns of early modern letter writers, many of whom were Londoners. In a series of books and articles they detail the results of their current project on variation and change in early modern English.[21] Although I shall draw attention to just one study, the development of the use of the pronoun *you*, and their emphasis on variation, Nevalainen and Raumolin-Brunberg and their research group have studied many more features than this, and in finer detail with more informants. My purpose here is to present their methodology (in a pared-down way) in order to show how they study their subject.

Nevalainen and Raumolin-Brunberg report the rates of introduction of the second person pronoun *you* in the subject function,[22] and the abandonment of the old nominative form *ye*, in the letters included in their *Corpus of Early English Correspondence*. (For example, the old, outgoing form, *ye are in good helthe*, as opposed to the new, incoming form *yow have not received hit*).[23] The first instances of *you* in subject

---

sociolinguistic model', *Language in Society*, 21, 1 (1992), p. 126; J. Milroy and L. Milroy, 'Linguistic change, social network and speaker innovation', *Journal of Linguistics*, 21 (1985), pp. 339–84; I. Tieken-Boon van Ostade, 'Social network analysis and the history of English', and 'Social network analysis and the language of Sarah Fielding', in I. Tieken-Boon van Ostade et al., eds, *Social Networks*, pp. 211–16, 291–301; I. Tieken-Boon van Ostade, 'Social network theory and eighteenth-century English: the case of Boswell', in D. Britton, ed., *English Historical Linguistics 1994* (Amsterdam and Philadelphia, 1996), pp. 327–37; T. Nevalainen, 'Mobility, social networks, and language change in early modern England', *European Journal of English Studies*, 4, 3 (2000), pp. 253–64.

[21] T. Nevalainen, *Historical Sociolinguistics: Language Change in Tudor and Stuart England* (London, 2003); T. Nevalainen and H. Raumolin-Brunberg, 'The changing role of London on the linguistic map of Tudor and Stuart England', in D. Kastovsky and A. Mettinger, eds, *The History of English in a Social Context. A Contribution to Historical Sociolinguistics* (Berlin and New York, 2000), pp. 279–337. See also the extensive lists posted under publications at http://www.eng.helsinki.fi/varieng/ from the Research Unit for Variation and Change in English at the University of Helsinki.

[22] T. Nevalainen and H. Raumolin-Brunberg, eds, *Sociolinguistics and Language History. Studies based on* The Corpus of Early English Correspondence (Amsterdam and Atlanta, 1996), pp. 65–6.

[23] Nevalainen and Raumolin-Brunberg, eds, *Sociolinguistics and Language History*, 63.

function appear in the fourteenth century, increase over the fifteenth century, and *ye* is finally superseded altogether in the sixteenth century. During the changeover period both *ye* and *you* forms could coexist in the same letter. Nevalainen and Raumolin-Brunberg divided the letter writers in their Corpus according to social rank. The social ranks consist of the nobility (15 writers, 34 004 words), the upper gentry (11 writers, 63 136 words), the lower gentry (13 writers, 9485 words), the upper clergy (six writers, 6350 words), merchants (four writers, 70 792 words), a group they label 'social climbers' (four writers, 80 085 words) and the non-gentry (ten writers, 13 976 words). They then divided the letters according to date. The first period, 1520–1550, showed the ratios indicated in Table 3.1.

*Table 3.1    Letter writers, by social rank, London*

| Rank | You (%) |
| --- | --- |
| Nobility | 8 |
| Upper gentry | 48 |
| Lower gentry | 36 |
| Upper clergy | 16 |
| Merchants | 25 |
| Social climbers | 26 |
| Non-gentry | 29 |

There were no instances of *ye* in subsequent periods, as *you* had completely taken over its function. In the period 1520–1550, the upper gentry had advanced furthest in their *you* usage at 48 per cent. By contrast, the nobility at 8 per cent, followed by the upper clergy at 16 per cent, were the most conservative and the least likely to use this incoming form. The merchants, social climbers and non-gentry all used *you* around a quarter of the time. One point, which may be salient, is that the nobility and the upper clergy frequently used secretaries to draft and copy their letters, which might account for their conservative usage.[24] However, in Nevalainen and Raumolin-Brunberg's earlier pilot study they found that royal usage – written by secretaries but signed by the monarch – showed a 49 per cent usage of *you*. Such a breakdown does not, of course, provide an explanation as to why the nobility might be so conservative whilst the upper gentry are so innovative. Moreover,

---

[24] Nevalainen and Raumolin-Brunberg, eds, *Sociolinguistics and Language History*, pp. 65–6.

that the upper gentry were innovative with regard to the introduction of *you* does not mean that they were innovative with regard to other grammatical features: each one has to be studied in its own right, and has its own social trajectory. The lesson to be drawn from this investigation is that early modern Londoners heard much variation in the speech of their fellow citizens, and they could sometimes use this variation to deduce social information about the speaker.

To conclude, there was much variation in the speech of early modern Londoners (as indeed there is today), and some of it came to be encoded for social class. This was a point of departure from previous centuries. Social network theory provides a mechanism for investigation, but it does not provide an explanation as to why this process came to fruition in the early modern period. In this essay, I have tried to present some information that might parallel historians' discourse of cultural transfer. Linguists regard cities as *loci* of development and change. They consist of numerous small, dense speech communities sites of collective memory with many weak-tie networks to speakers elsewhere. In some ways it could be argued that the difference between speakers in cities and small remote communities lies not so much in the numbers of speakers (because, in both cases, speakers live in dense, multiplex networks), but in the presence for city speakers of weak-tie networks to speakers elsewhere (be it hinterland, provinces, other cities, or other nations) and the corresponding absence for speakers in remote or small communities of weak-tie networks to speakers from elsewhere.

Early modern Londoners heard foreign language systems spoken in their city, both from within and outside Britain, and forms of English that were informed by other substrate languages, as in the *Proceedings of the Old Bailey*. They heard many different British dialects spoken by visitors from other regions, and from within the London region they heard both the London English dialect and accent, and the newly-emergent Standard English dialect with its unique forms. Historical linguists attempt to be sensitive to spoken language by identifying clusters of oral features (such as use of the first person pronoun, pragmatic and deictic markers, and so on, mentioned above); and by identifying potential contrasts, such as a choice of *you* rather than the alternatives *ye* or *thou*, which carried social information. Essentially the process of identification of all such features is one of comparison, which is increasingly made easier by the compilation of large databases of text types.

**Further reading**

T. Hitchcock and R. Shoemaker, eds, *The Proceedings of the Old Bailey* (http://www.oldbaileyonline.org).

R. Lass, ed., *1476–1776; The Cambridge History of the English Language*, vol. 3 (Cambridge, 1999).

R. Latham and W. Matthews, eds, *The Diary of Samuel Pepys: a new and complete transcription* (London, 1995).

L. Milroy, *Language and Social Networks*, 2nd edn (London and New York, 1987).

T. Nevalainen, 'Mobility, social networks, and language change in early modern England', in I. Tieken-Boon van Ostade, L. Caon and T. Nevalainen, eds, Special Issue: Social Networks and the History of English, *European Journal of English Studies*, 4, 3 (2000), pp. 253–64.

T. Nevalainen, *Historical Sociolinguistics: Language Change in Tudor and Stuart England* (London, 2003).

T. Nevalainen and H. Raumolin-Brunberg, 'Social stratification in Tudor English?', in D. Britton, ed., *English Historical Linguistics 1994: Papers from the Eighth International Conference on English Historical Linguistics* (Amsterdam and Philadelphia, 1996), pp. 303–26.

T. Nevalainen and H. Raumolin-Brunberg, eds, *Sociolinguistics and Language History. Studies Based on The Corpus of Early English Correspondence* (Amsterdam and Atlanta, 1996).

T. Nevalainen and H. Raumolin-Brunberg, 'The changing role of London on the linguistic map of Tudor and Stuart England', in D. Kastovsky and A. Mettinger, eds, *The History of English in a Social Context. A Contribution to Historical Sociolinguistics* (Berlin and New York, 2000), pp. 279–337.

L. Wright, ed., *The Development of Standard English, 1300–1800. Theories, Descriptions, Conflicts* (Cambridge, 2000).

L. Wright, 'The space of English: geographic space, temporal space and social space', in C. Tschichold and D. Spurr, eds, *The Space of English* (Tübingen, 2005).

# CHAPTER FOUR

# Engineering vision in early modern Paris

*Ulf Strohmayer*

The year was 1603. It is said to have been a daring undertaking, no less so for having been ventured by a king. Wooden planks had to be moved and fastened, access to the construction site had to be secured, and still some involved in the activities of the day fell into the river underneath. Yet Henry IV, King of France and self-appointed master builder of Paris, insisted on being the first person to cross what was in 1603 the fifth and newest bridge spanning the river Seine in its entire length.[1] Thus inaugurated, a year before being fully finished and becoming useful as a traffic thoroughfare, the Pont-Neuf connected the historically dissimilar north, or right (*droite*) and south, or left (*gauche*) banks of the city's main fluvial artery in a more or less direct fashion, touching the Ile de la Cité at its most westerly and marginal point.[2]

This anecdote involving Henry IV's determination would probably not have survived (or even been invented) had it not been for the fact that the Pont-Neuf was decidedly unlike the existing bridges in Paris. This essay analyses the many facets of this difference and deploys them in an attempt to contextualise an early, but vastly influential, form of modernity. Sensual perception, as we shall see, played a crucial role in this process, but was itself conditioned by, and contextualised within, novel spaces. By analysing and focusing primarily on the built environment of the city, the essay underscores the importance of material conditions for elementary, epochal changes. It argues that the invention of the city as a visually appreciated entity paved the way for a far-reaching reappraisal of 'the visual' within Western societies. The Pont-Neuf, as we shall see, was a key site implicated in this change, as well as facilitating it.[3]

---

[1] Pierre de L'Estoile in 1609, cited in H. de Carsalade du Pont, *La municipalité parisienne à l'époque d'Henri IV* (Paris, 1971), pp. 242–3.

[2] For contextual reasons alone, it is worthwhile remembering that the number rose to ten by 1635 alone: A. Fierro, *Histoire et Dictionnaire de Paris* (Paris, 1996), p. 1088.

[3] The vast amount of primary sources related to the construction of the Pont-Neuf – of which a large amount has been pre-selected and is now contained in P. de Lasteyrie, 'Documents inédits sur la construction du Pont-Neuf', *Mémoires*

The anecdote that opens this essay, although little more than an embellishment of the reign of Henry IV, highlights the importance ascribed to the Pont-Neuf by contemporaries and later generations alike. Although merely one of many royal construction sites within the city of Paris at that time, the Pont-Neuf occupied, and to some extent still occupies, a privileged position in the public imagination of the French capital. Part of this appeal is undoubtedly owed to its central position within the urban geography of the city. Few tourists can avoid seeing the Pont-Neuf when they visit Paris. Yet 'being seen' was arguably the least of the many concerns that guided the construction of the bridge. On the other hand, as we shall note shortly, the 'visual sense' was not altogether absent from those concerns.

In order to understand the particular opening towards modernity embodied by the Pont-Neuf, it is imperative that we place its construction within a larger context. The sixteenth century was one of change and unrest in France. Chief amongst the many causes of such upheavals were, arguably, the withering of royal powers through the spread of the Reformation within France, as well as non-religiously motivated forms of aristocratic insubordination. Crucially, both brought forth a remapping of loyalties and dependencies across France. The result was at least half a century of civil wars. The beneficiaries of these disruptions at the expense of both the Crown and the Church, especially during the second half of the sixteenth century, were chiefly the regional aristocracy. As well as religious divisions and the political posturing that was not uncommon in early modern Europe, there was a much wider European 'price revolution' which devalued many a commoner's savings in the wake of a massive and inflationary influx of precious metals from the Americas. Together, these broad tendencies shaped what has been described as *une civilisation de l'angoisse* (a civilisation of anguish) for the majority of French citizens living at that time.[4]

---

de la Société de l'Histoire de Paris et de L'Ile-de-France, 9 (1882), pp. 1–94, and Y. Metman, ed., *Le régistre ou plumitif de la construction du Pont-Neuf* (Paris, 1987) – has been presented and analysed in F. Boucher, *Le Pont-Neuf*, 2 vols (Paris, 1925); R. Pillorget, *Paris sous les premiers Bourbons, 1594–1661* (Paris, 1988) and, to especially profitable ends, in H. Ballon, *The Paris of Henry IV. Architecture and Urbanism* (Cambridge, Mass., 1991). In addition to these, I have consulted documents contained in the séries GAZ and VD at the Archives de Paris (pertinent especially to the later construction on the bridge), séries E35B, H², M 215–34 and Z at the Archives Nationales and numerous sources and descriptions at the invaluable Bibliothèque Historique de la Ville de Paris. I am grateful to everyone working at these and other truly central institutions for their constant help and assistance.
[4] R.J. Knecht, *The Rise and Fall of Renaissance France, 1483–1610* (London, 1996), p. 370.

These, and related developments, brought an end to a Renaissance culture only recently introduced to France during the reign of Francis I and hastened the demise of Humanist modes situating a new and partly secular understanding of humankind. At the same time, however, they contained within themselves the seeds of new times indeed: of new *things* to come. Nowhere did this nascent modern time show itself more clearly than in the city of Paris, the emerging principal city within a predominantly rural country. 'In Paris, France boasted the largest city west of Istanbul' in the early modern period,[5] the inhabitants of which increased 'from 250 000 to 450 000 between 1550 and 1650, during which period the kingdom's population registered no overall increase'.[6] It was here, in Paris, that a still embryonic capitalism created the first real proletariat in modern French history. It is thus no accident that these very same urban centres became the ground in which novel forms of technology took root within the everyday life of people. From late fifteenth-century printing presses to the merchant activities that were increasingly structured by, and around, novel forms of technological progress, life increasingly became governed by technical change.[7] New forms of capital emerged which created new classes and class conflicts which, together with a general secularisation of daily practices, led to a new appreciation of the present moment as something distinct from both antiquity and the more recent past.[8]

The place that created a fertile context for these momentous changes was itself far from a stable political entity: Paris had been the capital of France since 987, but it lost whatever 'capital' image it might have had during the Middle Ages following the defeat of the French crown at Agincourt and the ensuing retreat of the kings and nobles of France to

---

[5] P. Benedict, 'French cities from the sixteenth century to the Revolution: An overview', in P. Benedict, ed., *Cities and Social Change in Early Modern France* (London, 1989), p. 8.

[6] Benedict, 'French cities', pp. 24, 28.

[7] Mention of 'technologies' in this context should not be understood to imply the absence of 'technologies' of some kind in pre-modern societies. The modernity ascribed to the kind of technologies alluded to here – printing of books and paper money, map making, warfare – shares an emphasis, largely absent in pre-modern technologies, upon an abstract notion of 'reproducibility' that was granted by dismantling. Increasingly, the present worth or value of technologies depended on some absent potential needed to be realised for it to make its presence felt.

[8] This transition has been documented and analysed most competently in H. Heller, *Labour, Science and Technology in France, 1500–1620* (Cambridge, 1996). He also notes that the civil wars of the second half of the sixteenth century brought forth not so much a disruption of this 'technologisation' of everyday economic activities but a shift towards more practical and empirically relevant forms of learning about technologies (cf. pp. 97ff).

places other than the centre of the Ile de France. The last of the Valois kings of France, in particular, nourished such a dislike for Paris that for long periods in the sixteenth century the royal court embodied not a stationary but a displaced and peripatetic form of existence, travelling the length and breadth of the country for almost ritualistic relocations of court life. The legacy of the highly material imprint of these movements can still be encountered in the form of the castles and renovated chateaux, especially along the Loire valley in central France. All of this changed with Henry IV's decision to re-establish Paris as the undisputed capital of France. Following his entry into the city on 23 March 1594, nine months after having celebrated the famed mass that made his succession to the throne acceptable to the Catholic majority of France,[9] he decided to reside more or less permanently in the largest city of the realm.[10] This resolve in turn set off a flurry of building activities, with the aristocracy now eager to establish themselves permanently close to the centre of power, thus adding pressures to a revitalised real estate sector and furthering the aims of commerce and trade. Sully, Henry IV's choice for longer-term strategic planning, adapted the geography of Paris to cope with the changing political context by deciding to cultivate the Marais, a swampy area immediately to the east of the city, and by encouraging the construction of a large number of *hôtels* or aristocratic urban residences in this new neighbourhood. The still majestic ensemble on the present-day Place des Vosges (known as the Place Royale in the early seventeenth century) bears witness to the spirit and the needs of the time.

It is within this admittedly sketchy context that the construction of the Pont-Neuf acquires its significance. Conceived in 1578 under Henry III, the last Valois king of France, and begun during his reign,[11] the bridge was fully completed in 1604 under Henry IV, the first Bourbon king of France, after, as we have seen already, the disruptive influences caused by

---

[9] M. Wolfe (1993), *The Conversion of Henry IV. Politics, Power, and Religious Belief in Early Modern France* (Cambridge, 1993).

[10] D. Thompson, *Renaissance Paris: Architecture and Growth 1475–1600* (Berkeley, 1984), p. 50.

[11] H-L. Dubly, *Ponts de Paris à travers les siècles* (Paris, 1957), p. 118, notes that, in 1556, Henry II already contemplated the construction of a bridge at the site of what was to become the Pont-Neuf. According to this source, his scheme (for which I could not find any supporting evidence) never received any support from the *prévôt des marchands* (effectively the mayor of Paris); cf. B. Diefendorf, *Paris Councillors in the Sixteenth Century. The Politics of Patrimony* (Princeton, 1983), pp. 5–14, and was thus dropped. Knecht, *The Rise and Fall of Renaissance France*, furthermore states that 'the idea of linking the *bourg* Saint-Germain with the right bank of the Seine can be traced back to the reign of Charles V', p. 505.

years of civil unrest had come to a preliminary end. Officially, the bridge was required for a host of reasons, which ranged from the local (the bridge was part of the enlargement of Paris) to the global (increased inter-European traffic required larger and wider river crossings at crucial places like Paris). However, it is not for these reasons that the Pont-Neuf concerns us here. Its first and much noted significance derives from the fact that the construction of the bridge did not represent an individual achievement like other bridges before and after, but characterised one part of a consciously executed building programme for the modernisation of Paris. Henry IV and Sully, his superintendent for the reform of France's infrastructure, amongst other things, saw fit to reconfigure and indeed partially restructure Paris on a scale hitherto unknown in French history. The construction of the Place Dauphine right next to the Pont-Neuf, the Place Royale, the enlargement of the Louvre, the planning of the Hôpital Saint-Louis, the reinforcement of many river quays and other sites all owe much of their present state to the conscious injection of change and forward planning into the built environment during Henry IV's reign.[12] The implied birth of a national technocratic bureaucracy capable of planning and, in the case of Sully, of establishing the means to finance the implementation of plans,[13] was new indeed at the time within the confines of French society. As part of this programme, the Pont-Neuf marked a change in dynasties. Furthermore, it represented the materialisation of a series of tentative openings towards modernity at the crucial turning point between sixteenth-century humanism and its intellectual successor, a move towards science and method that was to mark the seventeenth century across the European map.

The most obvious of these openings – and we shall have reason to

---

[12] D. Buisseret, *Henry IV. King of France* (London, 1992), pp. 128–33. Arguably, this has to be seen as the 'political' conclusion of a trend set in motion earlier in the century by Machiavelli and Bodin. The rise of the modern state from these seeds and the accompanying emphasis on order, which led to absolutism a century later, inaugurated the quite modern idea of an 'active' law-giving sovereign. See Q. Skinner, *The Foundations of Modern Political Thought*, 2 vols (Cambridge, 1978).

[13] See D. Buisseret, *Sully and the Growth of Centralized Government in France, 1598–1610* (London, 1968), who counts the title of *géographe et ingénieur du roi* among those contributing to this new elite (p. 129); also M. Greengrass, *France in the Age of Henry IV: The Struggle for Stability* (London, 1984), esp. p. 131. While these *ingénieurs* were responsible for the transformation of the site later used for the construction of the Pont-Neuf, they were primarily concerned with building fortifications. Boucher, *Le Pont-Neuf*, vol. 1, pp. 72–3, describes how two smaller islands at the westernmost tip of the Ile de la Cité, both of which appear clearly on the majority of pre-seventeenth-century maps, had to be practically erased to allow for the structurally solid construction of the bridge.

address the nature of this 'obviousness' shortly – was the absence of houses on the Pont-Neuf. Towards the end of the sixteenth century, this 'absence' represented a physical novelty within Paris, which soon became established as the norm with which we are familiar today. In fact, the vast majority of bridges that are part (and often parcel) of our present-day urban arteries, railways or rivers were explicitly built *not* to have houses on them. At the turn of the sixteenth and seventeenth centuries, however, the novelty of this was clearly indicated, not just by maps of the French capital, but in the older styles of constructing and maintaining bridges that persisted well into the eighteenth century.[14] The principal reason for the persistence of this tradition is not difficult to gauge, for at that time the construction of houses on an urban bridge was the customary way to finance their construction. Like present-day real estate tycoons selling property from a blueprint, a city in early or pre-modern Europe would profit from a new crossing being financed by largely private means. The specific design of the Pont-Neuf ultimately resulted from a decision by Henry IV, who inherited an abandoned construction site for a bridge with built structures upon it. Henry, however, altered the original plans because only a bridge without houses would permit an unobstructed view of his royal palace, the Louvre, which in turn was undergoing an extensive building programme at the time.[15]

In other words, for the first time in the history of the French capital, a highly visual form of aesthetic was separated from other sensual forms of appreciation and as such privileged over and against any immediate financial or practical gain. What is more, the priority accorded to a visually justified urban plan came at a price that must have weighed heavily upon the mind of a king who had had to fight so long to be granted access to the capital city. Rather than being able to rely upon private investment as a means to finance the Pont-Neuf (like most other bridges in Paris), the new administration had recourse to a second modern motif: the use of direct taxation for the construction of a public building, more specifically, through a tax levied on wine.[16] Furthermore, deprived of the income customarily generated by the trade and

---

[14] Simultaneously with the construction of the Pont-Neuf, the Pont Marchant, named after its financier, Charles Marchant, was built (1598–1608) parallel to the Pont au Change on the northern bank of the Ile de la Cité. As was customary in Paris at the time, this bridge included financially lucrative houses. See H. Ballon, *The Paris of Henri IV*, pp. 299–301.

[15] Boucher, *Le Pont-Neuf*, I, pp. 106–7, also pp. 113–14; Pillorget, *Paris sous les premiers Bourbons*, p. 275; Ballon, *The Paris of Henri IV*, p. 117.

[16] Carsalade du Pont, *La municipalité parisienne*, p. 243. It is entirely appropriate that the main commerce on the bridge today is generated by an exquisite Burgundy wine bar named after Henry IV.

commerce that took place on the other four Parisian bridges, the Pont-Neuf clearly did not fit into an existing medieval streetscape. It comes as no surprise, therefore, to see it being the first bridge in Paris to be paved in its entirety, thus easing the flow of traffic so that commerce would prosper elsewhere. Facilitated by a visual logic, the Pont-Neuf thus became a space of reduced functionalities, an early modern space par excellence.

This 'modernity' bequeathed a legacy that became most evident in the emergence of novel visual discourses within and about the city as an emerging urban landscape became anchored in the Pont-Neuf. Not only was Henry IV's royal gaze integrated into the resulting aesthetic appreciation of the city, attested to in the great number of seventeenth- and eighteenth-century illustrations of views of, or from, the Pont-Neuf,[17] the river Seine itself was incorporated into the subsequent 'invention' and perpetuation of Paris as a landscape. In all of this, it is worth remembering that the same river only a generation before had carried the corpses of the St Bartholomew's Day Massacre downstream.[18] Hand-in-hand with this change we can witness a simultaneous rise in the number and quality of the maps depicting the capital of France.[19] Together, these changes amount to a paradigm shift of sorts: from now on, and increasingly frequently, depictions of the city derived their rhetorical power from their ability to invoke 'real life' as it could be observed from concrete vantage points and invoked in everyday narrative constructions, instead of from pre-modern, highly idealised forms of representation.[20] Here, on the Pont-Neuf, the city opened up to the gaze of differently positioned onlookers; a form of 'gaze' that was to be transformed yet again in the nineteenth century with the advent of mechanised forms of representation, but which was nonetheless invented in the seventeeth century.

---

[17] During the seventeenth and eighteenth centuries in particular, the Pont-Neuf became one of the focal points of public life in Paris, so much so that Dubly, *Ponts de Paris*, notes of this time: 'If it is true that Paris is a world in and of itself, then the Pont-Neuf clearly must be its capital', p. 121.

[18] Within the vast literature on the massacre, allow me to single out B.B. Diefendorf, *Beneath the Cross. Catholics and Huguenots in Sixteenth-Century Paris* (Oxford, 1991), pp. 93–106.

[19] B. Rouleau (1997), *Paris: Histoire d'un espace* (Paris, 1997), pp. 192–3; T. Conley, *The Self-Made Map. Cartographic Writing in Early Modern France* (Minneapolis, 1996).

[20] The classical text on this transformation is S. Alpers, *The Art of Describing: Dutch Art in the Seventeenth Century* (Chicago, 1983). In the course of the eighteenth century, this genre mutated into much more 'theatrical' forms of representation, eventually culminating in the panoramas of the nineteenth century. See R. Dubbini, *Geography of the Gaze. Urban and Rural Vision in Early Modern Europe* (Chicago, 2002), trans. L.G. Cochrane, ch.1.

The novelty of these urban landscapes, furthermore, lies in the absence of any overt celebration of power. In contrast to medieval depictions of the city and the centrality accorded to particular buildings and fortifications in them (see Figure 4.1), the seventeenth century witnessed the materialisation of notions of a 'physiognomy of the city' in its pictorial representations.[21] This is not to say that power was not part of the landscapes wrought out of the emerging and increasingly planned city. The construction and subsequent use of the statue commemorating Henry IV following his assassination in 1610 and its incorporation into the emerging pictorial canon after its inauguration in 1614, is ample evidence to the contrary. The use of this statue, the first of its kind in France, in many public displays of a newly developing national imagery, also lends credence to the claim that we are witnessing the emergence of a new kind of space right in the heart of the French capital.[22]

The Pont-Neuf was emblematic of, as well as materially involved in, all these changes: it was at once facilitator and accelerator of a new world in which images increasingly took on a life of their own and, as such, shaped the way that cities regarded themselves or were viewed by their citizens, bureaucrats and, particularly from the nineteenth century onwards, by tourists.

This initiated the tradition of 'seeing' and 'displaying' along a host of distinct yet interrelated axes, through both the planning phases and the eventual completion (and continued maintenance) of the bridge, which continued to mark the history of the Pont-Neuf. In the seventeenth century in particular, it became the most frequented place in Paris for the increasingly popular staging of street theatre, as well as a transitory home for the first, as yet, only moderately commodified, flâneurs of the

---

[21] Dubbini, *Geography of the Gaze*, p. 49.

[22] This form of public display of a 'political' imagery should not be confused with the pre-modern notion of symbolically laden 'sacred' places, which appears to have been consciously fostered by Henry himself during his lifetime. See Y-F. Tuan, 'Space and place: humanistic perspective', *Progress in Geography*, 6 (1974), pp. 233–46; F. Bardon, *Le portrait mythologique à la cour de France sous Henri IV et Louis XIII* (Paris, 1974), also Greengrass, *France in the Age of Henry IV*, pp. 133–4, and Buisseret, *Sully*, pp. 149–50. It has deservedly been the focus of many analyses eager to understand the use of images in modernity. We should not forget that it continues to be one of the defining characteristics of modernity that those themes we see developed in the construction of the Pont-Neuf inaugurated a tradition that was decidedly not contained in a narrowly defined 'political' arena. Instead, we can witness what Derek Gregory has rightly called the inauguration of a 'world-as-exhibition' view characteristic of modernity, a theme which, like so many others, accelerated in the nineteenth century: D. Gregory, *Geographical Imaginations* (Oxford, 1994).

Fig. 4.1   The Pont Neuf in Paris, view towards the Louvre, c. 1700: Musée Carnavalet, Paris

city.[23] Invariably, accounts of the bridge's history allude to this phase as the 'golden age' of the Pont-Neuf, and one is indeed reminded of the heterotopic qualities that are often ascribed to the not altogether distant Palais-Royal some 170 years later.[24] So much so that Sébastian Mercier's 1786 remark that 'The Pont Neuf is to the city what the heart is to the body: the centre of movement and of circulation' does not surprise us at all.[25]

As with many planned structures, the history of the Pont-Neuf did not live up to its initial billing. The reduction of its functions, in particular, which I have portrayed as going hand-in-hand with the elevation of the city to the status of a visual object, did not go uncontested after the completion of the bridge. It was in far too central and prominent a location *not to* attract commercial interest. Hence, from the middle of the eighteenth century onwards, we can document the construction of vending stalls on the bridge that were officially tolerated until 1855.[26]

These stalls (see Figure 4.2), portrayed by Marville just at the point of their disappearance as part of Haussmann's urban overhaul, made creative use of the halfmoon-shaped bays bordering the bridge for a diverse range of commercial activities.[27] For a long time they competed functionally with the one officially planned and often rebuilt facility on the Pont-Neuf, the so-called 'Samaritaine'. This was a pump designed to provide the nearby royal gardens at the Tuilleries with a stable supply of water from the Seine which, after it was dismantled in the late eighteenth century, passed on its name to the adjacent department store still doing business on the right bank of the Seine today.[28]

---

[23] Dubly, *Ponts de Paris*, pp. 126–30; J. Garms, 'Projects for the Pont-Neuf and the Place Dauphine in the first half of the eighteenth century', *Journal of the Society of Architectural Historians*, 26, 2 (1967), p. 102.

[24] K. Hetherington, *The Badlands of Modernity. Heterotopia and Social Ordering* (London, 1997), pp. 1–19.

[25] L.S. Mercier, *Tableau de Paris* (Paris, 1994 [1786]), p. 135.

[26] Boucher, *Le Pont-Neuf*, I, pp. 145–50; Lavedan notes precise rhythms in the middle of the seventeenth century: commerce in the morning, promenades in the afternoon: H. Lavedan, 'Le Pont-Neuf', *Revue des Deux Mondes*, 45 (1925), pp. 271–2.

[27] As Shelley Rice has documented, there is nothing accidental about the photograph either: it was used by Haussmann specifically to document the 'old' Paris before it disappeared forever. Marville bequeathed a series of consciously quaint photographs to the archives, deliberately highlighting the contrast with an emerging, 'new' Paris. See A. Braun's photograph of the same site, taken in 1855 after the demolition of the stalls: S. Rice, *Parisian Views* (Cambridge, Mass., 1997), p. 70.

[28] This usage of bridges is clearly a pre-modern survival. Up to this point, the majority of bridges in Paris incorporated a source of energy usage through water mills underneath. The fact that the expertise required for the construction of the

Fig. 4.2   *The Pont Neuf in Paris*, Marville photograph, 1852: Bibliothèque Historique de la Ville de Paris

Just as, ten years earlier, Sixtus V was to leave a particular imprint on the appearance of Rome,[29] Henry IV modernised Paris and turned it into a genuine 'capital' city.[30] Structures like the Pont-Neuf embodied both the absolutist power and the mercantile economies that were to characterise the following century. It was instrumental in the transition towards modernity in that it legitimated vision as a guiding principle of the new times. How fitting, then, that this bridge was, and continues to be, called the 'new' bridge;[31] even if in the late sixteenth century this name only signalled a temporary, rather than qualitative, difference.[32] How fitting, furthermore, that this 'new' bridge is today's 'oldest' bridge in an increasingly post-modern Parisian landscape which ironises 'vision' in many forms. Not surprisingly, the Pont-Neuf was, yet again, an index of this change when it was transformed, first in 1985, into a monumental piece of art conceived by the artist known as Christo, who wrapped and concealed it, and secondly, in 1989, into the temporary home of three homeless people in Leos Carax's film *Les Amants du Pont-Neuf*. I have yet to encounter a better object than the Pont-Neuf for concealment or functional deconstruction in such decidedly superficial and consciously ironic ways. *Faire le Pont-Neuf* was not without reason a proverbial saying in the seventeenth century for achieving something extraordinary.[33]

---

Samaritaine had to be imported from the Netherlands already points towards a more refined and international knowledge now deployed in the service of functionality (cf. Fierro, *Histoire et Dictionnaire de Paris*, p. 1086).

[29] On the modernisation of Rome under Sixtus V, see S. Giedion, 'Sixtus V and the planning of baroque Rome', *Architectural Review*, 3 (1952), pp. 217–26, and H.G. Koenigsberger, G.L. Mosse and G.Q. Bowler (1989), *Europe in the Sixteenth Century*, 2nd edn (London, 1989), esp. pp. 121–3.

[30] Buisseret, *Sully*, p. 26.

[31] *Pont-Neuf, 1578–1978*. Exhibition catalogue (Paris, 1978), p. 5.

[32] Before the Pont-Neuf was named the 'new' bridge, the present-day Pont Saint-Michel had already been known under this name in the fourteenth century but had to relinquish this signifier when 'our' bridge became the 'Pont-Neuf'. This time, the name stuck – and for good reasons, as I argue above. See Fierro, *Histoire et Dictionnaire de Paris*, p. 1087.

[33] N. Heinich, 'Errance, croyance, et mécréance: le public du Pont-Neuf de Christo', *L'Écrit-Voir*, 11 (1988), pp. 3–18. Elsen writes: 'Just as building the bridge about 1600 had changed Paris forever and caused its focus on the Seine, so too did Christo's art bring Parisians back to this focus. A new visibility was given to a handsome old structure and a great historic monument that had become invisible with time': A. Elsen, 'What have we learnt about modern public sculpture: ten propositions', *Art Journal*, 48, 4 (1989), p. 293. A similar analysis could be pursued with reference to Daniel Buren's pillars, built in the court of the Palais-Royal during the same period. On *Les amants du Pont-Neuf*, see U. Strohmayer, 'Practising Film: The Autonomy of Images', in D. Dixon and T. Cresswell, eds, *Les Amants du Pont-Neuf, Engaging Film* (London, 2002), pp. 193–208.

In many ways, the history of the Pont-Neuf is therefore in tandem with other major changes taking place in Western Europe during the early modern period. Inventions in the realm of optical instruments, advances in cartography and novel forms of representation developed in the arts all contributed to novel 'ocular' forms of communication and argumentation. Indeed, many a contemporary commentator sees fit to characterise the seventeenth century as the century that inaugurated an era of 'ocular-centrism' in Europe and, by colonial extension, within the world at large.[34] The views across the Seine and the recognition of their instant commercial potential in the forms of paintings and prints would certainly bear out such an interpretation. However, the connection between these various tentacles of a world waiting to be born is not as linear and lacking in complexity as the notion of 'ocular-centrism' would have us believe. In other words, the rise of 'seeing' in the context of the seventeenth century needs itself to be contextualised for us to make sense of history.

Again, the Pont-Neuf serves us admirably for this task. We can take the visually charged term 'theatre' as a starting point for such a contextualisation, for we have already seen it occupy a central stage in the history of the Pont-Neuf. Not only did the performing arts flourish in the period following the construction of the Pont-Neuf, but the word 'theatre' itself came to be used in conjunction with a rapidly increasing number of illustrations. These depicted both human and animal bodies, as well as machines and the territory of France through maps, at a level of detail which was previously unknown. Writers in the late seventeenth and early eighteenth centuries spoke of 'theatres' where the word 'representation' or 'display' might come more readily to the minds of present-day observers. Rhetorically at least, the theatre of the streets thus became linked to the world of the book and the universe of learning.

---

[34] For a splendid summary of the history of vision and the privileging of 'vision' over and against other forms of contact with the 'world' in general in modern times, see D.M. Levin, ed., *Modernity and the Hegemony of Vision* (Berkeley, 1993), especially its splendid introduction. One of the central questions of this collection of essays, the historical depth we can accord to vision – going back to the pre-Socratics or being indicative of a more recent modernity – can only be hinted at here. For a discussion of the philosophical traditions touched on in the mention of 'ocular-centrism', see H. Jonas, 'The nobility of sight', *Philosophy and Phenomenological Research*, 14, 4 (1954), pp. 507–19. Jonas mentions three distinct features of 'sight' which predestined it to dominate the field of both metaphor and knowledge since Plato: the 'simultaneity' of image; the 'dynamic neutralisation' of the contact with 'world'; and the retention of 'spatial distance' – all of which will become important features later on in this essay.

It was these latter, of course, which, in the context of the eighteenth-century Enlightenment, would redefine the world as a modern world through the invocation of knowledge as the supreme arbiter of all things public. 'Theatrical' forms of representation, while a necessary prerequisite to modern knowledge (we need only remember those wonderful drawings that would eventually fill the pages of Diderot and D'Alembert's *Encyclopaedie* in the eighteenth century), lacked what was to become the linch-pin of modern visions and of modernity as such: the onlooker or modern subject critically engaged with particular forms of representation. The link between representation and gaze, in other words, was not to be secured from the Point-Neuf alone. For the link to become a useful one, the gazing individual on the bridge, in the gallery, bookshop or (eventually) in the laboratory would have to change as well and become modernised to fit into modernised environments like the Pont-Neuf.

Rephrased slightly, the problem with any form of 'theatric' representation of the kind to which this essay has alluded was that, in and of themselves, they could not (as yet) guarantee knowledge. Representations could betray, just as the eye, which was after all their common place of origin, did at times deceive. If this was possibly lack of precision, which had not previously presented much of a problem, then its solution would herald the completion of a new era. It was Descartes, aware of the shortcomings of both scholasticism and humanism, who was to become instrumental in this most crucial of transitions.[35] No longer eager to derive knowledge or certainty simply from previously accepted certainties, whether dogmatic or literary, Descartes applied to both philosophy and science the kind of experimental 'cartographic writing' recently used by Tom Conley in his analysis of sixteenth-century maps and their design,[36] and which the latter contrasts with the kind of 'textual nomadism' characteristic of

[35] On humanism, see P. Desan, 'The worm in the apple: the crisis of humanism', in P. Desan, ed., *Humanism in Crisis* (Ann Arbor, 1991), pp. 11–34. Desan portrays humanism as a legitimate response to the crisis of the notion of a universal knowledge and morality in the wake of the Reformation. This response became itself subject to critique when a crisis in the content of humanist values, largely wrought from the destitution brought about by the civil wars, brought into question the very form of humanist discourse. Before Descartes, this resulted in a renewed interest in both the occult and utopias.

[36] Hauser notes that the meaning of the word 'science' itself underwent a change in meaning during the sixteenth century. From a tradition passed on to the following generation, 'it now designates a knowledge of what is, a knowledge of what one gains by looking at things': H. Hauser, *La modernité du XVIe siècle* (Paris, 1963), p. 21 (my translation).

Montaigne, among others.[37] More than a century before the Enlightenment perfected this ideal, most pertinently in the rich illustrative material printed in the *Encyclopaedie,* Descartes' famous 'Second Meditation' effectively gave 'vision' a home crucially, not in the landscape, nor in tradition, but in the eye of the critical and methodically writing beholder. Thus 'vision' emerged as the fixed place of knowledge; 'cartographic writing' was writing with a 'signature'[38] that was at once the most private and the most public of expressions.

Crucially, it was not the centrality of 'vision', in and of itself, nor its privileging at the expense of the other senses – however lamentable this might strike some of us – that should be identified as the 'modern' aspect of buildings like the Pont-Neuf, but the new image of human beings as individuals to which this 'vision' gave rise. However, at the same time, this new or modern individual was also a social individual, the prototype of what would be called much later a 'citizen'. As a citizen, the Cartesian *cogito* is demonstrably attached to this world by the communality granted to individual positions by way of perspective: able to converse about society from a spatially secured position, citizens can exchange what are not accidentally called 'points of view'. The Pont-Neuf is what facilitated and at the same time embodied this development towards a society of equals.

At the same time, however, this coupling of *cogito* and 'visibility' brought with it a certain ordering, and thus reassuring, impulse, which began to accompany modernity.[39] One could argue that the visions of the city we have analysed were successful precisely because they provided both an accessible reality and an agent capable of 'authorising' visions. Onlookers, just like the gazing individual from the bridge, could rest assured by what they perceived because what they saw was shared by many. Only the blind were excluded from the emerging spectacle that began as the city, but increasingly extended to society as a whole.

It is in this form that the eye pragmatically bridged the all too apparent 'mind'–'body' duality that had plagued Cartesian philosophy

---

[37] Conley, *The Self-Made Map*, pp. 279–86. On the difference between Montaigne's concept of the 'self' and that of Descartes, see Z.S. Schiffman, 'Humanism and the problem of relativism', in Desan, ed., *Humanism in Crisis,* pp. 69–83.

[38] Conley, *The Self-Made Map*, pp. 20–22, 301.

[39] We should not forget, however, that the translation of the derived form of certainty into the language of science and 'positivity' was an invention of the nineteenth century that was not prescribed in its concrete facets by the kind of transition I am analysing here. What was present at the time, however, was a nascent belief in progress which left an imprint on 'modern' discourses from the time of Descartes onwards and which was more often than not thought to be embodied in technological developments.

right from its beginnings. Published some 33 years after Henry IV first enacted 'freedom of choice' by looking across the city from the Pont-Neuf,[40] Descartes' *Discours* positioned the ability to see as the quintessentially modern faculty. To quote from Tom Conley's seminal work on the iconography of maps in early modern France:

> The self is visible only when it achieves the effect of totality, of having engineered a world through its own labours. Yet, at the same time, in order to bear a signature, the self has to appear to be gratuitous, total, or 'self-made' in a space that is granted to be its own.[41]

It was through built structures like the Pont-Neuf, as I have argued in this essay, that this central feature of modernity is inaugurated and maintained. Here, on the Pont-Neuf, each and every passer-by was positioned as an individual *cogito* through the recreation of a view akin to one of the many maps that prominently depicted (and displayed) its existence: within the bounds of vision, each 'gaze' was a gaze that reaffirms and, as such, created the 'optimism' that became instrumental for the 'scientific revolution' that was to come.[42] Hence the well-known dictum of Marx, according to which 'the forming of the five senses is a labour of the entire history of the world down to the present' must be amended to include the very *telos* of this formation the 'present' as well.[43]

## Epilogue

The contextualisation of the Pont-Neuf as a prime site for the rise of 'ocular' means of communication within the history of modernity leaves one critical aspect untouched. Far from being a neutral space of modernity, sites like the Pont-Neuf contributed significantly to shaping the way modern citizens interact with one another. The proliferation and eventual success of 'ocular' manners of argumentation with society at

---

[40] Jonas, 'The nobility of sight', p. 514.

[41] Conley, *The Self-Made Map*, p. 6. He continues: 'The self makes itself or is made to look self-like when it appears to be a simultaneous cause and effect of a creation that is both local and total. The self's emergence is evinced where discourse and geography are coordinated, and the self becomes autonomous only (1) when it is fixed to an illusion of a geographic truth (often of its own making) and (2) when it can be detached from the coordinates that mark its point of view, its history, its formation, and the aesthetics and politics of its signature.'

[42] J. Cottingham, *Descartes* (Oxford, 1986), p. 22.

[43] K. Marx, *The Economic and Philosophical Manuscripts of 1844* (New York, 1964), p. 141.

large is, for instance, indicative of changes within the construction of knowledge in the narrow sense of the word. It also exemplifies and materialises a change in the way modern communities will increasingly be constructed. Crucial to this change is a simple geographical observation: the Pont-Neuf was an eminently public site within the context of the French capital. As such, its structure did contribute to a developing sense of 'publicness' and thus to the continuing development of a civil society.

Commentators on the rise of modernity are well used to locating the origins of these 'public' and thoroughly normative aspects of modern life within the context of the bourgeois rise to a dominant position within Western societies. Jürgen Habermas's insistence on the importance of eighteenth-century Masonic lodges, cafés and literary salons, for instance, works implicitly from a spatial template that is pre-modern in all but name.[44] Spaces like the Pont-Neuf, however, while not yet involving the articulation of class or entrepreneurial interests, clearly set the scene for social and cultural changes to follow in later centuries. In fact, the French notion of a *mise-en-scène* and its cinematic connotations conveniently underscores the importance of the (urban) material for changes within society at large. Thus, crucially, when the modern 'public sphere' emerged in the enlightened eighteenth century, the context within which it developed was both older and originally more complex than has hitherto been thought.

According to Habermas and his many commentators, the dialectic that has been part of the 'public sphere', the structural relationship between its proto-democratic qualities and the restrictions that rendered the modern 'public sphere' a less than open forum, was already present in the Pont-Neuf. At once an open space, where access and the chance to view the city was denied to no one *and* a space where functional diversity was sacrificed for efficiency,[45] the Pont-Neuf was modern in a clearly recognisable way.

In conclusion, an analysis of material structures like the Pont-Neuf allows us to backdate the origins of a modernity that is still very much with us today. Not unlike Lisa Jardine's recent historicisation of 'consumerism',[46] we can thus assert a modernity both older, more complex and, by implication, less 'original' than has hitherto been

---

[44] J. Habermas, *The Structural Transformation of the Public Sphere* (Cambridge, Mass., 1989), trans. T. Berger.

[45] As opposed to the restriction of vision to the space of both palace and church in pre-modern times.

[46] L. Jardine, *Worldly Goods. A New History of the Renaissance* (London, 1996).

thought. If these conclusions are not intellectually comforting, we can at least take refuge in the realisation that they were never meant to provide such sustenance. At worst, we are back to where we started in the late sixteenth century before humankind posited itself as the necessary and sufficient condition of the possibility of both knowledge and liberation.

## Further reading

A. Baker, ed., *Ideology and Landscape in Historical Perspective* (Cambridge, 1992).

T. Conley, *The Self-Made Map. Cartographic Writing in Early Modern France* (Minneapolis, 1996).

D. Cosgrove, *Social Formation and Symbolic Landscape* (Totowa, NJ, 1984).

D. Cosgrove and S. Daniel, eds, *The Iconography of Landscape* (Cambridge, 1988).

R. Dubbini, *Geography of the Gaze. Urban and Rural Vision in Early Modern Europe* (Chicago, 2002), trans. L.G. Cochrane.

J. Duncan, ed., *Place/Culture/Representation* (London, 1993).

L. Marin, *Portrait of the King* (Minneapolis, 1988).

M. Ogborn, *Spaces of Modernity. London's Geographies, 1680–1780* (London and New York, 1998).

# PART TWO

# THE CULTURE OF CONSUMPTION

# CHAPTER FIVE

# Touching London: contact, sensibility and the city

## *Ava Arndt*

When Frances Burney's heroine Cecilia arrives in London, one of the first things she is asked to do is attend the liquidation sale of Lord and Lady Belgrade's estate. The couple has spent well past their means and the demands of creditors have forced the sale of all their possessions. While Cecilia is shocked by this event, her 'citified' female friends view it as commonplace and a chance to find a bargain:

> 'I am come,' cried she eagerly, 'to run away with you to my Lord Belgrade's sale. All the world will be there; and we shall go in with tickets and you have no notion how it will be crowded.'
> 'What is to be sold there?' said Cecilia.
> 'O every thing you can conceive; house, stables, china, laces, horses, caps, every thing in the world.'
> 'And do you intend to buy anything?'
> 'Lord no; but one likes to see other people's things.'
> Cecilia then begged they would excuse her attendance.
> 'O by no means,' cried Miss Larolles, 'you must go, I assure you; there'll be such a monstrous crowd as you never saw in your life. I dare say we shall be half squeezed to death.'[1]

As Cecilia herself notes in her attempt to decline the invitation, the mere fact of crowding seems an odd inducement to attend anything and she explicitly connects the 'attraction' of such a sale, as well as the crowd, with 'the polish of a long residence in the metropolis'. The episode is meant to be an example of the corruption of London, or at least to mark the difference between London and the countryside, and to signal Cecilia's naïveté compared with her friends. What is striking about this is not that it sets up a familiar dichotomy between country and city, but that it does so in terms of commotion, crowding and economics, rather than sexual liberty, drink or other forms of corruption previously used as signifiers of urban life. Going out in the city, as the sale Cecilia is induced to attend, meant crowding, moving, rubbing and touching

---

[1] F. Burney [1782], *Cecilia, or, Memoirs of an Heiress* (Oxford, 1988), bk 1, p. 31.

rather than simply watching.[2] And this, as I will argue, is a significant change.

In *Techniques of the Observer*, Jonathan Crary describes the eighteenth century's attachment to the use and function of the camera obscura, a large darkened box or enclosure with an aperture for projecting an image of external objects on one side or wall of the box, or on a screen placed inside the box. Crary contends that the use of the camera obscura, especially large, walk-in versions popular in the period, created a 'radical disjunction of eye from observer', removing the camera 'eye' from human vision; and transforming it, in Crary's words, into a 'disembodied cyclopean eye'.[3] I want to take this argument one step further and say that what the camera obscura does, and why it was so popular, is that it makes physical the process of vision, bringing it out of the head, out of an abstract conception of 'sight', and placing it in a structure one could experience in broad daylight, at times even something one could walk into. In the following I argue that this inscription of physicality in fact occurred on a much larger scale. The experience of the city, at least the conception in imaginary writing of the experience of the city, shifted during this period, from a primarily visual perception to one conceived of in physical, tactile terms. Touch replaced sight as the primary sense of urban space.

Much early eighteenth-century writing on the city shows this shift. Perhaps most famously, John Gay's *Trivia, or, the Art of Walking the Streets of London* (1716), Jonathan Swift's 'A Description of a City Shower' (1710) and Ned Ward's *The London Spy* (1704) seek to involve their readers in a tactile experience of the city. The style, in each, is immediate and reportorial; pervasive, and all-consuming rather than ocular and from above.[4] Thus Gay's *Trivia* begins with a discussion of the weather and advice about what kinds of things to wear in different seasons, immediately locating the reader physically in the poet's

---

[2] Steven J. Gores discusses *Evelina* at length in this context in his book, *Psycho-social Spaces: Verbal and Visual Readings of British Culture 1750–1820* (Detroit, 2000), where he also makes the argument for a culture of 'circulation' in eighteenth-century life, which he sees as highly visual, and informed by moments or events of 'spectacle'. My point here is somewhat different in that I see this new culture of circulation as tactile, and moving away from primarily visual understandings.

[3] Jonathan Crary, *Techniques of the Observer: On Vision and Modernity in the Nineteenth Century* (Cambridge, Mass., 1990), p. 15.

[4] See Ned Ward, *The London Spy, Complete in Eighteen Parts* (London, 1703), and John Gay, *Trivia, Or the Art of Walking the Streets of London* (London, 1716), as well as numerous imitators including *The Town Spy* (1725), *The Honest London Spy* (1779), *The New London Spy* (1794), *The Country Spy* (1730).

experience. He goes on to describe the very real contact one might expect to have on London's streets:

> Oft' in the mingling press,
> The *Barber's* Apron soils the sable Dress;
> . . .
> The little *Chimney-Sweeper* skulks along,
> And marks with sooty Stains the heedless Throng;
> When *Small-coal* murmurs in the hoarser Throat,
> From smutty Dangers guard thy threaten'd Coat:
> The *Dust-man's* Cart offends thy Cloaths and Eyes,
> When through the Street a Cloud of Ashes flies;
> The *Chandler's* Basket, on his shoulder borne,
> With Tallow spots thy coat; resign the way,
> To shun the surly *Butcher's* greasy Tray.[5]

The passage is about clothing and dirt, most obviously, but it is also about touch, particularly a kind of constant touch when walking the city streets. Similarly, Swift's 'Shower' poem begins by describing the weather; literally how to tell if it is going to rain, again locating the reader physically in the space of the city street.

In her book on writing in London after the fire of 1666, Cynthia Wall argues that some of these texts dealing with 'the street' in the late seventeenth and early eighteenth centuries worked to 'rebuild, rename and rewalk the streets', essentially to refashion a 'complete cultural space' and contends that 'walking the streets increasingly invades the prose literature in tempo with the proliferating street guides'. This movement into movement in eighteenth-century writing is part of what I want to address here. Wall argues that the novel or novels 'release' the motion of the street.[6] My argument is that they organise and replicate it, very much on the model of a garden 'tour', and more than this, that Eighteenth-century city writing, more generally, seeks to inscribe and understand motion and touch.

It seems to me that it cannot be a coincidence that the same period that saw the development of what we now call modern capitalist systems also developed an obsession with sensibility, or the senses, literally the ability to feel, whether it be streets and sidewalks or a character's tremulous pulse. The eighteenth-century 'cult' of sensibility was about being and becoming 'sensitive' to one's surroundings to an extreme degree. It sought to develop (and later to make fun of) the ability to feel

---

[5] Gay (1716), Book II, 2324 [BL edition: 992.k.9]. The poet further cautions on problems in crowding: 'Let due Civilities be strictly paid./The Wall surrender to the hooded Maid;/Nor let thy sturdy Elbow's hasty Rage/Jostle the feeble steps of trembling Age.'

[6] C. Wall, 'The Literary and Cultural Spaces of Restoration London' (Cambridge, 1998), p. 133.

and be felt, because this was thought to be able to cause or allow access to forms of artistic expression or the sublime. At the height of its popularity this translated into the production of tears, fainting spells and fits as demonstrations of sensitivity to one's surroundings, since 'degrees of sensibility betokened both social and moral status'.[7] This also translated into an emphasis on touch and physicality, both in the sense of being figuratively 'touched' and in the literal sense of producing tangible physical responses (weeping, fainting) to the sensation of being in the physical world. The culture of sensibility thus provided a vocabulary for articulating the ways in which the mind received information from the senses (by imprints, stamps or grooves), so that experiences were thought literally to mark themselves upon the person. As touch became the primary sensation through which writers described their experiences of city life, the same nervous system ascribed to the 'sensible' functioning of the human system was also ascribed to the world of things, and the culture of sensibility was extended and adapted to the world of objects and surfaces.[8]

If London was viewed, as in Burney's novels, as a place of movement, even overwhelming mobility and crowding, then it was also viewed as a place of learning. What the city seemed to offer in terms of corruption was also linked to a process of education, which was itself linked to contact. The advantage as well as the danger of urban life was precisely its increased, multifarious and fearfully indiscriminate possibilities for circulation. This combination of forces or effects is discussed most frequently in writing about London via metaphoric references to coins. Familiar from restoration comedy where coinage is often used to discuss polarisations of purity and debasement in female characters, these images reappear in later eighteenth-century writing in largely positive terms to signify experience, learning and the value of exchange especially in the context of city life. Arguably the most touched objects in any city, coins become not only markers of the extent of travel, or mobility, but also, as surfaces, recording spaces for information, education and experience, if not also debasement. Henry Mackenzie's novel, *The Man of Feeling* (1771), for example, opens with a coin metaphor to describe

---

[7] G.J. Barker-Benfield, *The Culture of Sensibility: Sex and Society in Eighteenth-Century Britain* (Chicago and London, 1992), p. 9.

[8] For an interesting discussion of this phenomenon see Miles Ogborn's chapter on pavements in London in his book, *Spaces of Modernity: London's Geographies 1680–1780* (London and New York, 1998), where he details the development of paving stones and attention to the feel of the street as being 'a mark of urban modernity'; also Laura Brown's chapter on city sewers in *Fables of Modernity: Literature and Culture in the English Eighteenth Century* (Ithaca and London, 2001).

a process of education: 'There is some rust about every man at the beginning; though in some nations . . . the ideas of the inhabitants, from climate, or what other cause you will, are so vivacious, so eternally on the wing, that they must, even in small societies, have frequent collision; the rust therefore will wear off sooner.'[9] On the next page, the narrator's interlocutor suggests the best method for rubbing off this rust might be travel, and the novel proceeds to describe the travels of its sentimental hero and the process of his education. As in *A Sentimental Journey*, this education is particularly shaped by movement and exchange, often in pseudo-economic, or outright economic form: 'rubbing off' 'polishing' or being 'worn [in]'.

This way of explaining urban experience is further recorded in a series of novels and short narratives appearing in newspapers, magazines and printed books throughout the second half of the century (and mostly in the 1770s and 1780s) that record travels through London from the perspective of objects rather than people. These 'object narratives' are interesting for different reasons, one being that the objects in question touch more places and people even than the narrators in Gay or Ward's accounts, the other being that the thread of the storyline and the structure of the stories themselves are based on touching, passing, and the exchange of the narrating objects. In this sense, like early newspapers and magazines, they seek to bring the tactile experience of the city into their readers' homes. They also combine several of the features of London city writing in the period I have been discussing so far: an emphasis on the tactile quality of experience, an obsession with inventories and things, and a new formation of spatial relations in urban life.

The first of these stories appeared in Joseph Addison's popular news magazine, *The Tatler*, in 1710.[10] The entry tells the story of a shilling coin that relates the history of its life and experiences. The coin describes its movements around the city as it is passed from one 'owner' to the next: herb-woman, butcher, brewer, wife and preacher. The impetus for the story, as Addison recounts it to his readers, is a discussion at a dinner party regarding the rate of 'busyness' of people in business and the expressed wish, by one of the guests, that they might be able to travel about at the rate of a shilling coin. The dinner party breaks up, Addison goes to bed and is later awakened by the shilling, animated and turned on its side in a flood of light. The shilling recounts its adventures and Addison duly publishes the narrative for his readers the following morning. The apparatus is noteworthy in that it directs our attention to

  [9]  H. Mackenzie, *The Man of Feeling* (London, 1771), pp. 1–3.
  [10]  Joseph Addison, *The Tatler*, no. 249, 'The adventures of a shilling', in D.F. Bond, ed., *The Tatler*, 3 vols (Oxford, 1987), vol. 3, pp. 269–73.

either religious or alchemical processes (flood of light, rising up) and because it specifically acknowledges the source of the tale as being about mobility and finance and the relation of humans to both of these things.

Other coin narratives followed in *The Tatler* and elsewhere, and Londoners were inundated with the life stories of banknotes, rupees, a three-pence piece, a silver penny, as well as those of other small objects: a pen, a mirror, waistcoat, petticoat, pincushion, watch, slippers and shoes. The coins and objects in these stories delight in their physical progress and process, inhabiting the city in a variety of ways. The majority follow a format similar to that of the shilling, recounting their travels and daily routes. In this way the tales provide a narrative for the secret life of the city itself: how objects and coins and even people get from point a to point b; how the unseen mechanics of the city work. The objects and coins in these tales take their information literally from 'making the rounds' of the city and touching its inhabitants and spaces at the same time as they are rendering and engraving their moves, both on their own 'bodies' and on those of others. Like the characters in Burney's novel or Gay's poem, they are rubbed and jostled as they lie side by side, 'sweating' amongst one another in pockets and overcoats, or closeted in banks or pawnshops, in chests or purses. Their experience, too, is one of crowding. In a sense, coins and banknotes acted like glue or connective material through which motion, speed and a 'new' exchange economy can be glimpsed. Quite obviously they also provided a physical connection to abstract ideas and offered a tactile experience not only of the economy but of places it would be more difficult for a human character to go. Likely the most touched object in the city, animated money gave form to financial transactions and provided a map, not unlike Gay's *Trivia*, for the motion of exchange.

Indeed, within the novels themselves, the relation of an object's circulation 'history' is viewed as educative, and therefore valuable material. The novels continually refer to each other and the relative merits of their travels and routes. *The Adventures of a Black Coat* (1760), for example, is set up as being a series of remarks an old sable coat, who is about to be retired, makes to its new young replacement that has just arrived in the closet. The old coat relates the history of its life and adventures explicitly as a form of 'education' for its younger replacement. The story begins with the elder coat recounting the beginning of its 'life' when it is consigned to a merchant in Monmouth Street: 'Here I may say I began to exist.'[11] Because the merchant is the owner of a rental house, existence

---

[11] Anon., *The Adventures of a Black Coat, Containing A Series of Remarkable Occurrences and Entertaining Incidents that it was Witness to in its Peregrinations Though the Cities of London and Westminster, As Related by Itself* (London, 1760), pp. 4–5.

for the coat, as for the coins, is aligned with trade. Similarly stasis, for the Sable, is 'worse than total dissolution, or the tormenting needle of a botcher, than which nothing is half so dreadful'.[12] After lingering in the shop for three months, watching mournfully as the other coats 'depart from out our prison of dust and moths, and enjoy liberty and fresh air', the Sable is finally able to begin its travels. So eager is the coat to be at liberty that it contrives to 'contract every thread' in order to clasp the next young gentleman who comes in to hire a coat, in order to ensure a perfect fit. Its efforts are successful and it soon leaves the shop on its first outing. Most of the coat's ensuing adventures are concerned with switches, impersonation and theft. In this context the status of objects, and the power of objects to endow status, are frequently commented on in the novel. For instance, the coat refers to its rental house companions as 'temporary gentlemen', so called because in most instances the coats are used to impose upon the world through their would-be-gentleman wearers. The Sable's own 'true' value is assessed at an early point in its story, when its tale is interrupted by the entrance of 'a vamper of old commodities' who is brought to assess its worth. This man concludes that he could not 'give anything for it', adding that 'it has been so much used that it would not hold together for a single day's wear'. He pronounces it too rotten to repair and claims it cannot even be converted into patches as, in fact 'it consisted of nothing else but patches' and, in short, advises the owner, 'to keep it as a curiosity'.[13] The story ends when someone opens the closet door to take the new young coat away, depriving the older coat of its audience, and thus ending the novel.

Such stories' collective function as guides and warnings about the perils and pitfalls of modern city life quickly became the reason for writing more. In the following example, two ladies discuss the fact that a hackney (rental) coach is likely to circulate widely and therefore *should* be made to relate what it has seen, in order that its knowledge be passed on:

> It is one hour the seat of pleasure; the next of anxiety: incidents innumerable it is a daily witness of disappointment often steps into it from a great man's levee with a heart full of anguish; pleasure takes a jaunt to Vauxhall with the syren of his ruin; the nuptial pair to be married; the disconsolate maid to her lover's funeral. In short, I don't know adventures, if naturally related, would prove a higher source of pleasure to the generality of readers.[14]

---

[12] *Black Coat*, p. 12.

[13] *Black Coat*, p. 26.

[14] *The Adventures of a Hackney Coach* (Dublin, 1781), pp. 2–4. It is perhaps worth noting that the use of transport vehicles seems to have been a popular version of these types of tales. Besides the *Hackney Coach*, there are 'The

A Pen likewise justifies the publications of its memoirs on similar grounds:

> A *Guinea* has given to the world, in the history of its life, four volumes of amusement; and a *HalfPenny* has related its adventures in a strain of sentiment and pleasantry: why then should not the pen (whose words are generally marked in more lasting characters) communicate to the public the great events of an active and industrious existence?[15]

The implication behind these statements is that objects (or persons, or coins) in circulation gain a species of knowledge otherwise unattainable and that this knowledge is worth having. It further demonstrates that there was a recognisable dialogue current in society about the recording and interpretation of these books. Often there even appears an element of jealousy of the objects in question. After all, many of the stories begin with the conceit that the objects or coins in question have a more exciting or complete experience of the world than their human counterparts, and a more complete understanding of modern city life. 'Who would *not* be a banknote,' asks the Banknote of its audience, 'to have such a quick succession of adventures and acquaintance?'[16]

Tellingly, the contemporary human reviewers of *The Adventures of a Hackney Coach* objected precisely to its *too* quickly changing passengers: 'Our coachman's fares (as the reader who takes the trouble to ride with him will easily perceive) are too short; and before any interesting story can be told, or any good character drawn of one person, he stops on a sudden and takes up another.'[17] This highlights, on the one hand, one of the inherent failings of the novels and, on the other, what might be pointed to as the original motivation for their being written in the first place: fear of mobility and a fear of touch. That is, the reviewers feel it is impossible to keep up, or to have any meaningful relationship with any of the novel's characters, because of the rate at which they come and go. Touching, especially this particular kind of environmental touch, as a socialising process for humans, was viewed as at best a precarious route. As even the objects show, there were very real dangers (and fears) of corruption, debasement, excess and fraud. Although the Black Coat

---

adventures of a stage coach', in *The Rambler's Magazine* (1788–89), *The Sedan, A Novel* (London, 1757), and *Travels of Mons. le Post-Chaise, Written by Himself* (London, 1753).

[15] 'The adventures of a pen', in *Walker's Hibernian Magazine or Compendium of Knowledge* (August 1806), p. 459.

[16] T. Bridges, *The Adventures of a Bank-Note*, 2 vols (London, 1770), vol. 2, p. 25.

[17] *The Critical Review, or Annals of Literature, by a Society of Gentlemen*, vol. 51 (1781), pp. 284–7.

longs for its freedom, even within the rental coat community circulation is spoken of as a harrowing if not physically harmful affair: 'many of our community frequently brought home with them marks of various disasters, sometimes being dragged through a horsepond, at other times rolled in a kennel, besides numerous canings and kickings'.[18] A *Rupee* cleverly concludes its own history by emphasising the advantages of reading about rather than participating in this tactility: 'If you have any brains ... you must be improved by my adventures, which will stand you in stead of experience and give you some knowledge of mankind, without impairing the good qualities of your heart.'[19] London in the eighteenth century saw the development of public space that had 'private' qualities: smallness, closeness and crowds. It also saw the beginnings of the wish to bring the qualities of that public space home, in the form of newspapers and magazines, which sought to recreate the experience of the coffeehouse on the printed page. Part of my argument here is that these stories are another, more graphic, version of those same phenomena. While Addison and Steele in their weekly *Spectator* or *Tatler* columns physically locate their 'letters' in space and time – 'from White's coffeehouse', 'at the Royal-Exchange' – these novels describe the insides of shirt pockets, the feel of seats or the rain pounding on pavement.

Though little known to modern readers, these stories about objects were immensely popular with their contemporary audience, so much so that, by 1781, *The Critical Review* began to complain of their ubiquity: 'this mode of making up a book, and styling it the *Adventures* of a cat, a dog, a monkey, a hackneycoach, a louse, a shilling or a rupee or anything else is grown so fashionable, that few months pass which do not bring one of them under our inspection'.[20] An inscription in the Huntington Library copy of Charles Johnstone's *Chrysal, or the Adventures of a Guinea* (1760), describes the novel as 'universally read at the time', and Lady Mary Wortley Montague calls Francis Coventry's *The History of Pompey The Little, or the Life and Adventures of a Lap-Dog* (1751), 'a real and exact representation of life as it is now acted in London, as it was in my time and as it will be (I do not doubt) a hundred years hence'.[21] The intense contemporary interest in these stories alone suggests a reappraisal of the connection to city life.

---

[18]  *Black Coat*, p. 7.
[19]  Anon., *The Adventures of a Rupee* (London, 1782), p. 264.
[20]  *The Critical Review*, vol. 52, December 1781, in *The Critical Review, or Annals of Literature, by a Society of Gentlemen*, 70 vols (London, 1756–90).
[21]  Huntington # 77295; Robert Halsbad, ed., *The Selected Letters of Lady Mary Wortley Montagu* (London, 1967), p. 228. The letter is to Lady Bute, February 1752.

Evidence for the change in world view I have been suggesting here, from a primarily visual to a primarily tactile orientation, is demonstrated by the combination of interest in localised travels, the delight in walking tours, the enormous popularity of object narratives and what might be called an obsession with size and shape. An obsession with motion, financial, fictive and corporeal, is arguably one of the major effects of a move into modern capitalism. That this mobility gave rise to a new means of experiencing the city is appropriate and unsurprising. The proliferation in physicality in writing about London during this period suggests that the process by which this new modernity was imagined was overwhelmingly tactile.

## Further reading

G.J. Barker-Benfield, 'Sensibility and the nervous system', in *The Culture of Sensibility: Sex and Society in Eighteenth-Century Britain* (Chicago, 1992).

P.J. Corfield (1990), 'Walking the streets: the urban Odyssey in eighteenth-century England', *Journal of Urban History*, 16 (1990), pp. 132–74.

J. Gay, *Trivia; or, The Art of Walking the Streets of London* (London, 1716).

S.J. Gores, *Psychosocial Spaces: Verbal and Visual Readings of British Culture 1750–1820* (Detroit, 2000).

E. Mackie, ed., *The Commerce of Everyday Life, Selections from* The Tatler *and* The Spectator (Boston and New York, 1988).

M. Ogborn, *Spaces of Modernity: London's Geographies 1680–1780* (London and New York, 1988).

T. Smollett [1771], *The Expedition of Humphry Clinker* (Oxford, 1984).

P.M. Spacks, *Privacy: Concealing the Eighteenth-Century Self* (Chicago, 2003).

# CHAPTER SIX

# Sewers and sensibilities: the Bourgeois faecal experience in the nineteenth-century city

*David Inglis*

Friedrich Nietzsche once noted that no one had yet written a philosophical treatise on the social and moral significance of the human nose. Yet, in recent years, there has been an explosion of scholarly interest across the humanities and social sciences in matters to do with smell and olfaction, as these impinge upon forms of social relationships and modes of social organisation. Smell has become a 'hot' topic in disciplines as diverse as cultural history, anthropology, sociology, cultural studies, psychology, geography and literary studies.[1] The focus in all of these areas has been on the sociocultural mediation of smell, regarding it, not as a biologically 'hard-wired' human universal, but as contingent upon variant modes of social and cultural ordering. The olfactory dispositions of particular sets of people located in particular times and places are viewed as functions of the specific olfactory orderings of their social and historical contexts. Quite simply, then, the emphasis in recent work has been on how the odorifically 'foul' and 'fragrant' are radically historically and socially context-specific. The task has been to identify differing modes of olfactory dispositions and to explain why particular

---

[1] For example, G. Glaser, *The Nose: A Profile of Sex, Beauty and Survival* (New York, 2002); T.P. Hannigan, 'Body odour: the international student and cross-cultural communication', *Culture and Psychology*, 1 (1995), pp. 497–503; D. Howes and M. Lalonde, 'The history of sensibilities: of the standard of taste in mid-eighteenth-century England and the circulation of smells in Post-Revolutionary France', *Dialectical Anthropology*, 16 (1991), pp. 125–35; D. Laporte, *History of Shit* (Boston, 2002); R.A. Lewin, *Merde: Excursions in Scientific, Cultural and Sociohistorical Coprology* (London, 1999); A. Le Guerer, *Scent: The Mysterious and Essential Power of Smell* (New York, 1992); W.I. Miller, *The Anatomy of Disgust* (Cambridge, Mass., 1997); P. Rodaway, *Sensuous Geographies: Body, Sense and Place* (London, 1994); J. Scanlan, *On Garbage* (London, 2004); D. Rollfinke and R. Rollfinke, *The Call of Human Nature: The Role of Scatology in Modern German Literature* (Amherst, 1986); A. Synnott, 'A sociology of smell', *The Canadian Review of Sociology and Anthropology*, 28 (1991), pp. 437–59.

sociohistorical circumstances produce particular sorts of olfactory practices.

In this essay, I will draw upon some of this recent work on the socio-historical creation of senses of smell, including my own contributions to the field, in order to ascertain the historical processes whereby modern Westerners have come to smell things, especially their own bodily wastes, in the ways that they happen to do so in the present day. My argument is that the Victorian city should be seen as the crucible in which such sensory dispositions were generated. More specifically, I will argue that it is the Victorian revolution in urban sewerage systems that is a key factor in the genesis of modern sensory dispositions, which revile both the smell *and* sight of human faeces. The mid-to-late nineteenth-century water-sluiced sewerage system and its corollary in the domestic sphere, the water closet, were not just 'neutral' technologies of waste disposal designed to meet the requirements of public health. They should also be regarded as symbolic entities that met other needs felt by elites of the time, needs which had been developing amongst west European elites since the early modern period.

I will argue that Victorian sewers and water closets were simul-taneously (1) expressions of bourgeois disgust at human wastes – and, by extension, the human body itself; (2) important factors in the further development of such feelings and sentiments amongst elites; (3) crucial means whereby bourgeois imperatives as to rendering human wastes 'socially invisible' (that is, invisible to the eye and inoffensive to the nose) were met; and (4) central conduits for the eventual extension of such dispositions, and the life style practices attendant upon them, to the broad mass of the population in the twentieth century. My focus in pursuing this argument will primarily be on English and French sources, especially as these pertain to London and Paris, but the account of the interplay between sewers and senses here outlined holds more generally for other large and medium-scale urban areas in north-western Europe in the same period.[2] I conclude by reiterating the importance of

---

[2] As a sociologist by training, rather than a 'historian' per se, I am interested in general trends vis-à-vis changing understandings of human wastes. This essay will reflect my intellectual dispositions, insofar as it will delineate general trends in urban sanitary governance that occurred throughout north-western Europe in the period under consideration, rather than focus in detail on a particular locale as a case study. Clearly, it is empirically the case that the trends towards the construction of water-based sewer systems I identify were stronger or weaker in different urban locales at different times. Local variations could arise for a multitude of reasons; for example, how strongly in favour of new sewerage systems were the powerful groups on particular local authorities. Moreover, larger conurbations such as London tended to undergo sewerage processes on a

understanding the crucial role nineteenth-century sewer systems have played in creating the senses of bodily propriety, particularly in odorific terms, that we feel in the present day.[3]

## The spread of sewerage

One of the defining aspects of the later nineteenth-century cityscape is that which lay beneath it: the complex network of sewers and drains that sluiced the urban environment. As Asa Briggs has noted, there was a profound contrast between the bourgeois state's management of wastes below ground, and the cityscape produced in an era of laissez-faire capitalism:

> Perhaps . . . [the] outstanding feature [of later nineteenth-century cities] was, hidden from public view, their hidden network of pipes and drains and sewers, one of the biggest technical and social achievements of the age, a sanitary 'system' more comprehensive than the transport system. Yet their surface world was fragmented, intricate, cluttered, eclectic and noisy, the unplanned product of a private enterprise economy developing within an older traditional society.[4]

Water-based sewer systems were regarded by contemporary observers as one of the great achievements of the age. They heralded an epoch of hygiene and salubrity, combating the locales that produced noxious diseases and foul emanations. The desire to eliminate diseases through the means of water-based sewerage led to the rapid construction of such systems in larger conurbations throughout the Western world in a relatively short period of time.

---

greater scale and sooner than provincial cities, and these latter tended to have more resources at their disposal than smaller towns (for the British case in this regard, see A.S. Wohl, *Endangered Lives: Public Health in Victorian Britain* (London, 1984); B. Keith-Lucas, 'Some influences affecting the development of sanitary legislation in England', *Economic History Review*, Second Series, 6 (1954), pp. 290–96. Given these caveats as to local particularities, this essay intends to set up an 'ideal typical' account of major trends towards the implementation of sewerage systems across north-western Europe in the later nineteenth century, so that we may discern the major contours of changing sensory dispositions towards human excreta in the period.

[3] The argument pursued here comes from my monograph on the changing nature of Western understandings of excreta: see D. Inglis, *A Sociological History of Excretory Experience: Defecatory Manners and Toiletry Technologies* (Lewiston, NY, 2001). Certain sections of the present essay derive from Chapter 5 of that book.

[4] A. Briggs, *Victorian Cities* (Harmondsworth, 1968), pp. 16–17.

For example, less than two decades after construction began in 1859, London had a system of 83 miles of modern sewers, which carried 420 million gallons of water a day. In a period of laissez-faire dogmas in other areas, this system cost the British state over four million pounds.[5] Other major British towns were given similar systems soon after.[6] The central organ charged with regulating British local authorities, the Local Government Board, noted in its 1875 Report that 'Sewerage and drainage [are] either very defective or wanting altogether'. But its 1886–87 Report noted that, in 'most populous places sewering had been completed'.[7] In Paris, the sewer system was enlarged from 87 miles in length in 1852, to 350 miles in less than twenty years.[8] By 1911, there were 759 miles of sewers beneath the city.[9] Berlin and many other major northwestern European cities received similar systems in the 1870s.[10] Both in Western Europe and in the United States, most large cities had extensive modern sewerage systems by the beginning of the twentieth century.[11] Smaller urban locales in these countries soon followed suit.

Sewer systems were felt by most contemporary observers in England and France from the third quarter of the nineteenth century onwards to be necessary elements in a functional and healthy urban environment. But if one wishes to comprehend why this viewpoint had become so entrenched by this period, and thus also why water-based sewer systems were developed so rapidly in the later nineteenth-century city, one must contextualise these developments within broader processes of social change, the roots of which stretch back several centuries.

### The prehistory of sewers: changing sensibilities

As we will see in more detail below, the *immediate* causes of the view that sewerage was an absolutely essential element of urban life were beliefs as to the medical and moral benefits of such systems. However, the more general and indirect reason behind the perceived need for

---

[5] L. Wright, *Clean and Decent: The Fascinating History of the Bathroom and the Water Closet* (London, 1960), p. 156.

[6] A.S. Wohl, pp. 107–8.

[7] Cited in W.M. Frazer, *A History of English Public Health 1834–1939* (London, 1950), pp. 128, 131.

[8] R.H. Guerrand, 'Scenes and places', in P. Ariès and G. Duby, eds, *A History of Private Life*, vol. 4 (London, 1990), p. 372.

[9] D. Reid, *Paris Sewers and Sewermen: Realities and Representations* (Cambridge, Mass., 1991), p. 35.

[10] G. Rosen, *A History of Public Health* (New York, 1958), p. 258.

[11] G.C. Winkler and R.W. Moss, 'How the bathroom got white tiles', *Historic Preservation*, 36 (1984), pp. 32–5.

sewerage systems at this time was the development of a particular set of sensory dispositions. These had increasingly over time come to characterise bourgeois understandings and perceptions of what could be visually and olfactorily tolerated and what could not. By the middle of the nineteenth century, bourgeois observers operated with a set of sensory sensibilities, which could only with great difficulty bear the sight or smell of human filth. As sewerage systems were thought to diminish the visual and olfactory presence of human wastes in the urban milieu, they increasingly were regarded as a *sine qua non* of effective urban governance.

This set of sensory dispositions had been developing amongst elite groups, both aristocratic and (upper) bourgeois, since early modernity.[12] According to Norbert Elias's well-known account of the 'civilising process', which he sees as characteristic of social development in Western Europe, defecatory practices and verbal references to excretory matters were both subjected to increasing levels of repression from the early modern period onwards.[13] In the medieval West, excreta and excretion could appear relatively unproblematically within the purview of people in all social strata.[14] In this context, both defecation and verbal reference to matters excretory were relatively free of forms of regulation. This was because, within the social relations characteristic of that time, 'interest in bodily secretions . . . [could] show . . . itself . . . more clearly and openly' than in the different social relational conditions of modernity.[15]

In the medieval West, a person could excrete relatively unproblematically not only in the presence of other people, but also in a wide range of socially legitimate locales. In most medieval towns and cities there were usually very few latrines for public use, and thus the streets were the most likely place for defecation.[16] People were 'compelled to relieve themselves anywhere, to urinate inside towers and casemates, or in the porches of private houses in the less frequented streets'.[17] A vivid story is told by Boccaccio in the *Decameron*, his collection of stories dating from

---

[12] Limitations of space do not allow me to discuss differences in attitudes towards 'cleanliness' between aristocratic and bourgeois groups in the period. For an indication of this situation as it played out in the French context, see G. Vigarello, *Concepts of Cleanliness: Changing Attitudes in France Since the Middle Ages* (Cambridge, 1988).

[13] See N. Elias, *The Civilising Process* (Oxford, 1995 [1939]).

[14] J.-P. Leguay, *La Rue au Moyen Age* (Rennes, 1984).

[15] Elias, *The Civilising Process*, p. 122.

[16] G.T. Salusbury-Jones, *Street Life in Medieval England* (Hassocks, Sussex, 1975), pp. 96–7; E. Sabine, 'Latrines and cesspools of medieval London', *Speculum*, 9 (1934), pp. 306, 335–53; R. Palmer, *The Water Closet* (Newton Abbot, 1973), p. 16.

[17] Leguay, *La Rue au Moyen Age*, p. 58.

the mid-fourteenth century. Having been tricked by a Neapolitan courtesan, the horse-dealer Andreuccio walks onto planks suspended above a ditch where excreta are collected, and then, losing his balance, falls into the filth. Such planks were suspended between two houses, thus creating a primitive form of latrine seat, which was open to wide public scrutiny.[18]

Despite the visual and olfactory ubiquity of human wastes, the medieval burgh was not (and did not seem to its inhabitants to be) overwhelmed by the sheer quantity of faeces to be disposed of, as would be the case several centuries later. This was reflected in the means that were in place to dispose of faeces and other refuse. Medieval attitudes to urban cleansing were on the whole limited to finding ways of moving refuse from central parts of the urban areas to the periphery. Urban dwellers disposed of excreta by removing them to ditches on the outskirts, or into rivers.[19] In the case of sewers per se, the medieval and early modern practice of emptying pots filled with detritus into the gutters meant that the urban streets were themselves sewer channels.[20] The medieval and early modern sewer was not, like its later counterpart, a covered channel sluiced by water and designed to carry away waste materials; rather, it was both understood and functioned as a drain to rid the streets of rain water.[21] In the medieval world, therefore, there was neither a strong set of imperatives to hide excretory acts or to dispose of human wastes in such a way that they were borne quickly from one's purview.[22]

From such relatively 'open' conditions of defecatory and verbal practice, the seventeenth and eighteenth centuries paid witness to a set of more strict demarcations of, firstly, where excretion could legitimately take place, and, secondly, the ways in which such products could be

---

[18] G. Boccaccio, *The Decameron* (Harmondsworth, 1995), p. 103.

[19] Salusbury-Jones, *Street Life in Medieval England*, p. 90.

[20] F. Braudel, *Capitalism and Material Life 1400–1800* (London, 1973), p. 225; J. Rawlinson, 'Sanitary engineering Part II: Sanitation', in C. Singer et al., eds, *A History of Technology, vol. 4, The Industrial Revolution* (Oxford, 1958), pp. 520–41; I. Darlington, *The London Commissioners of Sewers and Their Records* (Chichester, 1969).

[21] G. Kitson-Clark, *The Making of Victorian England* (London, 1962), p. 71.

[22] It would be wrong to suggest, however, that there was a completely laissez-faire attitude amongst medieval town authorities vis-à-vis the issue of waste management, at least in some cases. For example, the city authorities of Paris outlawed the dumping of detritus in the streets, part of which would have come from pots, in 1395. Indeed, Parisian authorities seem to have been particularly strenuous in promoting alternative forms of disposal to the pot. Laws of 1513 bade that every house have a 'privy', that is, a permanent means of disposal attached to a container such as a barrel or a cesspool. See J.G. Bourke, *Scatalogic Rites of All Nations* (New York, 1968 [1891]), p. 136.

referred to verbally.[23] The direction of such trends was towards both the progressive restriction of defecation into *privatised* locales, and greater levels of *indirect* forms of verbal referencing of excretory matters.

In terms of the latter process, the feelings of embarrassment and disgust that such topics increasingly engendered in the early modern speaker were 'mastered by . . . precisely regulated social ritual and by . . . concealing formulae'.[24] For example, Elias cites a French courtesy manual from 1774 that offers an example of the demand for verbal propriety vis-à-vis excretory matters: 'It is never proper to speak of parts of the body that should always be hidden, or of certain bodily necessities to which nature has subjected us, or even to mention them.'[25]

Likewise, in the same period throughout the Western world and in larger urban areas especially, increasing limitations were effected upon the set of places where excretion could legitimately occur. Defecation was to be carried out only in locales deemed to be 'private' spaces.[26] Such spaces were separated from arenas dedicated to other forms of practice, such that excreting persons could not be subjected to the feelings of embarrassment which they would undergo if caught in the gaze of other people viewing them while in the act. Furthermore, any potential members of the audience viewing such acts and the products thereof would not be exposed to the feelings of disgust such acts would provoke. Increasingly, it was the case that, when such acts were carried out in public, they provoked horrified reactions amongst observers drawn from elite groups. For example, in his travels in Italy in the 1780s, Goethe was horrified by the local habit of defecating and urinating in public places.[27] In like fashion, Tobias Smollett, offended by the practices of the French and Italians during his travels of the 1760s, exclaimed:

> There are certain mortifying views of human nature, which undoubtedly ought to be concealed as much as possible, in order to prevent giving offence: and nothing can be more absurd, than to plead the difference of custom in different countries, in defence of those usages which cannot fail giving disgust to the organs and senses of all mankind.[28]

Examples such as these suggest that demands for privatised defecation were well in place among north-western European elites by the time of

---

[23] K. Allen and K. Burridge, *Euphemism and Dysphemism: Language Used as Weapon and Shield* (Oxford, 1991).

[24] Elias, *The Civilizing Process*, pp. 155–6.

[25] Cited in Elias, *The Civilizing Process*, p. 109.

[26] J. Pudney, *The Smallest Room* (London, 1954).

[27] J.W. Goethe, *Italian Journey* (Harmondsworth, 1970 [1786]), pp. 62, 64.

[28] T. Smollett, *Travels Through France and Italy* (Oxford, 1992 [1766]), p. 33.

the French Revolution. Yet we should not view the new set of mores as taking hold of elite life styles completely at this period, or without resistance from the accumulated historical weight of previous attitudes and practices. Urination in public remained acceptable in many parts of Western Europe in the eighteenth century, even amongst those at the upper end of the social hierarchy. In the Paris of Louis XVI, for example, visitors to the Louvre and Palais de Justice openly urinated within these buildings, receiving no condemnation from public morality for their acts.[29] Likewise, when Frederick the Great of Prussia erected the palace of Sans Souci, it was felt necessary to place a notice on the great portico asking courtiers not to urinate on the stairs.[30]

Nonetheless, the identifiable trend in all north-western European countries in the period is towards even greater restrictions on where one could defecate and how one could talk about such matters. Put together, the twin processes of referring indirectly to excreta and physically excreting in privatised locales involved decreasing degrees of the *social visibility* of excretory phenomena. This situation, both practical and symbolic, reflected a social context in which people in general, and those in elite groups in particular, had come to feel much more uneasy about the waste-producing capacities of their own bodies than had their ancestors.

### Unbearable urban filth and the onset of faecal crises

Despite the examples as to the continued acceptance of public urination cited above, there is ample historical evidence to suggest that, by about the second or third decades of the eighteenth century, members of both the aristocracy and the upper bourgeoisie had begun to find the presence of human wastes in the urban environment a highly displeasing, if not downright distressing, state of affairs.[31] The very presence of faeces, accumulated as they were in the gutters and drains, piled high in dungheaps, or pungently lurking in cesspits, confronted the eyes and noses of persons in elite groups at every turn.

An early voice raised in censure of the dirt-ridden streets of the European city was that of Jonathan Swift, whose poetry and prose both demonstrate a fixation with faecal matters. The filthy manners and bodies of the uncivilized Yahoos in *Gulliver's Travels* were intended to hold up a mirror to what Swift regarded as the equally foul faecal

---

[29] Braudel, *Capitalism and Material Life*, pp. 48, 225.
[30] P.L. Berger, *The Capitalist Revolution* (Aldershot, 1987), p. 99.
[31] C. Fabricant, *Swift's Landscape* (Baltimore, 1982), pp. 24–30.

behaviour of modern city dwellers.[32] Swift, as is demonstrated amply in many of his other writings, was acutely aware of the urban situation around him. For example, in *An Examination of Certain Abuses, Corruptions and Enormities in the City of Dublin*, Swift declaims that in that particular city 'every person who walks the streets must needs observe the immense number of human excrements at the doors and steps of waste houses, and at the sides of every dead wall'.[33] If the streets of Dublin were particularly vile, as not only Swift but contemporary opinion in general believed, so to an almost equivalent degree were those of London.[34] Swift's *A Description of a City Shower* relates the nature of the flood of detrituses that ensues each time the city experiences a rainstorm:

> Filths of all hues and odours . . .
> Sweepings from butchers' stalls, dung, guts, and blood,
> Drowned puppies, stinking sprats, all drenched in mud,
> Dead cats and turniptops come tumbling down the flood.[35]

This condemnation of the inadequacies of London's sewer system vividly dramatises upper-bourgeois and aristocratic perceptions of the problems of urban living at this period. Swift's writings are, in effect, dramatisations of elite confrontations with the increasingly densely populated urban scene he and his contemporaries were compelled to dwell within. For Swift, the urban body politic was like a carcass 'swollen . . . five times greater than it should be'.[36] Elite observers in other national contexts shared these perceptions.

A contemporaneous Italian describes the town of Modena in like manner, viewing the urban locale from the viewpoint of an onlooker horrified by the threat of overwhelming filth: 'Upon corner stones / and by gateways everywhere / untidy and scattered mounds of old manure / . . . Odorous turds and heaps of chamber pots / upset and scattered about and lurid torrents / of urine and rank and foulsmelling broth / that you cannot walk without boots.'[37]

Confronted by all these visible and odorific horrors, social elites, both aristocratic and bourgeois, wished for a more salubrious urban environment. In his poem *Trivia*, written in 1716, John Gay makes an

---

[32] J. Swift, *Gulliver's Travels* (Harmondsworth, 1994 [1726]).

[33] Cited in J.M. Murry, *Jonathan Swift: A Critical Biography* (London, 1954), p. 438.

[34] Fabricant, *Swift's Landscape*, pp. 24–30.

[35] J. Swift, *The Complete Poems*, ed. P. Rogers (Harmondsworth, 1983), p. 114.

[36] Cited in C.H. Flynn, *The Body in Swift and Defoe* (Cambridge, 1990), p. 132.

[37] Cited in P. Camporesi, *The Incorruptible Flesh* (Cambridge, 1988), p. 86.

imprecation, which in effect expresses the desires of elites in general: 'O bear me to the Paths of fair Pellmell / Safe are thy Pavements, grateful is thy Smell!'[38] In essence, then, the social elites of the eighteenth century, unlike their medieval predecessors, strongly abhorred both the sight and smell of human wastes as these intruded into their purview in the urban environment. This situation was exacerbated in the later eighteenth century, especially in large urban areas such as London and Paris, by constantly increasing levels of population density.[39] As Anthony Wohl notes, increasing population density produced far greater levels of human wastes in urban areas throughout Western Europe than had previously been the case: 'Among the many problems which urban densities exacerbated, none was greater than the accumulation of excrement, both human and animal, which was the unavoidable by-product of urban growth.'[40]

By the end of the eighteenth century and on into the early decades of the next century, there existed a profound contradiction between what aristocratic and bourgeois elites desired in sensory terms, the absence of the sight and smell of human excreta, and the situation as it actually pertained in towns and cities, especially those which had very rapidly increasing and densely-packed populations. This situation of potential faecal crisis was made worse by contemporary fears as to the health-destroying properties of human detritus, especially in terms of the odours they gave off. Before the mid-eighteenth century, the odours of excreta were already to a significant degree regarded as both disgusting and inimical to health. This was a result, not only of medieval and early-modern medical knowledge, but also, in connection with the processes we noted above, the increasing moral affront to propriety faeces were felt to offer. Thus the phase in Western Europe from the later medieval period to the second half of the eighteenth century paid witness to a relatively *gradual* reduction in levels of tolerance for faecal smells.[41] But from the mid-eighteenth century onwards, the process of reducing tolerances for such odours became much more rapid and intense than had previously been the case.

The French cultural historian Alain Corbin contends that, from this period onwards, there was a progressive 'lowering of the threshold of the tolerance for stench' throughout north-western Europe.[42] Odours of all

---

[38] J. Gay, *Poetry and Prose*, ed. V.A. Dearing (Oxford, 1974 [1716]), p. 150.

[39] J. Clifford, 'Some aspects of London life in the mid-18th century', in P. Fritz and D. Williams, eds, *City and Society in the 18th Century* (Toronto, 1973), pp. 22–31.

[40] Wohl, *Endangered Lives*, pp. 92–3.

[41] Inglis, *A Sociological History*.

[42] A. Corbin, *The Foul and the Fragrant* (Leamington Spa, 1986), p. 85.

varieties were 'more keenly smelled' than hitherto, and thus became ever more of a focus for popular concerns on the one hand, and elite policy making in the realm of urban sanitary governance on the other.[43] Tolerances of many types of odour, such as stenches emanating from prisons or graveyards, were reduced because they were held to be threatening to health. There thus appeared over time dispositions towards ever lower levels of tolerance of types of odour previously inhaled relatively without qualm. Late eighteenth- and early nineteenth-century commentators began to be repulsed by aromas their ancestors had been much more sanguine about. The historical record of the time is littered with examples of this new odorific sensibility, which increasingly could not stand the fumes that assailed the urban dweller. For example, in the 1820s, Samuel Taylor Coleridge denounced the olfactory situation in the German town of Cologne in this way:

> In Köhln, a town of monks and bones,
> And pavements fang'd with murderous stones
> And rags, and hags, and hideous wenches;
> I counted two and seventy stenches,
> Ah well defined, and several stinks!
> Ye Nymphs that reign o'er sewers and sinks,
> The river Rhine, it is well known,
> Doth wash your city of Cologne;
> But tell me, Nymphs, what power divine
> Shall henceforth wash the river Rhine?[44]

At a slightly later date, in this case the 1830s, it was said that Queen Victoria found the Palace of Holyrood unbearable to live in, because of its proximity to Edinburgh's meadows, where the city's detritus was dumped and left to fester. Previous monarchs had expressed no such qualms.[45] If this is true, it shows the extent to which people in elite groups living in the later eighteenth and early nineteenth centuries possessed much lower levels of tolerance for faecal odours than did their ancestors.

Corbin argues that shifts in the direction of decreasing tolerance of odours were in large part due to the forms of medico-scientific knowledge which had arisen from around the middle of the eighteenth century, and which had become increasingly the dominant mode of comprehending phenomena in medical and natural scientific terms. Such knowledge involved what we may term *miasmic science*. Innovations in

---

[43] Corbin, *The Foul and the Fragrant*, p. 56.

[44] S.T. Coleridge, 'Cologne', in P. Driver, ed., *Poetry of the Romantics* (Harmondsworth, 1996), p. 66.

[45] E. Gauldie, *Cruel Habitations: A History of Working Class Housing 1780–1918* (London, 1974), p. 75.

the fields of medical and natural scientific knowledge in the second half of the eighteenth century produced a set of representations of *miasmas*, exhalations from decomposing matter, which both corrupted the surrounding air and were seen as the root cause of various forms of disease. As a result of such a view of the nature of disease, medical and scientific professionals increasingly deemed various types of odour as life-threatening.[46] Particular attention was given to odours given off by the human body and its effluvial products. To the miasmic mindset, putrefying fleshly smells were hazardous, not only for the continued survival of the individual whose body produced them, but also for the health of others, as such odours were ripe sources of disease.[47] The health of the human body thus could only be guaranteed if there was constant vigilance over 'effluvia, breath and body odour'.[48]

Thus, in the later eighteenth century, and on into the first half of the nineteenth century, faecal odours were condemned as they produced miasmic threats to health. Faecal odours were to be avoided as they could, quite literally, kill. Of particular concern were locales where putrefying excreta were left to linger, such as cesspools and dungheaps.[49] This new conceptualisation of the odours of excreta as life-imperilling threat meant that there now appeared new emphases in understandings of the nature of excreta per se. Not only were these materials viewed as *morally* dirty – as disgusting and shameful – but they increasingly became explicable as harmful to the health of the excreting person and those in his or her vicinity. Although this had previously been the case to a certain extent, from the middle of the eighteenth century onwards, excreta were seen as much as being *hygienically* dirty as they were seen as being disgusting and morally contaminating. Human effluvia were now, to an extent hitherto unknown, seen under the dual rubric of threats to social propriety and threats to health.

Given the increases in population density in large conurbations such as London and Paris in the early nineteenth century, it often seemed to contemporary observers as if the urban environment might soon be wholly overwhelmed by a flood of filth, which brought with it foul odours carrying the threat of death.[50] This sense of foreboding deepened as the nineteenth century progressed. The surveys of the dwellings of the very poor carried out by bourgeois observers in England from the 1830s onwards stressed both the sensory noxiousness of faecal odours and their

---

[46] Corbin, *The Foul and the Fragrant*, pp. 11–14, 58.
[47] Corbin, *The Foul and the Fragrant*, p. 21.
[48] Corbin, *The Foul and the Fragrant*, p. 47.
[49] Corbin, *The Foul and the Fragrant*, pp. 28–9.
[50] J.A. Banks, 'Population change and the Victorian city', *Victorian Studies*, 9 (1968), pp. 277–89.

potential threat to life and limb.[51] The voices of the reforming bourgeoisie denounced the effects of the 'odours of excrement and refuse' to be found in the slum areas of the big French and English cities.[52]

The horror felt by the contemporary bourgeoisie as to the dangers of faecal smells is well expressed in Engels' reportage of the conditions of Manchester and other northern English cities in 1844. In these locales, especially in the slums, bourgeois eye and nose were assailed by situations such as the dumping of excreta from privies straight into rivers, dung heaps piled up in yards, and small numbers of privies for large amounts of people.[53] Faecal dirt and its odours were understood as generating cholera, typhus and other contagious diseases, which not only diminished the labour power of the workforce, but also threatened the health and well-being of the bourgeoisie itself. As Engels pithily noted, if left unchecked, such filth could result in a situation where 'the angel of death rages in the ranks of the capitalists as ruthlessly as in the ranks of the workers'.[54]

It was not only the directly physical and medical dangers of human faeces that exercised the imaginations of bourgeois observers of the time. Living conditions deemed by state officials and social reformers as lacking in salubrity were understood to lead to feelings of discontent among the proletariat, and even to periodic outbursts of rebellion.[55] Moreover, faecal filth was associated in the bourgeois imaginary with the living of a morally reprehensible, improvident and lascivious lifestyle. For example, the cornerstone of early state intervention in sanitary matters in Britain, Edwin Chadwick's *Sanitary Report* of 1842, explicitly avowed that the state must act to combat faecal squalor in working-class areas of towns and cities, not just because of the great loss of labour power through disease and unsanitary conditions, but also owing to the deleterious moral effects these conditions led to:

> the annual loss of life from filth and bad ventilation is greater than the loss from death or wounds in any wars in which the country has been engaged in modern times . . . these adverse circumstances tend to produce an adult population shortlived, improvident, reckless,

---

[51] H. Mayhew, *Selections from 'London Labour and the London Poor'* (Oxford, 1965 [1851–2]); F. Engels, *The Condition of the Working Class In England in 1844* (Harmondsworth, 1987 [1845]).

[52] Corbin, *The Foul and the Fragrant*, p. 151.

[53] Engels, *The Condition of the Working Class*, pp. 80, 90, 98.

[54] F. Engels 'The housing question', in *Marx and Engels, Collected Works* (London, 1988), vol. 23, p. 337.

[55] H.J. Dyos, 'The slums of Victorian London', *Victorian Studies*, 9 (1967), pp. 5–40; J.H. Treble, *Urban Poverty in Britain 1830–1914* (London, 1979).

and intemperate, and with habitual avidity for sensual gratifications.[56]

Thus it was not just the hygienic aspects of human wastes that exercised the minds of bourgeois observers at this time, but also their moral aspects too. Left unconfined and unregulated, the excretory habits of the poor were seen to encourage an animal-like form of life that was barely human in nature. Corbin's argument vis-à-vis the French context applies to the English situation too. The ruling classes were obsessed with excretion. Faecal matter was an irrefutable product of physiology that the bourgeois strove to deny. Its implacable recurrence haunted the imagination; it gainsaid attempts at decorporalisation; it provided a link with organic life . . . The bourgeois projected onto the poor what he was trying to repress in himself. His image of the masses was constructed in terms of filth. The fetid animal, crouched in dung in its den, formed the stereotype.[57]

For the bourgeoisie of the early nineteenth century, it was not only the city above ground that was felt to be filthy. The primarily medieval sewers that served the urban environment were also sources of grave concern. The sewers operative in the early decades of the century allowed the accumulation of faecal deposits and were increasingly great causes of anxiety because they were seen to be harbourers of all sorts of maladies injurious to health. As Sir John Simon, London's first Medical Officer, wrote in 1848, 'part of the City might be described as having a cesspool city . . . under it'.[58] This problem of the 'cesspool city', the legacy of hundreds of years of relatively unplanned urban development, now had to be faced head-on, if diseases were to be brought under control. But it was not just the medical aspects of the ancient systems of sewers that caused concern at this time.

Not only did the medieval sewer seem to be a prime source of disease, it also seemed to pose a series of moral threats too. Writing à propos of Paris, Reid argues that the system of sewers below the city 'called to mind the diverse threats . . . social disorder presented to [bourgeois] civilization . . . Concerns about a disruptive world below helped give impetus to control and transform the subterranean'.[59] As Victor Hugo effectively dramatised the point in Les Misérables, the antique sewer was seen by the bourgeoisie of Paris and other cities as a refuge for criminals

[56] Cited in Frazer, History of English Public Health, pp. 18–19.
[57] Corbin, The Foul and the Fragrant, p. 144.
[58] Cited in E. Wilson, The Sphinx in the City: Urban Life, the Control of Disorder and Women (Berkeley, 1992), p. 26. See also Sir J. Simon, English Sanitary Institutions (London, 1970 [1890]).
[59] Reid, Paris Sewers and Sewermen, p. 3.

and other members of the promiscuous and shady lumpenproletariat, literally an 'underworld' where all sorts of despicable acts were carried out far from the gaze of the forces of order.[60]

It was not just conditions in the slum areas and in the sewers themselves that provoked alarm. In most north-western European cities in the decades spanning the middle of the nineteenth century, proletarian housing of all varieties generally tended to involve the sharing of privies and general washing facilities between members of different households and/or families. The sharing of such facilities was, by the standards of faecal privacy now held by the bourgeoisie, inimical to cleanliness, in terms both of hygienic standards and of moral rectitude.[61] The homes of the upper bourgeoisie in both France and England were by mid-century in part oriented around privatised locales where the excreting person was hidden away from the prying eyes of others. Thus it became particularly offensive to think of lower-class people voiding their wastes promiscuously and in full view of each other.

This stereotype made its way into much social commentary of the time. For example, the editorial column of the London newspaper *The Times* (2 March 1861) put the point this way: 'Such aggregations [of toiletry facilities] cannot be favourable either to public or to private morality. They must tend, not only to harbour, but to generate, dangerous classes.'[62] In a similar vein, the English social reformer John Glyde, writing in 1851, apropos the English town of Ipswich, argued:

> The demoralizing practice of providing but one convenience for several houses is . . . seen in full force . . . The deficiency of private receptacles for refuse must tend greatly to deteriorate the moral habits of the community . . . Are not these circumstances sufficient to destroy all modesty, to blight the beauty of the female character, and to banish all feelings of self-respect from the human mind; and do they not militate most powerfully against the comfort, decency and morality of the labouring population of the town? . . . Is it not hopeless to expect moral improvement of the working classes until the means of preventing such evils are provided?[63]

For this mindset, without thorough reform of the excretory habits of the working classes, civilization remained imperilled, not just in medico-hygienic terms but in moral terms too. Social order required regulated defecatory practices, particularly in terms of such acts being carried out

---

[60]  V. Hugo, *Les Misérables* (Paris, 1862).

[61]  Wohl, *Endangered Lives*, p. 87.

[62]  Cited in D. Rubinstein, ed., *Victorian Homes* (London, 1974), p. 147.

[63]  J. Glyde, 'The moral, social and religious condition of Ipswich in the middle of the Nineteenth Century', [1850] in Rubinstein, ed., *Victorian Homes*, pp. 113–14.

by individuals in private spaces, removed from public view. In the next few decades, defecation that met the imperatives of propriety would more and more be associated with 'water closets', mechanisms that involved water-borne means of excretory disposal. As a result, the water-sluiced sewer increasingly seemed to bourgeois opinion makers as an absolutely essential element in making working-class existence clean, in both hygienic and moral terms.

### The sewerage solution: safeguarding the sense of sight

By the third quarter of the century, both the hygienic and moral threats posed by human faeces had become so great that there was an increasing consensus amongst observers of many types, state officials, local government officers, engineers, social reformers and campaigners in both Britain and France, that serious steps had to be undertaken to recast the urban environment in a more salubrious direction. More and more, a system of water-sluiced sewers seemed to such observers to be the answer to the problems of faecal overload that large conurbations faced.

This type of sewer was a relatively novel invention, having only become a practical possibility on a large scale in the 1840s. It was in this decade that engineers, especially in England, developed a new form of piping, which was oval in shape and made of glazed earthenware. This novel type of piping allowed the flushing away of wastes by a high-speed water supply, and potentially taking them out of the urban environment and pumping them into rivers and other watercourses.[64] The firm of Henry Doulton, for example, began producing such piping for the burgeoning English local authority market from the late 1840s onwards.[65]

Perhaps the primary reason why this type of sewer was increasingly regarded as the great panacea of urban sanitation at this time was the contemporaneous rise of bacteriological science. The science of miasmas that held sway in most professional circles from the middle of the eighteenth century until around the 1860s held that the spontaneous generation of harmful elements from putrefying wastes was at the root of many diseases. Conversely, the bacteriological position that came to dominate biological and medical thinking from the middle of the nineteenth century onwards understood disease as the outcome of

---

[64] S.E. Finer, *The Life and Times of Edwin Chadwick* (London, 1952), pp. 221–2; J. Kennard, 'Sanitary engineering, Part 1: Water supply', in C. Singer et al., eds, *A History of Technology*, vol. 4, *The Industrial Revolution* (Oxford, 1958), p. 498.

[65] Palmer, *The Water Closet*, p. 57.

contagion by germs. Contagion of diseases such as typhus and cholera, both of which had recently struck major European cities, was now believed to occur through the transmission of germs by water-based means. This view involved a new twist to the understanding of excreta.[66] They were understood as prime sources of germs, and contagion was seen to occur through the means of uninfected people coming into contact with the wastes of infected persons.[67]

Given this shift in thinking away from miasmic odours as the root cause of diseases towards ideas centred on germs and contagion, forms of excretory disposal that had previously been tolerated and regarded as relatively unproblematic were now understood as themselves filthy and dangerous. For example, although the cesspool had hitherto been regarded as a locale that at least concentrated miasmic odours in one delimited area, for the bacteriologically informed mindset it seemed to be a prime breeding ground of germs. As water-borne theories of contagion gained ground, so too did evacuation of detritus through flushing sewers seem to be an extremely pressing necessity.[68] If germ-carrying excreta were put into these sewers, and such excreta were the cause of infection, then sewers were no longer places of disease *generation*, but rather areas of disease *transmission*. If sewers could be flushed by water so as to bear excreta to places where they could be rendered harmless, then disease transmission could be brought under control.[69]

Sewers of this kind were increasingly regarded by engineering and medical professionals in the 1860s, and after, as drastically reducing the probability of disease, and thus the death rate, in the areas where they operated.[70] By the late 1860s, there were widespread beliefs amongst bourgeois opinion-making groups in both England and France as to the benefits of water-based sewers, and their concomitant, water closets, in the prevention of disease.[71] State officials and other concerned parties of the time were deeply impressed by the possibilities offered by water-based sewers of rendering urban environments 'cleanly'. It was on this basis that the great projects of sewer building, described at the beginning of this essay, were undertaken by state officials from the 1860s onwards.

A particularly striking instance of state officials coming face-to-face with the urgent need for reform of detritus management systems is

---

[66] Vigarello, *Concepts of Cleanliness*, pp. 202–5, 209, 211.

[67] Wohl, *Endangered Lives*, p. 89; F. Brockington, *A Short History of Public Health* (London, 1966), p. 40; S.B. Smith and N. Young, 'Sewers past and present', *History Today*, 43 (1993), p. 9.

[68] Gauldie, *Cruel Habitations*, p. 78.

[69] Brockington, *A Short History of Public Health*, p. 41.

[70] F.B. Smith, *The People's Health 1830–1910* (London, 1979), pp. 245–6.

[71] Smith, *The People's Health*, pp. 245–6.

afforded by the English context. The exceptionally hot summer of 1858 caused what came to be known as the 'Great Stink'. In the heat, the Thames began more than usual to display its role as the main conduit out of London for the contents of many of the capital's ancient sewers. In the words of the engineer Joseph Bazalgette, who was charged by Parliament the following year to begin the construction of new, water-sluiced sewers that would not discharge directly into the river, the hot weather had caused a situation whereby the odour arising from the Thames had become 'absolutely pestilential'.[72] Denizens of the Houses of Parliament were appalled by the noxious fumes rising from the water and assailing their nostrils. As *The Times* reported at the time:

> Parliament was all but compelled to legislate upon the great London nuisance by the force of sheer stench. The intense heat had driven our legislators from those portions of their buildings which overlook the river. A few members, bent upon investigating the matter to its very depth, ventured into the library, but they were instantaneously driven to retreat, each man with a handkerchief to his nose.[73]

Here we have a particularly vivid example of the great and the good being assaulted by excremental odours, their olfactory dispositions now being much less resilient than that of their forefathers. In other national and regional contexts, the attack on the senses of those in a position to reform the nature of waste disposal was generally less immediate and dramatic than was the case in London. Yet this particular example vividly illustrates the extent to which, by around 1860, the issue of excremental refuse was no longer one that could be ignored by those whose sensory life was increasingly based on utter repugnance for such materials.

As we have already noted, the major projects of sewer construction from the 1860s onwards were not undertaken for purely 'scientific' reasons. Apart from the apparent bacteriological benefits of water-sluiced sewer systems, they also provided ways of meeting the imperatives of the defecatory mores that had been developing amongst elites since the early modern period, in the direction of decreasing levels of tolerance for the sight and smell of human wastes. Thus part of the increasing demand for large-scale, water-sluiced sewers from the middle of the century onwards resided in the fact that they were part of new techniques of waste evacuation that made faeces *invisible*. This was so in two ways.

---

[72] S. Halliday, *The Great Stink of London: Sir Joseph Bazalgette and the Cleansing of the Victorian Capital* (Stroud, Glos., 1999), p. 5.
[73] Halliday, *The Great Stink of London*, p. 71.

First, by being connected to the self-enclosed and privatised locale of the water closet, the sewer was part of a moral and technological nexus that encouraged defecation to occur in private spaces.[74] Second, as this technology voided wastes rapidly away from the purview of the person who had evacuated them, it allowed that person very little contact, either visual or olfactory, with the detritus produced by their own bodies.[75] As a result, the sewer may be seen as both resultant of, and contributing to, long-term processes of masking the fact that the human body does indeed excrete, processes that had begun to develop in Western Europe several centuries before.

The systems of sewers that operated underneath the city streets of major conurbations such as London and Paris from the 1860s onwards greatly reduced the amount of human wastes that could be seen on those streets. The sewer systems of the later nineteenth century met the imperatives of keeping excreta hidden from the gaze of the bourgeois who found such materials repulsive, for sewerage of this sort was a means of excretory disposal which primarily occurred *underground*. The stated aim of bourgeois sanitary reformers, such as London's chief Medical Officer Sir John Simon, was to keep the urban environment 'free from the excrements of the population'.[76] This was achieved by the transmission of excreta out of the home or workplace into subterranean spaces beneath the city streets, and thence by bearing them off to distant locales in order to be processed. The sewer system, despite being huge in scale, did not threaten bourgeois sensibilities, insofar as it operated unseen.

The sensibilities of the later nineteenth-century middle classes who lived on the surface were therefore safeguarded by the vast excretory disposal network that quietly functioned beneath their streets and homes. The functionaries of the bourgeois state which constructed and ran these vast systems of disposal were well aware that the benefits to be gained from underground water-based sewerage included the prevention of faeces being seen above ground. Baron Haussmann believed that the new sewers, and the army of sewermen who laboured unseen within them, would allow the banishment of excreta from the streets of Paris, along with the 'unsightly' cesspools and scavengers that had previously been the main means of collection.[77] Only specially trained cadres would now see massed accumulations of faeces on a daily basis, a sight previously open to the gaze of the public. Such cadres would experience

---

[74] Wright, *Clean and Decent*.
[75] Smith and Young, 'Sewers past and present'.
[76] Cited in Wohl, *Endangered Lives*, p. 94.
[77] Reid, *Paris Sewers and Sewermen*, pp. 72–80.

this horror, not under the cover of darkness, as had the scavengers and cesspool cleaners of previous centuries, but under the clear light of scientific rationality, in the well-lit sewer and the modern sewage-processing plant.[78]

The visual benefits of the new type of sewers were not restricted to hiding excreta from the people who had produced them. The sewer system also brought with it moral and political benefits. For the bourgeois mindset, bringing moral cleanliness to the city involved an *orderly* recasting of urban space. This mode of reforming space applied as much to subterranean locales as it did to the environment above ground.[79] In the British context, central government legislation from the 1840s onwards required that local authorities map out their existing sewer systems; the position of privies and cesspools had to be noted and approved by local authorities. Government officials were to 'draw up plans, inspect, measure, level, supervise work in progress, examine the course of sewers and drains, [and] inspect or fix boundaries'.[80] Rather than harbouring dangers to the bourgeois order, such as criminals and malcontents, the new systems of sewers could now actually be utilised by the state to strike back at demotic rebellions. For example, the English sanitary reformer Edwin Chadwick viewed the mapped-out sewers as means whereby the police could travel through the city unbeknownst to rampaging Chartists, taking the latter by surprise.[81]

Similar processes were at work in Paris at around the same time. From at least the Revolution onwards, the old system of sewers under the city were associated in the bourgeois mind with potential demotic unrest, for they were unsupervised and relatively unmapped, and a lascivious *demimonde* was felt to lurk within them.[82] State scrutiny, in the interests of rendering safe this putrid, tumultuous zone, was thus brought to bear on this underworld. Sewer mapping became the concern of successive bourgeois regimes.[83] Mapping of existing sewer systems brought them, as it were, into the light of day, allowing the gaze of the bourgeois state to penetrate into their deepest recesses. The building of new sewer systems by the state from the 1860s onwards, according to geometrically

---

[78] Wohl, *Endangered Lives*, p. 110; Reid, *Paris Sewers and Sewermen*, pp. 60–69.

[79] Vigarello, *Concepts of Cleanliness*, pp. 192–3, 230.

[80] Provisions of the 1848 Health Act, cited in L. Benevolo, *The Origins of Modern Town Planning* (London, 1967), pp. 95–7; see also W. Ashworth, *The Genesis of Modern British Town Planning* (London, 1954), pp. 25–6.

[81] R.A. Lewis, *Edwin Chadwick and the Public Health Movement 1832–1854* (London, 1952), note to pp. 89–90.

[82] Reid, *Paris Sewers and Sewermen*, pp. 23–4.

[83] Reid, *Paris Sewers and Sewermen*, pp. 18–19.

composed plans, further facilitated these trends towards the surveillance of the territories below ground. Thus, in Paris, the *cloaque* of the *ancien régime*, with its organic, intestinal associations, was replaced by the *égout*, which denoted a man-made construction, under human guidance and control.[84] The sewers of early nineteenth-century Paris were understood by the contemporary bourgeoisie to be 'feminine' in nature, for they were under the influence of Nature rather than Reason, and thus full of potentially subversive threats. Conversely, the sewers constructed by the state in the Haussmann period and after exhibited a 'masculine' rationality, allowing a predictable uniformity where Nature was harnessed rather than in control.[85]

The transformation of Parisian sewers under Haussmann meant that, far from being a site of threats from disease and lumpen-proletarian agitation, by the second half of the century they were a 'locus of health and public order'.[86] The equipping of all Parisian streets with sewers underneath was the corollary of the recasting of the streets themselves, in the form of long, straight boulevards along which barricades could but with difficulty be erected and defended. Such trends towards subterranean forms of control were exhibited in most major urban areas of Western Europe in the later nineteenth century and on into the next. The bourgeois state recast the nature of the urban environment above and below in terms of making faecal discontents increasingly invisible, thus bringing control, order and moral cleanliness to both simultaneously.[87]

## The war against odours

Just as the new systems of sewers allowed people to avoid viewing their own wastes and those of others, so too did they facilitate the bourgeois nose in its quest to evade the foul odours of excreta. This led to considerable technological problems for the cadre of engineers employed by the state. If the excrements of entire populations were to be cast into the newly established sewer systems, this rendered them potentially profoundly odorific sites, utterly antithetical to the lowered olfactory thresholds of the day. Indeed, the horror felt for the primarily medieval and early-modern sewers that had hitherto served the city was due to the perception that such locales were prime sources of foul odours and

---

[84] Reid, *Paris Sewers and Sewermen*, p. 36.
[85] Reid, *Paris Sewers and Sewermen*, p. 41.
[86] Reid, *Paris Sewers and Sewermen*, p. 36; see also E. Hobsbawm, *The Age of Capital 1848–1875* (London, 1995).
[87] Benevolo, *The Origins of Modern Town Planning*, pp. 110, 135.

disease. In order for excretory emanations to be brought under control in these areas, strategies of deodorification were developed to allow the spaces under the cities to smell as anodyne as, increasingly, did the urban environment above ground.[88]

Thus, in the later nineteenth century, both the French and British states were greatly concerned to apply new scientific and technological developments in the neutralisation of faecal odours, both in the sewers and on the urban surface.[89] Sewage-processing plants that could process faecal stenches increasingly replaced rivers as the favoured points of outfall for sewers. Stenches emanating from major watercourses such as the Thames (see above) had caused great concern at mid-century, and contemporary bourgeois norms increasingly denied the possibility of leaving untreated sewage in rivers, on both hygienic and sensory grounds.[90] At the very least, effluents dumped in rivers had to be chemically treated before being deposited so as, among other things, to rob them of their smell.[91] Sewage-processing plants allowed the treatment of foul smells so that the vast amounts of excreta produced by urban populations, which had so offended bourgeois sensibilities before mid-century, were now rendered odorifically harmless.[92] As an aside, we should here also note that the word 'sewage' from this time onwards began to operate as an effective euphemism for human wastes, indicating materials that had been rendered 'safe' by the water-sluiced sewer and the processing plant. The overall sewerage system therefore guaranteed not only physical health but verbal propriety too.[93]

The new system of sewers itself was subjected to strategies of deodorisation, just as the spaces above ground were subjected to techniques of reducing smells unpleasant to the bourgeois nose. Moreover, the sewer system was deemed to be highly salubrious for it kept faeces in circulation, just as Haussmann's boulevards kept the populace above ground in constant movement. Such movement was felt to be healthy for it was akin to the circulatory system of the human body itself. No accretions of excrements were allowed to linger and fester.[94] These processes of bringing previously uncontrolled areas under regulation and

[88] Reid, *Paris Sewers and Sewermen*, pp. 1, 17.
[89] Corbin, *The Foul and the Fragrant*, p. 123; Reid, *Paris Sewers and Sewermen*, pp. 37–52.
[90] Wohl, *Endangered Lives*, pp. 233–56.
[91] Frazer, *A History of English Public Health*, p. 225.
[92] Rawlinson, 'Sanitary engineering Part II: Sanitation', p. 518; Wohl, *Endangered Lives*, p. 110; Reid, *Paris Sewers and Sewermen*, pp. 60–69.
[93] Smith, *The People's Health*, p. 219.
[94] W. Schivelbusch, *The Railway Journey* (Leamington Spa, 1986), p. 195; Vigarello, *Concepts of Cleanliness*, pp. 216–17.

scrutiny was part of wider trends of bourgeois governance of surface urban areas, such as the policing of prostitution, in line with the dictates of bourgeois decorum.[95]

But as well as providing solutions to existing problems of odour management, the new sewer systems sometimes brought with them their own odorific problems. The corollary of the sewer was the 'water closet', which from the 1870s onwards became the favoured mode of excretory disposal in the private realm for middle-class people. The expectation of the water closet from this time onwards was that it would void excreta totally and quickly from the domestic environment. A French source of the 1880s illustrates that water flushing was expected to protect the excreting person from the noxious entity his or her own body had produced, and thus to deny as far as possible that it had ever existed: 'City dwellers must be carefully protected from their excretions from the moment they are produced. The waste outlet, normally kept sealed, should be opened briefly, and waste should be forcefully expelled from the residence by a powerful stream of water.'[96]

Although the corps of engineers employed to keep sewer systems functional and salubrious could ensure that the main sewerage thorough-fares were kept relatively odour free, they could not guarantee that the pipes leading up from the sewers to water closets in private homes and other locales would be free of faecal deposits and their attendant fumes. This was particularly a problem if, as was now the case, defecation in middle-class homes was restricted to small closet-like rooms. Whilst defecating in a delimited space afforded the sort of privacy that now was the toiletry norm, it was nonetheless a space that could easily be polluted by foul odours, not just of the wastes that had recently been voided by people using the facilities, but also by the accumulated filth that had remained lodged on the walls of the pipes leading to the sewers.

It was a particularly loathsome thought that faeces should be retained by a system specifically designed swiftly and efficiently to expel them. Writing in the British context in the 1870s, Stevens Hellyer, the best-known sanitary engineer of the day, warned, 'There are a "thousand gates to death!" Fewer are wider, or open more readily, than those in our own homes, when unlocked by noxious gases or bad air from drains.'[97]

Within such a situation, the householder had always to be vigilant against odorific invasions from the drains, Trojan horses of a still some-times problematic underground world, which would on occasion erupt

---

[95] C. Bernheimer, 'Of whores and sewers', *Raritan – A Quarterly Monthly*, 6 (1987), pp. 72–90; Corbin, *The Foul and the Fragrant*, p. 145; Reid, *Paris Sewers and Sewermen*, p. 41.

[96] Cited in Guerrand, 'Scenes and places', p. 372.

[97] Cited in Palmer, *The Water Closet*, p. 47.

into the cleanly environment of the private home. Thus the contemporaneous domestic manual *Cassell's Book of the Household* enjoined the reader to give the water closet 'constant attention', recommending that, in the cause of dispelling foul accumulations, 'two or three pailfuls of water should be thrown down the pan every day to clean the pipes'.[98]

Given these problems, one of the main problems of toilet design in the final decades of the nineteenth century was the creation of a trap that would allow water in and out of the closet's bowl, but which yet would prevent unpleasant emanations from the drains.[99] In England, the acknowledged homeland of advanced toiletry technologies, by the late 1880s expectations as to the technical efficiency of water closets had become very great indeed. For example, Stevens Hellyer derided previous closet designs for their woeful inadequacies in expelling faeces into the sewers while keeping any unpleasant odours from the latter out of the home environment:

> No water closet is perfect which does not get rid of every vestige of excrement after usage but with one pull of the closet handle, i.e., a water closet which is not completely cleansed together with its trap and soil-pipe by a fair flush of water, say three gallons, is not a perfect closet.[100]

Private manufacturers of toiletry wares rushed to meet such demands, which were held not just by sanitary professionals such as Hellyer but increasingly by ordinary bourgeois householders too. The firm of the appropriately named Thomas Crapper was widely praised by public opinion of the time for developing a water closet that allowed a strong flush of water with minimum effort on the part of s/he who pulled the chain.[101] Thomas Twyford's company brought out a 'washout closet' which attempted to extend flushing capacity by doing away with valves in the design altogether, an innovation which further limited the possibility of odorific escapes from sewer pipes.[102] The major final innovation of later nineteenth-century toiletry design was the 'washdown closet', which was vaunted by its designers as having a stronger flushing action than previous types.[103] This type of toilet heralded a new age of excretory experience. It was designed in such a way that the threat of noxious emanations from the subterranean world outside and below

[98] Briggs, *Victorian Cities*, p. 252.

[99] M.J. Daunton, *House and Home in the Victorian City: Working Class Housing 1850–1914* (London, 1983), p. 258.

[100] Cited in Rubinstein, ed., *Victorian Homes*, pp. 89–90.

[101] W. Reyburn, *Flushed With Pride: The Story of Thomas Crapper* (London, 1989).

[102] Palmer, *The Water Closet*, pp. 6, 39–41.

[103] Wright, *Clean and Decent*, p. 205.

the home was mitigated as much as possible, therefore sealing off the domestic arena from odorific invasion from without. This type of closet remains the norm today across many parts of the Western world. It figures as a lasting legacy of the Victorian obsession with expelling excreta as rapidly as possible from the private realm, and for rendering human wastes as invisible and as odorifically neutral as is physically possible.

## Conclusion

In this essay, I have examined the crises of urban faecal disposal faced in Western European cities up to the middle of the nineteenth century, the reasons for the developments of these crises, and the solutions offered to meet them. In terms of the crises of faecal disposal that faced elites of the period, the reasons for their development were a complex of both socio-cultural and medico-scientific factors. It was both the moral and hygienic aspects of human wastes that were seen to be the problems that could be dealt with through state-sponsored sewer projects. Such projects sought, not only to reduce the generation and spread of disease in urban areas, but also to reform both the environment of proletarian areas and the moral economy of the people who dwelled therein.

Moreover, the sewer ensured that, for citizens in general, the great affront to the senses posed by human wastes was diminished, both in visual and olfactory terms. In this way, citizens were allowed to disassociate themselves from their excreta as soon as they had defecated. Faeces no longer lingered within sight or smell of the excreting person, but were quickly borne away, via the water closet, into the sewers, to be seen no more. Feelings of embarrassment and disgust provoked by excreta, dispositions which had been developing for several centuries beforehand, were thus mitigated by denying the visibility of these materials above ground in the public sphere, and bringing them under the watchful scrutiny of state employees below ground. The water-sluiced sewer mode of excretory disposal thus pushed to its apotheosis the imperatives of excretory invisibility that had been developing in the West since the early modern period.

The sewer systems of the latter half of the nineteenth century are not only a great source of interest to the historian of this particular period. The study of how Westerners today have come to think about their bodies, especially the defecatory capacities thereof, must be related to the construction of large-scale sewer systems across Western Europe from the 1860s onwards. Our modes of sight and smell, as well as our conceptions of cleanliness and socially acceptable bodily comportment, are to a large extent derived from that peculiar constellation of sensory and material factors that the later nineteenth-century city sewer system both embodied and further developed. The sewer of a century and a half ago should thus be seen as the generative site for many of the peculiarities of Western corporeal thought and practice prevalent today.

## Further reading

C. Classen et al., *Aroma: The Cultural History of Smell* (London, 1994).

A. Corbin, *The Foul and the Fragrant* (Leamington Spa, 1986).

S. Halliday, *The Great Stink of London: Sir Joseph Bazalgette and the Cleansing of the Victorian Capital* (Stroud, Glos., 1999).

A. Hart-Davis, *Thunder, Flush and Thomas Crapper* (London, 1997).

J. Hassan, *A History of Water in Modern England and Wales* (Manchester, 1998).

D. Inglis, *A Sociological History of Excretory Experience: Defecatory Manners and Toiletry Technologies* (Lewiston, NY, 2001).

L. Lambton, *Temples of Convenience and Chambers of Delight* (London, 1998).

D. Laporte, *History of Shit* (Boston, 2002).

R.A. Lewin, *Merde: Excursions in Scientific, Cultural and Sociohistorical Coprology* (London, 1999).

W.I. Miller, *The Anatomy of Disgust* (Cambridge, Mass., 1997).

D. Reid, *Paris Sewers and Sewermen: Realities and Representations* (Cambridge, Mass., 1991).

# CHAPTER SEVEN

# 'We demand good and healthy beer': the nutritional and social significance of beer for the lower classes in mid-nineteenth-century Munich

*Kim Carpenter*

## Introduction

On 1 May 1844, thousands of lower-class men gathered in breweries and pubs throughout Munich, the capital of Bavaria, to celebrate the first of the month. This date celebrated warmer weather and heralded good cheer by marking the beginning of the city's summer beer sales. This was a special day, and Munich's residents traditionally flocked to the streets to partake in the 'joy and pleasure' of the summer beer garden experience.[1] This year, however, the summer sales rapidly turned violent when beer – in terms of both price and quality – became a flashpoint for crowd resentment and anger.

Early in the day, several low-ranking soldiers, who were stationed at the local barracks, entered the Maderbräu, one of the city's largest breweries and one that was especially popular with working-class men. Incited by an 8 per cent increase in the beer price, the soldiers ordered a round of beer and then loudly refused to pay for it. Gendarmes who had been stationed in the brewery to prevent such disturbances immediately intervened and tried to 'talk some sense into the soldiers' by convincing them that the beer price had been 'irrevocably fixed'. Their attempt to calm the situation proved useless. Influenced by the soldiers' refusal to pay, the 'rabble' in the brewery quickly joined the confrontation and threatened to destroy 'everything' in the Maderbräu unless the beer price decreased and the quality increased.[2] Patrons then smashed their glasses

---

[1] Bayerisches Hauptstaatsarchiv. Ministerium des Innern (MInn) 46128. Munich Police Director Karg-Bebenburg to Bavarian Interior Ministry, Munich, 10 June 1844.

[2] Staatsarchiv München. Staat Appellationsgericht 4961. (Sta. App. Ger.) Munich, 18 October 1844.

together, opened the brewery's kegs and broke tables and chairs.[3] Within minutes, the violence spilled into the street as the 'dregs' of Munich's society swelled the numbers of angry patrons and bystanders. Men shouted that they wanted 'cheaper, higher quality beer' and that they would use violence to lower the beer price themselves.[4]

By now, the situation had grown beyond the control of city authorities. The number of protesters included what gendarmes on the scene estimated to be thousands of men. For five hours, these crowds carried out sustained violence against breweries and taverns throughout Munich. Despite the combined efforts of the police and military, the lower classes renewed their attacks during the following two days and continued to demand higher quality beer at cheaper prices. After three days of intense rioting, protesters had damaged property in all of Munich's 33 breweries. On 4 May, the Bavarian government and the city's brewers capitulated to the crowds' demands and agreed to lower the summer beer price.

When the Bavarian Interior Ministry summoned Munich's Police Director to explain why the lower classes had reacted so violently to the increase in the beer price, the latter summarised briefly: 'The Bavarian *Volk* . . . is extremely loyal to its king and dynasty . . . Only in one area of his life can the Bavarian be wounded. Specifically, the Bavarian really enjoys eating good food and a lot of it . . . The Munich citizen especially insists upon good and healthy beer.'[5] Other public officials and politicians shared this sentiment. Bavaria's District President, widely derided by the lower classes for his lack of sympathy with their problems, stated that, when it came to beer, Munich's public demanded both quantity and quality. It was unwilling to compromise either.[6] Even the French ambassador stationed in Munich could not resist commenting on what he considered an extreme lower-class fondness for beer. Following the riots, he wrote to his superiors in Paris: 'this beverage [beer] is a primary necessity for the Bavarian population. For a large segment of the working class, beer is the principal food, and it is considered as nourishing as bread itself.' The ambassador additionally remarked that this dependence upon beer was a Bavarian 'peculiarity'.[7]

---

[3] MInn 46128. Bavarian Praesidium to King Ludwig II, Munich, 30 May 1844; MInn 46128. Police Director to Interior Ministry, Munich, 14 June 1844.
[4] MInn 46128. Compagnie für die Haupt-und Residenzstadt to Gendarmerie Corps Commando, Munich, 3 May 1844.
[5] MInn 46128. Police Director to Interior Ministry, Munich, 10 June 1844.
[6] MInn 46233. Royal Proclamation, Munich, 13 May 1843.
[7] French Embassy to Paris; Baron de Bourgoing to Guizot, Munich, 4 May 1844. See A. Chroust, ed., *Gesandschaftsberichte aus München 1814–1848. Abteilung I: Die Berichte der französischen Gesandten. Band V. Die Berichte aus*

This essay accordingly analyses the 'peculiar' attachment that lower-class Munich residents had to their beer throughout the first half of the nineteenth century. Beer was far more than an alcoholic beverage; it was a *fließendes Brot*, a 'liquid bread' that both nourished and sustained them. Beer also brought these people together in breweries and taverns, and drinking beer in these public places allowed for social interaction and camaraderie.

To establish the framework for understanding beer's significance in Munich at this time, the first part focuses on the history of brewing in both Munich and Bavaria and the government regulations that arose to control this beverage's production, distribution and consumption. The complex web of legislation, quality controls and monitoring that developed illustrate just how critical city officials believed it was to protect beer's quality and pricing. Moreover, the evolution of beer production and quality control indicate just how critical authorities and brewers alike believed this staple commodity to be for lower-class consumers. Although Munich's system for regulating beer normally functioned quite well, the 1844 riots demonstrated that it nevertheless had weaknesses that contributed to its temporary break-down.

The second part focuses on the critical role that beer played for Munich's lower classes on a nutritional, economic, psychological and cultural level. Beer proved to be a central element in the city's development from a small, provincial capital into a modern city, because it did more than just nourish the lower classes: beer enabled the lower classes to establish a new sort of public, urban life. As taverns and breweries took on added social functions, drinking traditions were established and rules for socialising evolved.[8] The consumption of beer occurred during circumstances that facilitated relaxation, networking and ultimately social bonding. As the nineteenth century progressed, a definitive *Bierkultur* (beer culture) began to develop that would become a permanent fixture of the city's urban culture, one that persists until today. As Peter Stearns has observed, 'drink [in Europe] was the lubricant that helped [the] working-class shift from customary community to the new gregariousness with workmates and neighbours'.[9] For this reason, lower-class men living in Munich widely perceived beer

---

*der letzten Zeit des Ministeriums Abel und bis zur Thronentsagung König Ludwigs. vom September 1843 bis zum März 1848* (Munich, 1936), p. 57.

[8] F. Kaiser, 'Einleitung', in *Wirtshäuser in München um 1900. 'Berge von unten, Kirchen von außen, Wirtshäuser von innen'* (Munich, 1997), p. 9.

[9] P. Stearns, 'The effort at continuity in working-class culture', *Journal of Modern History*, 52 (1980) pp. 628–46.

as *the* 'drink of the people', the unofficial *Volksgetränk* that defined the very essence of what it meant to be living in the Bavarian capital.[10]

## A brief history of beer production and legislation in Munich and Bavaria

In 1840, a beer expert commented on the superiority of Bavarian beer, particularly that brewed in Munich: 'The English, French and most German beers spoil when they are exposed to air; this does not happen with Bavarian lagers; they can stay in full and half-filled kegs without becoming sour and without compromising their character at all.'[11] Other experts further argued that, since water so greatly affected taste, beer brewed in Munich was bound to taste noticeably better than any beer produced outside the region of the Alps.[12] In part, this exalted reputation stemmed from the city government's long and complicated control over the brewing process. Ironically, beer production predated the founding of the Bavarian capital by over three centuries. Freising, a small village, which later became a Munich suburb, produced the area's first beer in 815.[13] Officially, however, the Bavarian brewing tradition did not begin until the late fifteenth century, when Bavaria itself was still a small dukedom. In 1487, the Munich government introduced the *Reinheitsgebot*, an ordinance that brought brewing under the control of city authorities. In an effort to protect both beer's production and quality, this law stated: 'Beer brewers and others are not allowed to use anything in brewing, except: malt, hops and water: furthermore, these same brewers, and those who sell beer, may not add anything else to beer, under penalty of corporal and financial punishment.'[14] The

---

[10] U. Walter, 'Bierpaläste', in Kaiser, ed., *Wirtshäuser in München um 1900*, p. 23.

[11] W. Abel, *Stufen der Ernährung. Eine historische Skizze* (Göttingen, 1981), p. 54.

[12] During the nineteenth century, the demand for Bavarian beer grew so high that brewers could barely meet it. Although it cost four times as much as Saxon beer, consumers in Leipzig often preferred Bavarian beer. In the late 1800s, the German *Reichsnahrungsmittelgesetz* acknowledged Bavarian beer's superiority, compared, for example, with Prussian beer, which often included malt substitutes. MInn 46406. Ministerial Conference, Munich, 2 August 1846.

[13] G. Merk and H. Sieber, *Das Münchner Bier. Wer's braut, Wie's schmeckt, Wo's fließt* (Freising, 1991), p. 8; A. Zatsch, 'Die Brauwirtschaft Westfalens: Ein Wegbereiter modernen Getränkekonsums', in H-J. Teuteberg, ed., *Durchbruch zum modernen Massenkonsum. Lebensmittelmärkt- und Lebensmittelqualität im Städtewachstum des Industriezeitalters* (Münster, 1987), p. 239.

[14] Zatsch, 'Die Brauwirtschaft Westfalens'; E. Schmauderer, 'Die Beziehungen

*Biersatzordnung* of 1493 went a step further by professionalising the brewing industry.[15]

Typically, Munich's brewers offered two seasonal beers. During summer months, brewers served a 'white' beer designed to quench the thirst; a heavier 'brown' beer was reserved for the winter.[16] Although some brewers liked to consider their craft a 'magical art', with results dependent upon a capricious blend of 'water, wind and scent', seasonal harvests largely determined the brewing process, and brewing practices remained essentially the same for centuries until the early 1820s, when several important technical innovations began to have an impact on beer production.[17] Gabriel Sedlmayer, one of the city's leading brewery owners and entrepreneurs, has long been credited with initiating the industrialisation of beer production in Bavaria, because he travelled to England to learn how to use steam engines in the brewing process. During brewery tours, Sedlmayer and a colleague became 'nothing other than "industry spies"', by using bottles hidden in their canes to take secret samples of English beer for analysis.[18] Upon his return to Munich, the brewer employed steam engine machinery along with thermometers in his Spaten brewery. By the late 1840s, he had successfully industrialised Bavaria's brewing process.[19] Such advances quickly revolutionised control over beer production throughout Munich. Breweries no longer functioned as small businesses, but rather developed into 'factories' with high volume and booming sales.

By the 1850s, Munich boasted 33 breweries. The majority were located near workshops, barracks and the train station, where they attracted lower-class men who comprised the majority of their clientele. Popular breweries such as the Spaten, Augustiner, Pschorr and

---

zwischen Lebensmittelwissenschaft, Lebensmittelrecht und Lebensmittelversorgung im 19. Jahrhundert', in E. Heischkel-Artelt, ed., *Ernährung als Ernährungslehre im 19. Jahrhundert. Vorträge eines Symposiums am 5. und 6. Januar 1973* (Göttingen, 1976), p. 158.

[15] W. Behringer and C. Schäder, 'Münchner Großbrauereien. Vom Aufstieg kleiner Braustätten zu weltbekannten Bierfabriken', in Kaiser, ed., *Wirtshäuser in München um 1900*, p. 56.

[16] They also offered *Hausbier*, a weaker, cheaper beer. See H-J Teuteberg, 'Die Nahrung der sozialen Unterschichten im späten 19. Jahrhundert', in Heischkel-Artelt, ed., *Ernährung als Ernährungslehre*, p. 280.

[17] MInn 46406. Ministerial Conference, Munich, 2 August 1846.

[18] W. Behringer, *Die Spaten-Brauerei 1397–1997. Die Geschichte eines Münchner Unternehmens vom Mittelalter bis zur Gegenwart* (Munich, 1997), p. 162.

[19] B. Eckelt, *Biergeschichte(n). Bayerns fünftes Element* (Rosenheim, 1999), p. 55; MInn 44449. Interior Ministry, '*Concerning the relations of brewers to Munich's public*', Munich, 17 February 1846.

Hackerbräu were either in the middle of the city or on the east banks of the Isar River, where the soil was particularly good for building cellars that kept beer at appropriately cool temperatures. A number of smaller breweries, such as the Franziskanerbräu and Bürgerbräu, also established their businesses in this area. The Löwenbräu settled in the busy Nymphenburgerstrasse, and a number of other breweries made Stiglmaierplatz a major quarter for the brewing industry.[20] At this time, however, the royal Hofbräuhaus tended to have the highest rate of beer production, and even larger breweries had difficulty keeping pace with the king's own brewery.[21]

Political and economic reforms complemented these industrial advances. Bavaria's transformation into a modern economy began during the late 1700s and gradually continued over several decades. In 1799, the dukedom abolished the feudal beer constraint known as the *Bierzwang*. Until this time, the state had required all proprietors selling alcoholic beverages to purchase their beer from specific brewers, a practice that rendered it too costly for most small tavern owners to survive.[22] After repeal, brewers sold their beer to taverns at competitive prices, which enabled proprietors to select their own brewery contracts and regulate beer supplies more efficiently.[23] Tavern owners began competing for customers in an atmosphere of free trade. This led to a proliferation of taverns throughout Munich and, by the middle of the nineteenth century, there were close to 200 taverns and cafes registered in the Bavarian capital.[24]

The founding of the Kingdom of Bavaria in 1805 also indirectly triggered changes within the brewing industry by transforming Bavaria from a small dukedom into a growing, modernising kingdom.[25] Establishing Bavaria's sovereignty permanently altered Munich from a quiet

[20] W. Hardtwig, 'Soziale Räume, Stadtentwicklung, Städtebau. Soziale Räume und politische Herrschaft. Leistungsverwaltung, Stadterweiterung und Architektur in München 1870 bis 1914', in W. Hardtwig and K. Tenfelde, eds, *Soziale Räume in der Urbanisierung. München im Vergleich 1850–1933* (Munich, 1990), p. 73.

[21] U. Laufer, 'Das bayerische Brauwesen in frühindustrieller Zeit', in R.A. Müller, ed., *Aufbruch ins Industriezeitalter*: vol. 2, *Aufsätze zur Wirtschafts-und Sozialgeschichte Bayerns 1750–1850* (Munich, 1985), p. 288.

[22] Laufer, 'Das bayerische Brauwesen', p. 294.

[23] MInn 44451. *Gesetzes Entwurf*, Munich, undated 1846; Behringer and Schäder, 'Münchner Großbrauereien', p. 57.

[24] Bayerisches Hauptstadtsarchiv, Regierungsakt ('RA') 15829-7. Interior Ministry to Magistrat, Munich, 9 November 1843.

[25] H.W. Schlaich, 'Der Bayerische Staatsrat. Beiträge zu seiner Entwicklung von 1808/09 bis 1918', *Zeitschrift für Bayerische Landesgeschichte*, 28 (1965), p. 463.

city founded by monks in the twelfth century to the rapidly expanding capital of a new monarchy on Europe's political landscape.[26] In one of his first acts as king, Max Joseph secularised Bavaria. Beginning even before he took the throne, he abolished both male and female cloisters in their entirety in 1802. The government then sold Church lands and buildings to generate state revenue. Although many cloisters were re-established in subsequent decades, brewing for profit had become a lay endeavour.[27] The government now reserved the *Braurecht,* or 'right to brew', as a privilege for Munich's wealthier brewers, who were among the most elite artisans in Bavaria. These men were in the capital's upper tax bracket, and they enjoyed their reputations as some of Munich's wealthiest businessmen.[28]

With the support of his leading ministers, Max Joseph also began to liberalise the economy by abolishing market privileges traditionally enjoyed by guilds. This move simultaneously allowed him to bring state control over all trades. Beginning in 1807, the government nullified previous ordinances that had limited the number of apprentices and journeymen working in breweries. Brewers could now employ as many men as they needed, a development that led to the significant expansion of the brewing industry.[29]

Bavaria's second king, Ludwig I, continued his father's economic reforms. The 1825 Freedom of Trade Law mandated that all guilds become free trades. The regulation of guild qualifications was now transferred to the state, with education, guild admission and production all becoming government-regulated.[30] The government also monitored masters, who no longer controlled their own members. Systematic

---

[26] By 1815, Bavaria was the third largest German-speaking kingdom, ranking only behind Prussia and Austria. It also became part of the German Federation, which guaranteed a leading role in German affairs. In less than two decades, the Wittelsbachs had transformed themselves from a minor nobility in Austria's shadow to a respected and politically powerful dynasty. See E. Weis, 'Die politischen und historischen Auffassungen Ludwigs I. in der Kronprinzenzeit', in J. Erichsen and U. Puschner, eds, *Vorwärts, vorwärts sollst du schauen. Geschichte, Politik und Kunst unter Ludwig I* (Munich, 1983), p. 14; H. Reiter, *Die Revolution von 1848/49 in Altbayern* (Munich, 1983), p. 5.

[27] W. Zorn, 'Gesellschaft und Staat im Bayern des Vormärz', in W. Conze, ed., *Staat und Gesellschaft im deutschen Vormärz 1815–1848* (Stuttgart, 1962), p. 117.

[28] K-P. Ellerbrock, *Die Entwicklung der Lebensmittelüberwachung in Dortmund im 19. Jahrhundert. Ein ernährungsgeschichtlicher Beitrag zur 'Sozialen Frage' in Dortmund* (Dortmund, 1985), pp. 80–81.

[29] Behringer and Schäder, 'Münchner Großbrauereien', pp. 57–8.

[30] M. Birnbaum, *Das Münchner Handwerk im 19. Jahrhundert (1799–1868): Beiträge zu Politik, Struktur und Organisation des städtischen Handwerks im beginnenden Industriezeitalter* (Munich, 1984), pp. 44–7, 141–4.

ordinances brought further uniformity to the previous confusion in city trades and helped businesses rise to more efficient levels. The Interior Ministry granted concessions only to those industries critical for feeding Bavaria's population.[31]

Such strict constraints on traditional guild order and discipline resulted in the beer industry's inability to control internal quality.[32] The proliferation of producers, middlemen and traders added to the difficulty of properly monitoring and controlling food quality. Although regulating beer quality had long influenced Bavaria's domestic policy, addressing this issue took on added importance in the nineteenth century.[33] Beer was becoming an increasingly important staple for Munich's growing lower-class population, and authorities endeavoured to establish quality norms as well as to prevent the addition of harmful ingredients. The government also wanted to ensure that beer remained affordable. During the 1820s, the state therefore created an organisation that would both monitor and enact strict controls to regulate production and quality.[34]

In August 1829, the Interior Ministry and Munich's city council created an organisation of *Viktualien-Polizei*, or 'food police', that assumed responsibility for monitoring food prices and quality.[35] As a branch of the police, the *Viktualien-Polizei* not only guaranteed food safety throughout the capital, it also satisfied the public's desire for high quality, reasonably priced food. Since city officials were acutely aware of how food prices and quality could influence public opinion, the 'food police' played important economic and cultural roles.[36] The monarchy therefore perceived the *Viktualien-Polizei* as critical for maintaining consumer good will, keeping the urban peace and protecting its own stability.[37]

An integrated system that included farmers, brewers, vendors,

---

[31]  Zorn, 'Gesellschaft und Staat im Bayern', p. 118.

[32]  MInn 46464. *Zur Geschichte der Bierproben*, 1835; Ellerbrock, *Die Entwicklung der Lebensmittelüberwachung*, pp. 80–81.

[33]  S.W. Mintz, 'Die Zusammensetzung der Speise in frühen Agrargesell-schaften. Versuch einer Konzeptualisierung', in M. Schaffner, ed., *Brot, Brei und was dazugehört. Über sozialen Sinn und physiologischen Wert der Nahrung* (Zürich, 1992) p. 16.

[34]  Birnbaum, *Das Münchner Handwerk*, p. 144.

[35]  MInn 46304. *Verordnung*, Munich, 16 August 1829.

[36]  H-J. Teuteberg, 'Die Ernährung als Gegenstand historischer Analyse', in H. Kellenbenz and H. Pohl, eds, *Historia Socialis et Oeconomica. Festschrift W. Zorn* (Stuttgart, 1987), p. 187.

[37]  MInn 46233. Interior Ministry to Regensburg Government, Munich, 28 June 1843; RA 15829–7. Praesidium to Landgericht, Munich, 4 November 1844.

consumers and state authorities accordingly developed.[38] Officers in the *Viktualien-Polizei* recorded monthly prices for grain, flour, bread, meat and beer, and they carefully monitored their quality. Food police especially directed this supervision at beer. Officials wanted to ensure that beer remained *wohlfeil* (healthy). As one high-ranking official in the Bavarian parliament commented: 'Bad beer is poison, a mixture not against, but rather for sickness. Inferior beer quality can result in anything from infections, to dehydration, to haemorrhoids.'[39]

Before the government would allow breweries to sell their beer, a taster rated the quality of their kegs. Only after beer received a minimal designation of 'good' could brewers then sell it to tavern owners and brewery patrons. When brewers failed to meet government standards, the *Viktualien-Polizei* issued fines payable to the city magistrate. If beer lacked proper hops or malt quantities, for example, a brewer received a fine of between fifteen and fifty Florin, a sizable sum that could represent several months' worth of profits.[40] In rare cases, a brewer could receive a jail sentence for selling 'unhealthy' beer. To ensure that quality remained high after the initial rating, beer 'visitors' randomly tasted beer throughout Munich.[41] Inadequate cooling facilities often caused beer to spoil quickly, which turned it into a sour drink.[42] Brewers and tavern owners sometimes attempted to mask this flavour with a variety of ingredients ranging from chicory to caraway seeds, practices blatantly in violation of the *Reinheitsgebot*. Surprise quality checks known as *Visitationen* therefore enabled the *Viktualien-Polizei* to rate beer quality even after the initial inspection.[43]

Ordinarily, the *Viktualien-Polizei* made surprise visits to thirty brewers and roughly one hundred tavern owners every month. They 'visited' between 6 and 9 a.m. or 5 and 8 p.m. After producing identification, they tasted the beer and then filed a visitation report. In general, the *Viktualien-Polizei* ranked Munich's beer quality as 'good' and 'very good' throughout the first half of the nineteenth century.[44]

---

[38] Schmauderer, 'Die Beziehungen zwischen Lebensmittelwissenschaft, Lebensmittelrecht und Lebensmittelversorgung', p. 154.

[39] Abg. Dr. Schwindl, *Verhandlung der Kammer der Abgeordneten der Stände-Versammlung des Königreichs Bayern im Jahre 1846*, Munich, 11 May 1846.

[40] MInn 44451. *Biertaxregulierung Verordnung*, Munich, 11 April 1811.

[41] MInn 46399. Regensburg Stadtkommissariat to Praesidium. Regensburg, 29 November 1845.

[42] Walter, 'Bierpaläste', p. 23.

[43] H-J. Teuteberg, ed., *Durchbruch zum modernen Massenkonsum. Lebensmittel-Märkte und Qualität im Städtewachstum des Industriezeitalters* (Münster, 1987), p. 11.

[44] RA 15829/7. Magistrate to Praesidium, Munich, 5 January 1844.

Such strict government regulation over beer quality triggered one journalist in Paris to comment: 'Nowhere, not even in England is so much beer consumed as in Bavaria's capital. The government therefore monitors the production of this national drink and the police even test the beer kegs every month.'[45] Neither brewers nor the public, however, regarded the *Viktualien-Polizei* reports as highly as foreign observers: brewers could bribe beer police too easily, and the public often viewed official tasters as incompetent.[46]

Beer tasters, though, remained a minor issue, with the government's control over the beer price causing the majority of criticism among Munich's lower classes. Fiscal interests had long prompted the government to tax beer production, since beer revenues alone provided one-sixth of Bavaria's annual income.[47] In this regard, the Bavarian beer price had 'always been a political price'.[48] Munich's leading ministers dismissed criticism of beer price regulation, noting that some form of beer taxation had existed for centuries in Bavaria. Even more importantly, they argued that government control over the pricing structure remained critical for regulating a staple food as important as beer.[49]

Ordinances from 1806 and 1811 codified this regulation during the nineteenth century. The 1806 introduction of the *Malzaufschlag* enabled the government to tax brewers and tavern owners according to the amount of malt used in beer production. Since brewers did not always report accurate malt amounts, the government further declared in 1811 that no more than seven kegs of beer could be produced from one bushel (222 litres) of malt.

Since beer production was limited to producing two seasonal beers for summer and winter, the Interior and Finance Ministries fixed a biannual beer price for what they designated a 'normal *Maß*' (approximately one litre) in Munich and its local districts. The amount that brewers could charge for beer was based on harvest prices. In addition to establishing the price, the government also wanted to regulate competition among breweries. By setting maximum prices, authorities hoped to protect smaller breweries and tavern owners. On average, beer tended

---

[45] *Der Bayerische Volksfreund*. Munich, 7 May 1844.
[46] Laufer, 'Das bayerische Brauwesen in frühindustrieller Zeit', p. 289.
[47] W.K. Blessing, 'Konsumprotest und Arbeitskampf. Vom Bierkrawall zum Bierboycott', in K. Tenfelde and H. Volkmann, eds, *Streik. Zur Geschichte des Arbeitskampfes in Deutschland während der Industrialisierung* (Munich, 1981), p. 110.
[48] K-J. Hummel, *München in der Revolution von 1848/49* (Göttingen, 1987), p. 343.
[49] MInn 46406. Ministerial Conference, Munich, 2 August 1846.

to cost between five and five-and-a-half Kreuzer, depending on the season.[50]

To put these prices into perspective, a comparison of average wages and other staple prices is useful. At this time, the Bavarian currency was in Florin and Kreuzer. One Florin equalled sixty Kreuzer or 240 Pfennige, and four Pfennige equalled one Kreuzer.[51] The average lower-class carpenter earned a daily wage ranging between 40 and 42 Kreuzer, excluding room and board. A mason earned approximately the same. Workers employed on Munich's public construction sites, the city's major employers, earned 48 Kreuzer a day. An enterprising journeyman might earn up to 160 Florin annually. In contrast, some master masons and carpenters earned as much as 55 Kreuzer daily. Members of the bourgeoisie earned even more. A professor or public official, for example, could earn an annual salary ranging from 400 to 1200 Florin. Lower-class men living in Munich spent approximately five Florin annually on clothing. If legally registered, they paid between 20 Kreuzer and one Florin annually in taxes. Food in the capital, however, remained the biggest cost concern affecting daily life. Bread cost between three and six Kreuzer, depending on the type (rye versus wheat).[52] If men could afford to eat in pubs and restaurants, they might spend anywhere between 24 and 36 Florin annually on their meals.[53] Beer, however, accounted for a significant portion of a worker's budget. A lower-class man most likely spent between 15 and 20 Kreuzer daily for beer, an amount that not infrequently amounted to almost half his wages. During the 1840s, those relying on beer as their primary nutritional source spent roughly 90 Florin annually. These amounts varied depending on how much men needed to drink beer in order to supplement their diets as well as on how much they were able to afford.

Officials computed the winter beer price (*Winterbiersatz*) by averaging costs for barley and hops in November and December. They used October, November and December grain price averages to arrive at the summer beer price (*Sommerbiersatz*). The official price for winter beer began on 15 October; the summer beer price took effect on 1 May. Summer beer required a longer brewing period than winter beer, and its price usually registered one half Kreuzer more.[54]

---

[50] Based on public notices released in the *Königlich Bayerischer Polizey-Anzeiger von München*, 1840–43.

[51] K. von Zwehl, ed., *Aufbruch ins Industriezeitalter*, vol. 3, *Quellen zur Wirtschafts- und Sozialgeschichte Bayerns vom ausgehenden 18. Jahrhundert bis zur Mitte des 19. Jahrhunderts* (Munich, 1985), pp. 57, 68–70.

[52] MInn 46242. Food Price Listing, Munich, 31 May 1843.

[53] von Zwehl, *Aufbruch ins Industriezeitalter*, p. 65.

[54] MInn 46406. Biertaxregulierung Verordnung, Munich, 25 April 1811.

Because grain prices were so critical for determining the *Biersatz*, Munich's magistrate warned grain merchants to report accurate prices and instructed police authorities on how to calculate accurate averages.[55] If averages rose or fell by two Florin per bushel, the government increased or decreased beer prices by one Pfennig per *Maß*. If the grain price fluctuated beyond this limit, the change likewise affected the beer price.

In 1811, the government set the base price for beer at six Pfennige. Using the *Malzaufschlag* as a base, it added another four Pfennige tax on each Bavarian *Maß*. This brought the base price of a *Maß* to ten Pfennige.[56] For six decades, this formulation enabled the Bavarian government to receive five Florin for every bushel of malt used in the brewing process.[57]

This base price, however, did not remain static in Munich. In the 1830s, the Bavarian parliament allowed brewers to add a so-called *Minuto-Verschleiß* to production costs. This permitted brewers to put two Pfennige onto the beer price to cover any waste incurred during the brewing process. Additionally, the city government added a *LocalAufschlag* of two Pfennige, which functioned as a city tax. The base price for a Munich *Maß* thus rose to 14 Pfennige after 1831.[58]

The Interior and Finance Ministries further differentiated between a *Ganterpreis* and a *Schenkpreis*. Brewers sold their kegs to tavern owners at the *Ganterpreis*, which grain and production costs determined. Both brewers and tavern owners then sold beer to consumers at a *Schenkpreis*. This price typically stood at two Pfennige above the *Ganterpreis*. Once the Ministries determined the new price for summer or winter beer, the city magistrate recorded the official *Biersatz*, and Munich's police authorities issued public notices in conjunction with the royal Hofbräuhaus. The new beer price also appeared in city newspapers, and brewery and tavern owners posted the new *Schenkpreis* throughout their establishments.[59]

In accordance with the beer tax ordinance, all breweries and tavern owners were supposed to charge the same *Schenkpreis*. Although the magistrate allowed some businessmen to sell beer slightly below the

---

[55] MInn 44451. Interior Ministry to Police Authorities, Munich, 28 July 1817.
[56] G. Döllinger, *Sammlung der im Gebiete der inneren Staats-Verwaltung des Königreichs Bayern bestehenden Verordnungen* (Munich, 1839), Article 9.
[57] Laufer, 'Das bayerische Brauwesen in frühindustrieller Zeit', pp. 294–5.
[58] *Kammer der Abgeordneten der Stände-Versammlung des Königreichs Bayern im Jahre 1846*, Munich, 11 May 1846.
[59] For example, RA 15894. Royal Hofbräuhausamt, Munich, 14 July 1843.

*Schenkpreis*, it forbade them from selling above this limit.[60] Despite this provision, many brewers often charged between half and one Kreuzer above the *Schenkpreis*, a practice that led many consumers to complain that brewers did what they wanted without any regard for the public's well-being. The lower classes further believed that Munich's brewers had been growing wealthy at consumer expense for years. They resented the *Minuto-Verschleiß* and complained that brewers often did not pay the entire four Pfennige *Malzaufschlag* and pocketed the difference as profit.[61] The lower classes further resented the monarchy using beer taxes as a way to fund the king's pet projects.[62]

The government's focus on beer's production, quality and pricing indicates strongly just how important beer had become to the general population. From beginning to end, officials felt it necessary to oversee every detail relating to beer, from the brewing process to the beverage's very consumption. By the 1850s, beer had clearly become one of the most critical commodities within Munich's lower-class culture. On a variety of intriguing complex and interwoven levels, beer consumption underscored just how much a nutritional staple could shape the public sphere of a nineteenth-century city.

### The nutritional and social properties of Bavaria's '*fließendes brot*'

Since the Middle Ages, beer had played a critical role in the daily lives of Bavarians. It was both the most popular beverage, a *Volksgetränk* (people's drink), and a main nutritional staple, a *Volksnahrungsmittel* (people's food). The lower classes in particular viewed their beer not so much as an intoxicant but rather as a *fließendes Brot*, or 'liquid bread'.[63]

In contrast, the middle and upper classes preferred wine to beer, with the former costing three times as much.[64] They also tended to gravitate toward non-alcoholic drinks such as coffee and tea, which promoted greater sobriety and a stricter work discipline.[65] Since hygiene and sanitation practices were poor, public water was also frequently polluted. Although nothing was yet known about bacteria, people nevertheless

---

[60]  See Döllinger, *Sammlung*.

[61]  *Kammer der Abgeordneten der Stände-Versammlung des Königreichs Bayern im Jahre 1846*, Munich, 11 May 1846.

[62]  MInn 46128. Police Director to Interior Ministry, Munich, 14 June 1844.

[63]  Blessing, 'Konsumprotest und Arbeitskampf', p. 109.

[64]  Abel, *Stufen der Ernährung*, p. 53; R. Sandgruber, *Bittersüße Genüsse. Kulturgeschichte der Genußmittel* (Vienna, 1986), p. 36.

[65]  Walter, 'Bierpaläste', pp. 22–3.

noticed that drinking water precipitated illnesses.[66] Such factors promoted beer consumption and, throughout the nineteenth century, physicians even recommended that children, the elderly and the sick drink beer.[67] Indeed, drinking beer had become so critical for maintaining good health that, by the close of the 1700s, one astute observer aptly remarked: 'We Bavarians live in a country where beer, as it were, is represented as the fifth element.'[68]

During the first half of the nineteenth century, beer became the drink of choice for many members of the underprivileged classes throughout Germany.[69] Beer was often the most nutritional beverage available, and German lower-class beer consumption tripled in the 1800s.[70] The average Bavarian lower-class man, however, consumed anywhere between 165 and 333 litres of beer annually, more than four times what his northern German counterpart drank.[71] By the mid-1840s, beer consumption had become so central in the diets of Munich's lower-class population that the Police Director estimated that at least 40 000 people in and around the city received their nutrition primarily from beer and bread alone.[72] Such high rates of consumption prompted one Munich physician and beer expert to observe that beer was so important for lower-class nutrition that people did not simply desire it; they considered beer 'most necessary'.[73] Another expert additionally commented that 'in Bavaria, beer is not drunk; beer is eaten'.[74]

Even politicians concurred. A representative to the Bavarian parliament commented: 'Beer the pure grain force from the goddess Ceres . . . is a noble means for providing energy for the working classes, a true need for the people. Without these mildly powerful drinks, the body would quickly decay. Good beer, moderately consumed, is the best thing for fanning the flames of life.'[75]

---

[66] Eckelt, *Biergeschichte(n). Bayerns fünftes Element*, p. 8.

[67] MInn 46464. *Zur Geschichte der Bierproben*, 1835; Teuteberg, 'Die Nahrung der sozialen Unterschichten, p. 280; H. Spode, *Alkohol und Zivilisation: Berauschung, Ernüchterung und Tischsitten in Deutschland bis zum Beginn des 20. Jahrhunderts* (Berlin, 1991), p. 63.

[68] V.D. Laturell, *Volkskultur in München. Aufsätze zu Brauchtum, Musikalische Volkskultur, Volkstanz, Trachten und Volkstheater in einer Millionenstadt* (Munich, 1997), p. 48.

[69] Walter, 'Bierpaläste', pp. 22–3.

[70] Teuteberg, 'Die Nahrung der sozialen Unterschichten', p. 230.

[71] Zatsch, 'Die Brauwirtschaft Westfalens', p. 240; Behringer and Schräder, 'Münchner Großbrauereien', p. 58.

[72] Munich's population in the mid-1800s was roughly 200 000.

[73] MInn 46464. Zur Geschichte der Bierproben, 1835.

[74] MInn 46464. Bavarian Bierprobe, undated. (Early 1840s.)

[75] Abg. Dr. Schwindl. Verhandlung der Kammer der Abgeordneten der

This increased reliance on beer was triggered, in part, by what one historian has described as a nineteenth-century 'nutritional revolution'. Throughout Europe, every aspect of consumption from the time of the evening meal to holiday celebrations underwent some type of change during the 1800s. Changes in consumption affected norms and conventions surrounding food as well as how people of all classes felt about what they ate and drank. To be sure, eating and drinking had always functioned as symbolic and socially communicative acts, with food and drink providing for social distinctions. Cultural traditions, social hierarchies, customs and traditions all influenced class preferences. Fluctuations in household size, prices for staple foods, employment and wages, as well as the ability to provide adequate substitutes, also biased these choices. Additional social forces, such as occupation, age and gender further determined what and where people ate and drank.[76]

For Europe's lower classes, the advent of mass consumption had particularly far-reaching effects.[77] In Munich, increased traffic and transportation accompanied the dismantling of state regulations on breweries and taverns. Technological advances in the brewing industry meant not just greater production but also higher beer quality. The Bavarian economy also improved following the Napoleonic wars, enabling the lower classes to increase the amount of income spent on beer. In general, good harvests throughout the first half of the nineteenth century kept beer prices consistently low.[78]

Such developments resulted in changing demands, and Bavarians, particularly those residing in the capital, altered their attitudes about what constituted acceptable food and drink. By the 1850s, the average lower-class home consumed, in order of importance: meat and sausage; bread and baked goods; milk; and beer. Lower-class Bavarians also depended on cabbage, beets, carrots, cucumbers and onions, and they particularly loved 'Sauerkraut and white, stubbly beets mixed with carrots and green beans'.[79] Beer, however, was at the top of the list for many lower-class men, who no longer just demanded beer; they demanded *wohlfeiles*, or healthy and satisfying, beer.[80] Drinking

---

Stände-Versammlung des Königreichs Bayern im Jahre 1846, Munich, 11 May 1846.

[76] Teuteberg, 'Die Ernährung als Gegenstand', pp. 182–3, 198, 234.

[77] U.A.J. Becher, 'Die Nahrung der sozialen Unterschichten im späten 19. Jahrhundert', in Heischkel-Artelt, ed., *Ernährung als Ernährungslehre*, pp. 73–4.

[78] Blessing, 'Konsumprotest und Arbeitskampf', p. 110.

[79] Teuteberg, 'Die Nahrung der sozialen Unterschichten', pp. 230, 259.

[80] A. Lüdtke, 'Hunger, Essens-"Genuß" und Politik bei Fabrikarbeitern und Arbeiterfrauen. Beispiele aus dem rheinisch-westfälischen Industriegebiet, 1910–1940', *Sozialwissenschaftliche Informationen*, 14 (1985), pp. 118–26.

watered-down, spoiled beer was unacceptable even to the poor. Times of failed harvests, such as the 1816–17 'hunger years' and 'the hungry forties', failed to alter this new perception. Bavarians continued to believe that they had a right to demand high quality, reasonably priced beer.[81]

Perhaps the most important factor that influenced beer consumption, however, was Munich's transformation from a provincial capital into a modern city. Since the late eighteenth century, Bavarians had begun moving in greater numbers from their small, rural communities to Munich in an attempt to improve the quality of their lives.[82] In 1810, Munich's population stood at 40 000. By the middle of the century, this number more than doubled to 100 000 residents.[83]

Young men in particular arrived in the Bavarian capital seeking employment, and they often made Munich their permanent base.[84] The majority of them worked as journeymen, apprentices or day labourers.[85] New living and working rhythms influenced both what and where these men ate and drank. Traditionally, journeymen had relied on guilds and unorganised communities of fellow artisans to aid in managing basic needs, such as finding lodging and employment. In 1800, almost all apprentices and journeymen resided with a master. Others simply stayed for a few nights in a boarding house while on the way to their next position. By the middle of the century, this arrangement had become the exception.[86]

Social restructuring and new work requirements further affected lower-class mealtimes. For example, the traditional 'breakfast pause', which a master or farmer granted his workers, became much shorter or

---

[81] H. Medick, 'Hungerkrisen in der historischen Forschung. Beispiele aus Mitteleuropa vom 17–19. Jahrhundert', *Sozialwissenschaftliche Informationen*, 14 (1985), pp. 95–103.

[82] M. Spindler, ed., *Bayerische Geschichte im 19. und 20. Jahrhundert 1800–1970. Erster Teilband. Staat und Politik. Zweiter Teilband. Innere Entwicklung, Land, Gesellschaft, Wirtschaft, Kirche, geistiges Leben* (Munich, 1974–75), p. 686.

[83] This increase was especially considerable since the entire Bavarian population grew by only 21.5 per cent between 1818 and 1848: Hummel, *München in der Revolution von 1848/49*, pp. 258, 261.

[84] M. Doege, *Armut in Preußen und Bayern: 1770–1840* (Munich, 1991), p. 114.

[85] The construction, metal, lumber, cloth and food industries provided the main sources for Munich's lower-class employment: Hummel, *München in der Revolution von 1848/49*, p. 286; Birnbaum, *Das Münchner Handwerk*, pp. 22, 32.

[86] W. Kaschuba, 'Vom Gesellenkampf zum sozialen Protest in den Vormärz- und Revolutionsjahren', in U. Engelhardt, ed., *Handwerker in der Industrialisierung* (Stuttgart, 1984), p. 389.

disappeared altogether. The separation of consumption from the workshop and the master's home meant that eating and drinking now cost money and lower-class men were now almost entirely responsible for themselves and their meals.

Even though the lower classes in general had greater choices regarding their food, most lower-class men contended with insufficient and bad food at one time or another. Improved food variety may have changed taste preferences, but choices still depended upon income and status.[87] Frequently, available food was too expensive and/or poor in quality. Sometimes workers could not even afford spoiled vegetables or mouldy bread.[88] Almost half the Bavarian population experienced difficulty at some point when purchasing food during the first half of the nineteenth century. A full 25 per cent lived on the edge of poverty and barely provided for their subsistence.[89] If lower-class men could not purchase bread, they therefore had little choice but to opt for Bavaria's 'liquid bread', which was both inexpensive and healthy.

In comparison to other available beverages, beer, or *Gerstensaft* ('barley juice') as it was often called, was highly nutritional. Beer consumption often provided men with their daily calories and contributed to otherwise inadequately met energy needs.[90] At this time, the typical litre of beer contained between two and four hundred calories, depending on its strength. For this reason, beer often dulled hunger pains and reduced the amount of food working men actually needed. Indeed, beer consumption could provide for up to 30 or 40 per cent of an average man's energy needs without leading to intoxication.[91]

Drinking beer also had the additional attraction of providing relief from the monotony of the work environment. Beer added flavour to otherwise mundane meals and offered welcome breaks from bland and repetitive food. Regular beer consumption therefore helped to compensate for 'real' foods on a psychological level.[92] In this regard, drinking beer helped to make economic hardships more bearable,

---

[87] G. Wiegelmann, 'Tendenzen kulturellen Wandels in der Volksnahrung des 19. Jahrhunderts', in Heischkel-Artelt, ed., *Ernährung als Ernährungslehre*, p. 16.

[88] C. Lipp, 'Uns hat die Mutter Not gesäugt an ihrem dürren Leibe. Die Verarbeitung von Hungererfahrungen in Autobiographien von Handwerkern, Arbeitern und Arbeiterinnen', *Beiträge zur Historischen Sozialkunde*, 2 (1985), pp. 54–8.

[89] Doege, *Armut in Preußen und Bayern*, p. 130.

[90] Teuteberg, 'Die Nahrung der sozialen Unterschichten', p. 277.

[91] J.S. Roberts, 'Drink and working class living standards in late 19th century Germany', in W. Conze and U. Englehardt, eds, *Arbeiterexistenz im 19. Jahrhundert* (Stuttgart, 1981), p. 83.

[92] Teuteberg, 'Die Nahrung der sozialen Unterschichten', p. 280.

especially since nutritional uncertainty affected most lower-class men at some time or another.[93]

By the middle of the century, the average middle-class man living in Bavaria drank approximately one-half litre of beer daily.[94] In contrast, a lower-class man typically consumed at least two or three times as much since beer was his main beverage if not the meal itself. Many of these men were single and had fewer, if any, family ties, factors that tended to encourage high rates of consumption. Single men also depended more on breweries and taverns for their meals.[95] Rough estimates therefore place average daily lower-class beer consumption as at least two to three litres per day.

Estimating beer's alcohol content during the nineteenth century remains tricky at best, but it was most likely 90 per cent water.[96] Table 7.1, first published in 1835, lists beer with the following alcohol percentages:[97]

*Table 7.1    Alcohol content of Bavarian beer*

| Beer | Alcohol content (%) |
| --- | --- |
| Doppelbier | 68 |
| Starkes Bier | 36 |
| Mittelbier | 1.53 |
| Dünnbier | 0.81.5 |

Here, *Doppelbier* and *Starkes Bier* refer to stronger winter beers such as *Bockbier* and *Salvatorbier*. Although beer was filling, its alcohol content remained relatively low. The lower classes therefore integrated beer into the working day with relatively few problems, and alcoholism, or *Trinksucht*, did not appear to be a significant problem, at least one that was not widely discussed, until after the middle of the century.[98]

Since beer served such an important nutritional function for lower-class men, the Bavarian parliament enacted a measure in 1831 designed

---

[93] G. Bollenbeck, 'Zur Bedeutung der Ernährung in den Arbeiter-Lebenserinnerungen', *Sozialwissenschaftliche Informationen*, 14 (1985), pp. 110–17.

[94] von Zwehl, *Aufbruch ins Industriezaitalter*, p. 65.

[95] Roberts, 'Drink and working class living standards', p. 77.

[96] Zatsch, 'Die Brauwirtschaft Westfalens', p. 248.

[97] MInn 46464. Zur Geschichte der Bierproben, 1835.

[98] H. Spode, *Alkohol und Zivilisation: Berauschung, Ernüchterung und Tischsitten in Deutschland bis zum Beginn des 20. Jahrhundert* (Berlin, 1991), p. 34.

to mediate price increases for specific segments of the population. Soldiers and lower-ranking civil servants were granted a cost-of-living allowance, or *Theuerungszulage*, for beer. The Interior Ministry hoped that these *Bierzulage* would help quell any discontent, especially in Munich's barracks. In the early 1840s, soldiers stationed in Munich's barracks received a daily *Bierzulage* of two Pfennige. The Interior Minister proudly noted that Bavaria had introduced the commonly used term '*Theuerungszulage*' to the rest of Germany.[99]

How lower-class men felt about their beer at this time is somewhat more difficult to chronicle than beer's nutritional merits. Mealtime as a component of lower-class culture included the notion of community. Eating and drinking brought people together not just to satisfy hunger but also to spend time with one another.[100] Sharing meal times fostered a sense of belonging and built group identification. As important as beer was nutritionally, drinking with others served a critical social purpose that satisfied intense psychological needs.[101] As one historian has noted in his examination of nineteenth-century Bavaria, beer simultaneously provided for 'consumption, communication and recreation', with all three proving integral to daily life among Munich's lower classes.

For generations, beer consumption had possessed an unusual significance within Munich's atmosphere of *Geselligkeit* (sociability) and *Gemütlichkeit* (amiability).[102] Drinking beer had worked as a ceremonial and symbolic form of traditional interaction in the artisan's pre-industrial world, and Bavarian peasants even believed that men had a *Kruggerechtigkeit*, or a 'right to receive drinks'.[103] Communal drinking also marked holidays, celebrations and informal meetings. Many rituals, such as *Krugtag* ('Beer Glass Day') or *Blauer Montag* ('Blue Monday'), featured alcohol consumption.[104] These drinking customs set rules for personal exchanges, and it was not unusual for young men from the country to bring these traditions and drinking habits with them to Munich.

Economic policy makers expressed concern that such artisan traditions disrupted both work schedules and the public peace. To make businesses more productive, the central government attempted to

---

[99] Hummel, *München in der Revolution von 1848/49*, p. 343.

[100] Becher, 'Die Nahrung der sozialen Unterschichten', p. 73.

[101] Teuteberg, 'Die Ernährung als Gegenstand historischer Analyse', p. 185.

[102] Blessing, 'Konsumprotest und Arbeitskampf', pp. 109–10.

[103] U. Wyrwa, *Branntwein und 'echtes' Bier. Die Trinkkultur der Hamburger Arbeiter im 19. Jahrhundert* (Hamburg, 1990), p. 37.

[104] This custom originated with weaver apprentices, who had Mondays free while waiting for dye to turn wool blue: P. Oppenheimer, ed., *Till Eulenspiegel* (Oxford, 1995), p. 50.

separate work and free time. City officials and the new ranks of burgeoning businessmen no longer tolerated customs such as *Blauer Montag* and *Krugtag* by making them illegal. Despite attempts to curtail drinking holidays, however, the general attitude toward alcohol consumption remained indulgent. Clearly, the lower classes considered beer as 'one of the good things in life, something to be enjoyed rather than deprecated, something to be refined as living standards improved rather than curtailed'.[105]

For men such as journeymen and day labourers, drinking beer together was also connected to social prestige and belonging within the lower-class hierarchy.[106] Since beer consumption had a central place in their daily lives, where these men gathered to drink was frequently just as important as the beer itself. In the middle of the nineteenth century, this place was usually the neighbourhood brewery and tavern. While coffeehouses had gained popularity between the seventeenth and eighteenth centuries, they generally attracted merchants, businessmen and civil servants. Until after the 1850s, Munich's upper classes tended to patronise 'finer', more expensive establishments where wine was often featured above beer.[107]

In contrast, lower-class men frequented breweries and taverns almost exclusively. Since they now provided for their own nourishment, workers came here for their daily meals.[108] Additionally, most rooms in boarding houses were extremely cramped, dismal and uncomfortable, and men 'fled' their living quarters as often as they could. Before the advent of inexpensive concert halls and sports arenas, breweries and taverns offered reasonably affordable ways to socialise for the lower classes, who lacked access to other recreational alternatives.[109] In these places, music and singing often accompanied drinking, and seasonal festivals were even celebrated in a number of popular breweries.[110] Not surprisingly, lower-class men depended heavily on these places for almost all their social interaction and integration, and breweries and taverns became their 'second homes'.

As in most German industrial quarters, the majority of Munich's

---

[105] Roberts, 'Drink and working class living standards', pp. 79–80.
[106] Teuteberg, 'Die Nahrung der sozialen Unterschichten', p. 207.
[107] Eckelt, *Biergeschichte(n). Bayerns fünftes Element*, p. 99.
[108] U. Tolksdorf, 'Nahrungsforschung', in R.W. Brednich, ed., *Grundriss der Volkskunde. Einführung in die Forschungsfelder der Europäischen Ethnologie* (Berlin, 1988), p. 180; Teuteberg, 'Die Nahrung der sozialen Unterschichten', pp. 335–6.
[109] Behringer, *Die Spaten-Brauerei 1397–1997*, p. 21.
[110] Walter, 'Bierpaläste', p. 26; Eckelt, *Biergeschichte(n). Bayerns fünftes Element*, p. 99; Sandgruber, *Bittersüße Genüsse*, p. 48.

drinking establishments were located predominantly in the lower-class section, close to both living and working quarters. Although women and children patronised breweries, many lower-class taverns remained predominantly male domains. These places were especially important now that young men remained separated from their families and communities. With the exception of beer maids and prostitutes, patrons could be almost entirely men. These dark, crowded and smoke-filled spaces allowed men to socialise and exchange ideas while relaxing over their beer.[111] Men also forgot, if only momentarily, their workplace drudgeries, repetitive tasks and low wages.[112] Regulars often complained about their poor living and working conditions, high food costs and luxurious noble life styles. Given the level of trustful camaraderie, they were able to vent these frustrations freely, without fear of endangering or compromising their employment. For many, the attractiveness of taverns therefore lay in the 'element of male bonding'.

Perhaps even more importantly, taverns functioned as communication centres for lower-class men, and beer consumption signalled the acceptance of newcomers into established groups.[113] Arriving in a rapidly expanding city, strangers used neighbourhood taverns to make contacts. Here they had their first opportunity to become acquainted with their surroundings and meet others from Munich by establishing circles for networking and socialising. Before renting rooms, it was thus not unusual for men to spend their first nights in tavern halls or attics. Fellow lodgers regularly celebrated a new tenant's arrival at a boarding house by drinking beer.[114]

The environment of regular customers also allowed men to deal with any loneliness, particularly for young, single men without established social circles. Even casual communication helped alleviate homesickness or depression. Being invited to join a group at a *Stammtisch* (reserved table) could therefore make free time enjoyable, making one's acceptance into a tavern far more important than merely finding a regular place to drink.

In this context, selecting a tavern conferred a certain amount of respect on lower-class men, and most had a *Stammkneipe*, a place they frequented almost exclusively.[115] Munich's artisans and soldiers, for example, favoured the popular Maderbräu, and workers and day labourers tended to frequent the Bockkeller. Personal beer mugs

---

[111] Wiegelmann, 'Tendenzen kulturellen Wandels', p. 14.

[112] Becher, 'Die Nahrung der sozialen Unterschichten', pp. 104–5.

[113] Sandgruber, *Bittersüße Genüsse*, pp. 21, 44.

[114] Wyrwa, *Branntwein und 'echtes' Bier*, 52; Teuteberg, 'Die Nahrung der sozialen Unterschichten', pp. 210–11.

[115] Roberts, 'Drink and Working Class Living Standards', pp. 81–2.

indicated their distinctive status as 'regulars'. The practice of keeping tabs or accounts for patrons further established these taverns as special places for lower-class men.[116]

The gestures and mimicking that occurred during drinking were also tightly bound up with social belonging. These customs fostered a sense of *Bruderschaftstrinke* (drinking brotherhood) among beer drinkers. When a guest visited a pub, he entered a world replete with symbolic meanings and unwritten laws. For example, a man often knocked three times on a table to gain 'admission' into a pub's regular society.[117] Saying *Auf die Gesundheit trinken, zum Wohl* (both essentially 'to your health') and *Prost* (cheers) while clinking glasses brought drinkers together and unified them on both personal and social levels. Since distrust concerning people who did not travel in the same work circles ran high, these rituals could be crucial for gaining acceptance. Participation was mandatory, unwritten though the code of conduct may have been.

Since a brewery or tavern was one of the few places men could spend their time pleasantly, meeting there after work also eased artisans' transitions into their roles as workers.[118] Institutions of socialisation and education had traditionally included the family, the school and the workplace, all of which prepared artisans for becoming model members of society. As fewer artisans resided with masters, however, education and socialisation occurred more frequently in drinking establishments. Here regular patrons continued obsolete guild traditions by founding societies and clubs to fill the gaps created by guild deregulation.[119] These initiatives developed informal systems for assisting one another in which organisers addressed common matters with great efficiency. Men took up collections to aid the sick or injured, paid for the funerals of 'members' and supported the disabled. Unemployed men found out about job opportunities as well as positions that offered better wages and working conditions.[120] In this regard, gathering in a *Stammkneipe* helped men cope with rapid social and economic changes by serving much needed corporative purposes.

Young workers also learned social behaviour in their regular taverns and received their political indoctrination there, taking instructive cues from older patrons. Regulars often exchanged the latest political news and current gossip, with class resentments beginning around reserved tables.[121] Such political discourse educated young lower-class men and

---

[116] Teuteberg, 'Die Nahrung der sozialen Unterschichten', pp. 280–81.
[117] Wyrwa, *Branntwein und 'echtes' Bier*, p. 159.
[118] Wyrwa, *Branntwein und 'echtes' Bier*, p. 25.
[119] Eckelt, *Biergeschichte(n). Bayerns fünftes Element*, p. 99.
[120] Sandgruber, *Bittersüße Genüsse*, p. 44.
[121] Sandgruber, *Bittersüße Genüsse*, p. 42.

prepared them for the working-class movement. To a certain degree, what began in the back room of the local *Stammkneipe* eventually emerged as a public forum for working-class rights. Contemporaries even described local pubs as the *Volkhochsschulen des Proletariat* (schools of the proletariat).[122]

Given beer's central role in the lower-class diet and social world, it is relatively easy to understand why higher prices and poorer quality triggered the rioting chronicled in this essay's introduction. If a lower-class man wanted to fit into Munich's lower-class society and remain in good health, it was impossible for him *not* to drink beer. Refusing to drink was out of the question, since beer provided for a man's nutritional, recreational and social needs. A journeyman or day labourer could not turn down a drink without risking being ostracised.[123] For many men, moving to Munich was therefore inextricably linked with beer consumption, and drinking beer set the tone for one's social life in the Bavarian capital.

## Conclusion

By the late 1850s, breweries and taverns began to lose their special status as the communication places of the lower classes. After the middle of the century, these places were where all Munich's residents gathered to spend their free time.[124] The Romantic Movement, which kindled an interest in the Middle Ages, was part of the reason behind beer's greater acceptance by all members of society. The spirit of Romanticism encouraged the upper and middle classes to 'rediscover' the 'traditional' Bavarian beer culture, and the wealthy no longer frowned upon the public consumption and enjoyment of beer.[125] In fact, drinking beer was encouraged, with this beverage becoming the leading drink among all social classes.[126]

Growing prosperity, increases in real wages and shorter working days also made it possible for beer to develop into a drink 'of the first order'.[127] In 1854, the changing attitude toward beer caused one observer to reflect on the 'democratising power of beer'. Even the 'most common of workers knew that the noble born prince and count could create no better [drink] than beer'. In this respect, the 'equality' of the national drink eventually contributed to the lessening of the emphasis on

---

[122] Wyrwa, *Branntwein und 'echtes' Bier*, p. 158.

[123] Wyrwa, *Branntwein und 'echtes' Bier*, p. 64.

[124] Walter, 'Bierpaläste', p. 48.

[125] Walter, 'Bierpaläste', pp. 22–3.

[126] Behringer, *Die Spaten-Brauerei 1397–1997*, p. 13.

[127] Walter, 'Bierpaläste' p. 23.

social distinctions. For example, once the warm weather arrived, people of all social classes gathered in the beer gardens, a mixture the 'like of which was never seen in Berlin'.[128] Drinking beer had thus evolved from the 'historical drink of the common people', the true *Volksgetränk*, to the Bavarian *Nationalgetränk* (national drink).[129]

Although beer's nutritional and social significance was culturally specific to Bavaria, this essay has, it is hoped, demonstrated how important a specific type of commodity could be for a city's development during the nineteenth century. Beer was and remained intricately bound up with the *Alltagskultur* (everyday culture) of Munich's lower-class citizens, and it was while drinking beer that these residents established norms for conversing, relaxing and exchanging information. For these reasons, beer consumption played a highly significant and determining role in creating an enduring sense of public life. Taverns and breweries were places where people lived their 'public lives', and these places became the true 'salon of the little people'.[130] In this regard, Munich's 'sense of place' was to a large degree created by beer and its inherent ability to provide for high levels of sociability. Not surprisingly, then, this beverage continued to define the Bavarian capital's public sphere for the remainder of the 1800s, to such a degree that those living in Munich would become infamous for their high rates of beer consumption.

This nineteenth-century Bavarian reverence for beer has proved enduring, and beer continues to represent the cultural history of Munich in profound ways. Drinking beer still has an unusual significance within an atmosphere that is best described as *gemütlich*, and Munich citizens are publicly proud of their beer and all the traditions and rituals that accompany its consumption.[131] Even today, 'a summer without a visit to the beer garden is no summer at all' for those living in or visiting Munich, and beer persists as one of the commodities most closely bound up with the Bavarian sense of national identity.[132]

### Further reading

F. Adam, ed., *Wirtshäuser in München um 1900*. '*Berge von unten, Kirchen von außen, Wirtshäuser von innen*' (Munich, 1997).
W.K. Blessing, 'Konsumprotest und Arbeitskampf. Vom Bierkrawall zum Bierboykott', in K. Tenfelde, ed., *Streik* (Munich, 1998).

---

[128] Laturell, *Volkskultur in München*, p. 87.
[129] Walter, 'Bierpaläste', pp. 22–3.
[130] Kaiser, 'Einleitung', p. 9.
[131] Laturell, *Volkskultur in München*, p. 55.
[132] Laturell, *Volkskultur in München*, p. 48.

B. Eckelt, *Biergeschichte(n). Bayerns fünftes Element* (Rosenheim, 1999).

S. Göttsch, 'Hungerunruhen – Veränderungen im traditionellen Protestverhalten', *Zeitschrift für Volkskunde*, 80 (1984), pp. 170–82.

V.D. Laturell, *Volkskultur in München. Aufsätze zu Brauchtum, Musikalische Volkskultur, Volkstanz, Trachten und Volkstheater in einer Millionenstadt* (Munich, 1997).

J. Roberts, 'Drink and working-class living standards in late nineteenth-century Germany', in W. Conze, ed., *Arbeiterexistenz im 19. Jahrhundert* (Stuttgart, 1981), pp. 74–91.

B. Speckle, *Streit ums Bier in Bayern: Wertvorstellungen um Reinheit, Gemeinschaft und Tradition* (Münster and New York, 2001).

# CHAPTER EIGHT

# Boulevard culture and advertising as spectacle in nineteenth-century Paris

*Hazel Hahn*

In *La Vie des boulevards: Madeleine-Bastille* (1896), the journalist Georges Montorgueil wrote that 'the movement of advertising and journalism towards the Boulevard was inevitable.'[1] He then asked rhetorically: 'Isn't it after all the purpose of journalism to be at the centre of activity?' The Grands Boulevards, which formed a semicircle on the right bank from the Madeleine to the Bastille, were the geographical centre of news, entertainment, fashion and advertising in nineteenth-century Paris. Also known simply as 'the Boulevards' or 'the Boulevard', they date from the seventeenth century when the old ramparts were converted into a promenade.[2] Newspaper headquarters and advertising brokers were located in the area throughout the nineteenth century, making the Grands Boulevards into a centre for news and communications that reached its peak at the *fin-de-siècle*. The animated telegraph rooms of the newspaper headquarters attracted large crowds while the newspapers themselves not only reported in minute detail on events on the Boulevards, but were read in the cafés along the street so that much of what was advertised was available just around the corner. The proximity of the places where newspapers were read to the boutiques, department stores, theatres and café-concerts advertised in their pages underscored the centrality of information and consumption to life on the Boulevards.

This essay explores the dynamic between advertising as a form of spectacle and the commercialised, urban culture of the Grands

---

[1] G. Montorgueil, *La vie des boulevards: Madeleine-Bastille* (Paris, 1896), p. 42.

[2] The eleven Boulevards were Boulevard de la Madeleine, Boulevard des Capucines, Boulevard des Italiens, Boulevard Montmartre, Boulevard Poissonnière, Boulevard Bonne-Nouvelle, Boulevard Saint-Denis, Boulevard Saint-Martin, Boulevard du Temple, Boulevard des Filles du Calvaire and Boulevard Beaumarchais. The singular term, 'the Boulevard', designated a particular section of the Grands Boulevards, usually the western portion. However, the term also often referred to the Grands Boulevards in their entirety.

Boulevards, out of which a unique sensibility and culture emerged. Scholars have argued that, in the second half of the nineteenth century, advertising formed a new and distinctive form of visual culture, with its own, totally new, mode of communication. Thomas Richards, in an analysis of Victorian advertisements, has shown that a new way of representing commodities first occurred at the 1851 Crystal Palace exhibition and that advertising continued this trend of showcasing commodities, forming a culture based on the exchange of material goods.[3] While this essay affirms the view that French advertising of the same period similarly increasingly showcased commodities, the focus of this essay is not so much the content of advertisements but rather advertising as urban spectacle. The ways in which French advertisements were conceived, displayed and perceived show a great deal of influence of boulevard culture. Vanessa Schwartz has shown that boulevard culture was an important aspect of the new mass culture of *fin-de-siècle* Paris in which features of everyday life became transformed into 'spectacular realities'.[4] The commercial attraction of the Grands Boulevards, however, meant they were not just sites of amusement, but also of consumption. Their distinctive culture was articulated from early on, since the 1840s, in a visual sensibility manifested in a fascination with the rapidly changing scene constituted by the combination of shop window displays and diverse passers-by. Advertisements reinforced boulevard commercial culture; countless advertisements depicted stores located on the Grands Boulevards full of people looking into shop windows. At the *fin-de-siècle* this orientation towards the visual culminated in a phenomenal outpouring of images in the form of distinctive and

---

[3] Thomas Richards, *The Commodity Culture of Victorian England: Advertising and Spectacle, 1851–1914* (Stanford, Calif., 1990). For an excellent historiographical overview on advertising, see C. Wischermann, 'Placing advertising in the modern cultural history of the city', in C. Wischermann and E. Shore, eds, *Advertising and the European City: Historical Perspectives* (Aldershot, 2002), p. 131. This is the first volume that places advertising in urban contexts.

[4] V. Schwartz, 'On the Grands Boulevards', *Spectacular Realities: Early Mass Culture in Fin-de-Siècle Paris* (Berkeley, 1998). See also D. Caillaud, ed., *Les grands boulevards*, exhibition catalogue (Paris, 1985) and B. Landau, C. Monod and E. Lohr, eds, *Les Grands Boulevards: un parcours d'innovation et de modernité*, exhibition catalogue (Paris, 2000). On Haussmannisation, see J. des Cars and P. Pinon, *Paris-Haussmann: 'Le Paris d'Haussmann'* (Paris, 1991); D.P. Jordan, *Transforming Paris: The Life and Labors of Baron Haussmann* (Chicago, 1995); M. Carmona, *Haussmann: His Life and Times, and the Making of Modern Paris* (Chicago, 2002); F. Loyer (1988), *Paris Nineteenth Century: Architecture and Urbanism* (New York, 1988), trans. Charles Lynn Clark; and G. Duby, *Histoire de la France urbaine*, vol. 4 (Paris, 1983).

colourful illustrated posters. The strategies adopted in the latter were recognised as distinctively French and were focused on presentational techniques designed to catch the attention of passers-by suggesting that French cities, particularly Paris, were more image-oriented at this period than London, Berlin or New York.[5]

## The visual culture of the Grands Boulevards

The Grands Boulevards had been regarded as a site of diversion and amusement since the mid-eighteenth century. An 1814 English guidebook declared that here could be found whatever that 'can divert the lounger and the idler, theatres, musicians, rope-dancers, coffee-houses, Vauxhalls, and restaurateurs … fan-menders, bead-stringers, beggars, quacks, tumblers, and showbooths'.[6] A form of visual culture began to emerge on the Grands Boulevards in the 1840s when they first began to be explicitly celebrated for providing a unique, continually changing, spectacle of new amenities and sights that were considered refreshing to the eye and a stimulus to reflection. They became a place to see and be seen. Observers during the period of the July Monarchy viewed the parts as elements of a panoramic whole, as in Balzac's 1845 description of the hourly changes taking place along the Boulevards. At nine o'clock 'the boutiques open their eyes showing a terrible interior disorder'. At eleven 'cabriolets run along' and different types of people appear. From two to five, according to Balzac, activity on the Boulevards is at its peak, staging a 'FREE grand show. Its three thousand boutiques scintillate, and the grand poem of window displays sing stanzas of colour from the Madeleine to the Porte Saint-Denis'.[7] Balzac was impressed above all by the boutiques and commercial bustle. The extraordinary array of people and alluring shops were distinctively urban attractions, the colourful façades and windows of the latter forming a pleasing and harmonious spectacle.

The reputation and 'unique aesthetic' of the Grands Boulevards were created by their 'intense life', atmosphere and animation rather

---

[5] On Berlin, see P. Fritzsche, *Reading Berlin 1900* (Cambridge, Mass., 1996) and S. Kracauer, *The Mass Ornament: Weimer Essays* (Cambridge, Mass., 1995). On New York, see D. Henkin, *City Reading: Written Words and Public Spaces in Antebellum New York* (New York, 1998).

[6] L. Tronchet, *Picture of Paris* (London, 1814), p. 191.

[7] H. de Balzac, 'Histoire et physiologie des boulevards de Paris. De la Madeline à la Bastille', in A. Prevost, E. Renard, G. Possion, H. de Balzac et al., *Panorama des grands Boulevards: Paris Romantique* (Paris, 1980), p. 91. Originally published in *Le Diable à Paris* (1845).

than their magnificent architecture.[8] The commercial success of the Boulevards underlined the growing importance of consumer goods intended to appeal to the visual sense. Certain parts became marked out as areas devoted to female consumption, delineated as such by fashion magazines and commercial establishments. The columns in fashion magazines urged readers to visit shops on the Boulevards and in nearby areas, such as the rue de la Paix, which were also noted for their fashionable shops and dressmakers. A fashion columnist for *Les Modes parisiennes* wrote in 1845 of a week's shopping excursions during which she and her companions went 'often to the boulevard'.[9] This, and similar representations of joyous yet diligent excursions through the most fashionable boutiques of Paris, elicited in the reader a desire to follow in the steps of the columnist and visit the shops in vogue. Such columns, which were most likely paid advertisements written as articles, were intended to appeal to the reader's visual imagination and her desire for beautiful goods by providing detailed descriptions of dresses, accessories and other consumer items, thereby contributing to the formation of the Boulevards' unique visual culture.

During the Second Empire, Baron Haussmann created a network of wide boulevards modelled on the original set of Grands Boulevards which, however, remained largely intact, apart from a couple of piercings. One of these, on the western side, linked the Boulevards to the new Place de l'Opéra, while the creation of today's Place de la République, off the eastern part of the Boulevards, caused the disappearance of the Boulevard du Crime, a celebrated part of the Boulevard du Temple that was home to numerous popular theatres. Nevertheless, the Grands Boulevards remained the absolute centre of Parisian commerce, entertainment, news, tourism and spectacle, in other words, of urban modernity.

As the atmosphere became more lively, Paris became increasingly cosmopolitan and the Boulevards the prime destination for tourists who revelled in their unique atmosphere. In the 1860s, there was a big increase in the number of people on the streets, many of whom felt as if they were partaking in one of the rapidly changing street spectacles. The variety of the latter was often described as 'infinite'. The staging of these

---

[8] E. Renard, cited in 'L'esthétique des grands boulevards', in Bibliothèque Historique de la ville de Paris, Anciennes Actualités (BHVP, AA, 38), 11 Mar. 1832.

[9] *Les Modes parisiennes* (5 Jan. 1845), p. 418. On urban change and consumption in the July Monarchy, see N. Green, *The Spectacle of Nature: Landscape and Bourgeois Culture in Nineteenth-Century France* (Manchester, 1990).

varied thematically according to the time of day.[10] From two o'clock the wide pavements were 'literally packed with men and women promenading', and the animation was great in the late afternoon when newspapers came out.[11] At six, working-class women descended on the Boulevards.[12] By seven o'clock, restaurants were empty and people were moving towards cafés.[13] An American woman observed in 1859 that, during an evening walk, 'innumerable varieties of costume, of language, of face, and of manner, follow each other in quick succession, and keep one's attention alive for hours'.[14] This spectacle of real life was so appealing because, despite all the transient and unexpected variations, it could be comfortably and safely observed from the cafés and because, amid the Haussmannian transformation of Paris, the Grands Boulevards provided a sense of continuity that blended tradition with modernity.

The Boulevards had some lesser rivals that also contributed to the formation of the city's visual culture. The regime of the Second Empire excelled at creating spectacular publicity for itself. Its court, full of beautiful women, received much publicity, staging a wide variety of ceremonies and rituals, including the inauguration of the new boulevards.[15] However, throughout the early twentieth century, it was the Grands Boulevards that continued to be the showcase of Paris. One Londoner observed in 1911 that the 'Grands Boulevards might be called the showrooms of Paris', that in 'London one may live for years and never see a Londoner' as 'London has no showrooms for their display'.[16] To be sure, London was full of shows to see, but no street in London, or any other European city, became a visual spectacle that could match that of the Grands Boulevards.[17]

### Information, advertising, street furniture and magic lanterns

The Grands Boulevards attracted advertising from an early date. In the

---

[10] A. Delvau, *Les Plaisirs de Paris: guide pratique et illustré* (Paris, 1867), pp. 18–19.

[11] J. McCabe, *Paris by Sunlight and Gaslight* (Philadelphia, 1870), p. 661.

[12] Delvau, *Les Plaisirs de Paris*, p. 21.

[13] McCabe, *Paris by Sunlight and Gaslight*, p. 661.

[14] M. Sweat, *Highways of Travel: or a Summer in Europe* (Boston 1859), p. 48.

[15] See M. Truesdell, *Spectacular Politics: Louis-Napoleon Bonaparte and the Fête Impériale* (New York, 1977).

[16] E. Lucas, *A Wanderer in Paris* (London, 1911), p. 179.

[17] On entertainment in London, see R. Altick, *The Shows of London* (Cambridge, Mass., 1978) and L. Nead, *Victorian Babylon: People, Streets and Images in Nineteenth-Century London* (New Haven, 2000).

1820s, sandwichmen and the 'elegant-models' of the tailors' shops appeared on fashionable promenades.[18] In 1849, an entrepreneur proposed setting up gas candelabras on the Boulevards that would also serve as vehicles for advertising.[19] One entrepreneur declared in 1858 that 'advertising pursues you everywhere', especially on the Grands Boulevards.[20] Handouts were so common that a caricature, entitled *Le spectacle dans la rue* (1861) protested against the 'rage of brochures' on the Boulevards that had become a 'spectacle' in its own right.[21] At the same time, traditional itinerant hawkers and entertainers were increasingly displaced, replaced by modern commercial enterprises such as photography studios.[22]

Advertising was a controversial issue in the Second Empire. As the 'embellishment' of Paris spread and created new, elegant and luxurious neighbourhoods and monumental vistas, the sight of haphazardly placed posters came under attack and led to greater regulation of advertising. Temporary construction walls, for example, were leased out for organised advertising and in the 1860s a set of 'street furniture', such as newspaper kiosks, urinals and toilettes, was built to display posters. Kiosks and urinals had existed earlier, but now their number increased and a hundred and fifty Morris Columns were built to accommodate posters for theatres and other spectacles.[23] Posters were almost always commercial, rather than political, in nature, as severe censorship was exercised against those criticising the government. The beauty and charm of the Grands Boulevards was an important issue in the debate about street advertising. The critic Louis Lazare called for the municipality to give advertising media elegant and tasteful appearances.[24] Designed to fit into the newly embellished surroundings, items of street furniture were part and parcel of Haussmannisation. However, while the furniture increased the uniformity of the streets, it also contributed to the

---

[18] *Le Provincial* [1824], cited in J. Grand-Carteret (1893), *XIXe siècle en France, classes, moeurs, usages, costumes, inventions* (Paris, 1893), pp. 684–5.

[19] Archives de la Police de Paris (hereafter APP) D/b1 204, *Affichage* (1849), Report by the Direction of Sanitation and Lighting, file Delion, 11 Nov.

[20] Anon., *La publicité au point de vue industriel et commercial* (Paris, 1858), p. 3.

[21] Biscotin, *Le spectacle dans la rue: grande revue nouvelle de l'année 1861* (Paris, 1861).

[22] F. Denoyelle, 'De l'atelier au temple de la photographie', in B. Landau et al., *Les Grands Boulevards; un parcours d'innovation et de modernité* (Paris, 2000), p. 179.

[23] APP D/b1 513, *colonnes d'affichage dans Paris. Le Moniteur Universel*, 4 May 1868. Later models of the Morris Column and newspaper kiosks are currently seen in San Francisco.

[24] L. Lazare, 'Promenades dans Paris', *Revue municipale*, 236 (1857), p. 43.

privileging of the Grands Boulevards as a centre of information and advertising since the majority was placed along the axis of the Boulevards and the Boulevard Sebastopol. In 1911, the majority of 478 kiosks were still concentrated in the older parts of Paris, while only a few existed in the outer *arrondissements*.[25]

In the second half of the century, spectacular advertisements proliferated on the Grands Boulevards. Buildings along the Boulevards were used for publicity with maximum effect. Newspaper buildings, ornate and covered with banners, billboards and screens, were lit at night. *Le Temps*, *Matinées espagnoles*, *L'Événement*, *Gil Blas*, *Le Voltaire*, *L'Éclair*, *Le Journal* and *Le Gaulois* were all located near to the Grands Boulevards and the Stock Exchange.[26] The building of *Le Petit Journal* and *Le Journal illustré* on the boulevard Montmartre featured the Frascati gallery, a popular destination. Named after the celebrated gaming house that used to be there, it housed a bazaar, an aquarium and painting exhibitions.[27] An illustration (see Figure 8.1) on the front page of *Le Journal illustré* from 1864 not only shows that newspaper headquarters were prominently featured in the news, but also demonstrates a method of self-promotion by publicising the newspaper's own building. Advertisements for newspapers often depicted the newspaper buildings on a busy street filled with people and traffic, emphasising the central position of the newspaper headquarters in the city. *Le Petit Parisien* established a museum of celebrities on the boulevard Montmartre.[28] The popular wax museum, Musée Grévin, opened in 1882 on the boulevard Montmartre and was a locus of *actualités* (current events).[29] Illuminated screens on the façades of buildings flashed the latest news, becoming the focal point of a highly charged atmosphere on election nights. At times of sensational events or crises, panic-stricken crowds besieged newspaper kiosks.[30] Once success was assured, newspapers needing more space often relocated to streets nearby. In 1878, *Le Figaro* inaugurated its telegraph room and started a trend. A continuous flow of the curious visited it, turning it into a space

---

[25] Archives de Paris 1304 w p.j. 30 dossier 15, *Concessions des édicules sur les voies publiques* 1906–1923; report of 29 May 1911.

[26] Montorgueil, *La vie des boulevards*, pp. 37, 42; P. Albert, 'Journaux et journalistes', in Landau, *Les Grands Boulevards*, p. 201.

[27] E. Dubief, *Le Journalisme* (Paris, 1892), p. 21.

[28] Montorgueil, *La vie des boulevards*, p. 36.

[29] P. de Moncan, *Les Grands Boulevards de Paris: de la Bastille à la Madeleine* (Paris, 1997), p. 95. On the Musée Grévin, see Schwartz, *Spectacular Realities*, and M. Sandberg, *Living Pictures, Missing Persons: Mannequins, Museums, and Modernity* (Princeton, 2003).

[30] Louys (*c.* 1914), 'Le Boulevard', clipped article, BHVP, AA 38.

Fig 8.1   *Le Journal Illustré*, 20 March 1864, p. 1, 'Aspect de l'angle du Boulevard Montmartre et de la rue de Richelieu le jour de l'apparition d'un numéro du *Journal Illustré*': © Photothèque des Musées de la Ville de Paris

devoted as much to advertising as to information.[31] The great hall of *Le Figaro* was frequently crowded with women and men placing classified ads.[32] Newspapers also gave away countless gifts such as photographs, mineral water or tickets, and *Le Figaro* invented the free supplement.[33]

At Lent, *mardi gras*, or on the occasions of visits by foreign dignitaries, there were parades on the Boulevards.[34] The Boulevards were also the most coveted route for advertising vehicles. Suppressed since 1847 and reintroduced in the 1870s, they quickly became flamboyant. The carriages of *Le Petit Journal*, pulled by five horses and decorated with flags and insignias, were accompanied by ten people in costumes who distributed the paper along the Boulevards throughout the day and night.[35] Postilions in livery riding horses, Amazons guiding triumphal chariots, 'magnificent carriages' with turning kiosks, carriages with three-metre-high turning pyramids, five-metre-long carriages displaying products, all crowded the Boulevards.[36] The ubiquitous, strange, huge, red vehicle of the tailoring shop, Old England, attracted much satire.[37] The police authorised only a fraction of the requests for advertising vehicles put in by entrepreneurs yet, although only ten to twenty versions of each model were allowed to circulate in an already congested street, their numbers quickly multiplied, until they were completely suppressed in 1900. Advertising experts did not consider such methods as particularly effective, but they were very popular and were obviously encouraged by the reputation of the Boulevards as the best place to display to potential customers.

The theatrical atmosphere of the Boulevards promoted and reinforced the attention-seeking strategies characteristic of French advertising. In 1875, Villiers de l'Isle-Adam wrote a celebrated short story on the use of the sky as a gigantic canvas for 'celestial advertising' made with stars. Soon his vision seemed to have become reality as, in the evening, well-lit signs and screens competed for attention. In the 1880s, neon signs replaced mechanically moving boards.[38] Illuminated advertising on celluloid resembled a magic lantern show and attracted 'thousands and

---

[31] Montorgueil, *La vie des boulevards*, p. 36.

[32] J. Grand-Carteret, *XIXe siècle en France, classes, moeurs, usages, costumes, inventions* (Paris, 1893). See figure 40.

[33] Dubief, *Le Journalisme*, pp. 188–9.

[34] APP D/a1 127, *Voitures de publicité*, file Delalande, 1879–1880.

[35] Ibid.

[36] G. Bastard, *Paris qui roule* (Paris, 1889), p. 174.

[37] APP D/a1 62, *Voitures de publicité*, files Peinte, Taullard, Hefty, Villard, and Maugras and Montaut; Musée de la Publicité, Centre de Documentation, P. Bruyant, 'Fiacres-réclame à demi-tarif'. File Old England, 1881–87.

[38] *Le Soleil*, 9 Jan. 1889, cited in M. de Thézy (1976), *Paris, la rue. Le mobilier urbain du Second Empire à nos jours* (Paris, 1976), p. 71.

thousands of *badauds'* in the 1880s.[39] One shop was famous for its ten windows with changing transparencies that displayed portraits of a dramatic heroine.[40] In the 1910s, cinematography, accompanied by advertisements and news, was projected onto screens along the Grands Boulevards that were up to thirty metres square in size.[41] Writers expressed their ambivalence about the crowds who watched with 'hypnotised eyes'.[42] Spectacular advertising flourished on a street long famed for its visual attractions and intensified the process of commercialisation, enhancing its 'modern' reputation. Eventually, however, as competition turned the Boulevards into a battleground, the advertising came be seen as excessive.

The fame of the Grands Boulevards contributed to the reputation of Paris as the 'world's pleasure city', second to none in liveliness and sparkle.[43] Edmondo d'Amicis, visiting Paris for the 1878 Universal Exposition, declared that 'the spectacle that the picture of life on the fashionable Boulevards presents is absolutely unique' for here 'everything is open, transparent, and exposed to view',[44] the 'horses pass in troops, and the crowd in torrents. It is a rivalry of magnificence and stateliness which borders on madness'.[45] His perception of the Boulevards as a source of overwhelming stimuli is very different from the views expressed during the July Monarchy. Instead, emphasising leisure and the reflections produced by pleasurable sensations during a *flâneurie*, he focuses on the relentless lure of the visual and a general commotion directed towards the promotion of consumption that seemed especially powerful at night. An image (*c.* 1885), titled 'Paris le soir: les cafés du Boulevard Montmartre', shows a throng of elegantly dressed men and women densely packing the pavement, most of them standing before a brilliantly lit café.[46]

---

[39] J. Pâle, *Croquis Parisiens* (Paris, 1897), p. 103; *La Publicité*, 106 (1912), p. 215; Montorgueil, *La vie des boulevards*, p. 37.

[40] E. Fournier, *Histoire des enseignes de Paris* (Paris, 1884), p. 441.

[41] APP D/b1 204, *Etude sur la publicité industrielle et commerciale*, June 1917, p. 42; H. Gaisser, ed., *Annuaire général de la publicité et des industries qui s'y rattachent* (Tours, 1914), p. 253.

[42] R. Coolus, 'Affiches lumineuses', in O. Uzanne, ed., *Badauderies parisiennes. Les rassemblements: physiologies de la rue* (Paris, 1896), p. 115.

[43] E. de Amicis, *Souvenirs de Paris*, cited in E. Reynolds-Ball, *Paris* (London, 1900), p. 188.

[44] Amicis, *Souvenirs de Paris*, p. 189.

[45] Amicis, *Souvenirs de Paris*, pp. 187–8.

[46] Jules Pelcoq, illustrator, Musée Carnavalet Estampe Topo PC 042 B. On the night in Paris, see S. Delattre, *Les douze heures noires: la nuit à Paris au XIXe siècle* (Paris, 2000); and J. Schlör, *Nights in the Big City: Paris, Berlin, London, 1840–1930* (London, 1998).

The close link between consumption and sensation on the Boulevards was not lost on Henry James, who noted in 1876 that the Boulevards were 'a long chain of cafés, each one with its little promontory of chairs and tables projecting into the sea of asphalt' that were filled with sensation-seekers by night and day, in this 'best lighted capital in the world'. In the summer, it could get very hot, as gas lighting 'heats and thickens the atmosphere'.[47] In 1890, he described the Boulevards as the 'night aspect of Paris which represents it as a huge market for sensations', with 'a profusion of light and a pervasion of sound' and people crowding 'all over the broad expanse of the asphalt'. James underlined the Boulevards' theatrical ambiance, animated with visual and aural stimuli that were 'tokens of a great traffic of pleasure'. The very architecture, bathed in light, appeared ornamental, like a stage set: 'the Madeleine rose theatrical, a high artful *décor* before the foot lights of the Rue Royale'.[48] This staged ambiance did not sit well with some of James's characters. In *The Portrait of a Lady* (1881), Isabel Archer, the young, intelligent American visitor, is advised against going on the Boulevards. In *The Tragic Muse* (1890), Nick Dormer protests against 'the publicity and vulgarity' of a café on the Boulevards.[49] Like Amicis, James implied that the onslaught of sensations numbed, rather than encouraged, the capacity for reflection, that the intensely attractive ambiance of the Boulevards was ultimately superficial.

### *Faits divers* advertising

A curious episode highlights the dynamic of advertising on the Grands Boulevards. In 1881, camels carrying kiosks appeared on the Boulevards, attracting a crowd of 250.[50] The police not only banned the practice, reasoning that 'the number of camels existing in Paris is increasing daily', but also prohibited the sale and reproduction of camels in all extended French territories. A newspaper article, bemoaning the demise of camel advertising, argued that the extremely severe response of the Prefect had to do with a recent disastrous French military campaign in Algeria; the camel, as a symbol of Africa, caused embarrassment for the authorities.[51]

---

[47] H. James, *Parisian Sketches: Letters to the* New York Tribune *1875–1876* (London, 1856), pp. 189–90.

[48] H. James, *The Tragic Muse* (London, 1995), p. 74.

[49] James, *The Tragic Muse*, p. 113.

[50] APP D/a1 127, *Voitures de publicité 1876–1885*, file Maugras et Montaut, 1881–82.

[51] D. Tapin, 'La guerre au chameau', *Le Clairon*, 10 Jan. 1882 in APP D/a1 127.

The camel incident is emblematic of the politics of street advertising. Usually, any press coverage that turned it into a current event was welcome. However, the penchant for advertising as street spectacle meant that advertising was vague on the specifics of products being publicised.

Fascination with the minute details of everyday life in Paris turned *faits divers* and *actualités* into two of the staples of the popular press. *Faits divers* were short, episodic news and were instrumentally applied to advertising techniques. In *faits divers*, current events could end with the names and addresses of shops where one could buy products mentioned in the stories. Such techniques were popular with the *boulevardier* press. One of them, *The Boulevard*, an English-language weekly, declared that its advertisements would be 'pretty, graceful, and artistic'. It lamented the condition of English and American advertising, which was 'in a most barbarous and shocking state. English advertisements are so hideous and unimaginative that they repel attention'.[52] The paper implied that French advertising was more artistic and clever, more visually aesthetic than the English or American equivalent.

*Faits divers*, as Vanessa Schwartz points out, reproduced seemingly incredible stories that were in fact true and thereby contributed to the construction of everyday life as a spectacle.[53] Whereas *faits divers* in *Le Petit Journal* focused on sensational events such as crimes or accidents, those in *Le Figaro* focused on high-society activities. *Le Figaro*'s *fait divers* advertising was based on the idea that consumers would want to emulate the behaviour of other consumers and particularly the life style of the rich, a view supported by Thorstein Veblen's *The Theory of the Leisure Class* (1908). The target audience was mostly women. Posters depicted elegant women reading newspapers, as did an 1895 poster (see Figure 8.2) for *L'Éclair*. *Le Figaro*'s *faits divers* column, 'Nouvelles Diverses', was full of editorial advertisements. A typical item featured a visit by foreign royalty, the clothes the ladies wore, and the shop selling the clothes. An article on a plant exhibition urged readers to visit a greenhouse.[54] 'Un Conseil par Jour', for medical products, aperitifs and cosmetics, and an illustrated column titled 'Le Modèle du Jour' were also columns for advertisements in *Le Figaro*. The latter was often read on the Boulevards in cafés and hotels, with easy access to the shops. These readers were often women, since *Baedeker's Paris* of 1900 specified that

[52]  G. Murray, 'A paper for the happy', *The Boulevard*, 25 Apr. 1879, p. 5.

[53]  Schwartz, *Spectacular Realities*, pp. 26–44. Also see D. Kalifa, *L'encre et le sang: récit de crimes et société à la Belle Époque* (Paris, 1995).

[54]  *Le Figaro*, 6 Apr. 1883, p. 2.

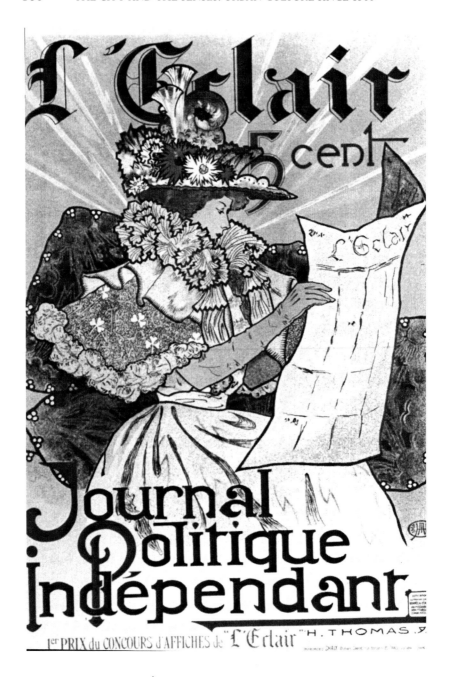

Fig 4.2    Poster for *L'Éclair*, 1895. Roger Marx, *Les Maîtres de l'affiche*, Paris: Chaix, 1896–1900

the 'best cafés may with propriety be visited by ladies'.[55] While editorial advertising in France courted continuous controversy, many experts recommended it. According to one authority, Emile Mermet, advertising in *Le Figaro* was 'excellent, regardless of where it is placed', including foreign news.[56] According to *Le Figaro*, the art of editorial advertising was that it 'insinuates a commercial recommendation where it would seem impossible to slip it in, in a work of literature, fantasy, even politics'.[57]

Textual and visual advertising in France shared similar strategies. Foreign critics noted that neither the *réclame*, often in 'elegant and classical style', nor the French poster had 'any direct link with the announced object'.[58] The iconography of the illustrated poster often depicted an enigmatic scene, as in a poster (*c.* 1895) for a medication named 'La Pertuisine' for hair growth. The poster depicted a glamorous woman with a decolleté dress seated in a balcony at a theatre, accompanied by a male admirer. The image appears at first enigmatic, since there is no obvious connection between the advertised product and the image, until one grasps the narrative. Surveying the scene of spectators, most of whom happen to be bald men, the woman is commenting, 'What do you see? Nothing but bald heads!' While the poster makes it clear that the spectacle to watch is not the play but the voluptuous woman, the image also bestows the power of the gaze on the woman.

This cinematic sensibility *avant la lettre* can be seen also in Toulouse-Lautrec's poster for a shop, 'Artisan Moderne', which depicts an artisan barging in to find the lady of the house still in bed in her negligée, and the maid looking scandalised. Such an image forced the viewer to spend some time to understand what was being advertised. Multi-media campaigns, using a combination of posters and *faits divers* advertisements, constructed carefully orchestrated, intriguing visual narratives. This phenomenon also underlines the way that textual advertising, instead of being replaced by images, created scenes into which the reader could insert herself, reinforcing the visual element of these campaigns.

From the 1880s, colourful artistic posters filled the streets with images of women and led to the 'poster mania' that lasted from 1895 to 1900. Jules Chéret, the most popular poster artist, attained fame for his 'formula of exterior decoration' with posters mostly depicting images of a seductive female known as *chérette*. He designed about a thousand

---

[55] K. Baedeker, *Paris and Environs. Handbook for Travellers* (Leipzig, 1900), p. 290.

[56] E. Mermet, *La publicité en France: guide-annuaire* (Paris, 1883), pp. 620–21.

[57] Anon., 'La réclame et l'art,' *Figaro illustré*, 183, Jun. 1905, p. 14.

[58] *American Advertiser*, cited in *La Publicité moderne*, 1 (1905), p. 16.

posters in ten years.[59] The supporters of the poster art saw it as fulfilling 'the need to feel vivid sensations and intense emotions, rapidly blunted to be revived again'.[60] Such an idea reaffirmed the association of modernity with the experience of constantly renewed surface sensations. Critics placed new emphasis on the physiological and psychological need for sensations, especially those that induced pleasure rather than reflection. Poster art, according to Jules Claretie, provided 'the education of everyone through the retina ... instead of a bare wall, the wall attracts, as a kind of a chromolithographic Salon'.[61] Although the poster was valued above all for its art, it appealed to the vision and the psyche through colourful, pleasing forms, usually the forms of vibrant young women. In this, the illustrated poster supported the tendency of French advertising to focus on attractive and amusing presentation and images, rather than on direct, informative communication.

## *Camelots* and sandwichmen

One of the favourite topics of *fin-de-siècle faits divers* was that of the *camelots* on the Boulevards. *Camelots* sold *articles de Paris*, objects manufactured in Parisian workshops that included everything from fans to artificial flowers. *Camelots* often created a fashion for particular goods and even flooded the Boulevards with one item. They were famed for their ability to gather and amuse crowds through their clever selling pitches.[62] Newspaper columns on Parisian events and scenes (*chroniques*) described *camelots* as 'essentially Parisian, indigenous to the faubourgs' and that, 'chased by the police, their obsessing *pittoresque* fills terraces'.[63] The very fact that the *camelots* were not authorised by the police enhanced their romantic mystique.

---

[59] G. d'Avenel, 'La Publicité', *Le Mécanisme de la vie moderne* (Paris, 1902), p. 176. On Chéret, see S. Le Men, *Seurat et Chéret: Le peintre, le cirque et l'affiche* (Paris, 1994) and B. Collins, 'The poster as art; Jules Chéret and the Struggle for the Equality of the Arts in Late Nineteenth-Century France', in D. Doordan, ed., *Design History, an Anthology* (Cambridge, Mass., 1995), pp. 17–27.

[60] A. Mellerio, 'Le renouveau de l'estampe', *L'Estampe et l'affiche* (1897), pp. 45–6.

[61] J. Claretie, 'Quelques opinions sur l'affiche illustrée', *La Plume*, 15 Nov. 1893, p. 495.

[62] APP D/b1, E. Frébault, 'Curiosités parisiennes. Les industries de la rue', *L'Histoire*, 26 May 1870, p. 197, *Camelots, crieurs, distributeurs*. On *articles de Paris*, see W. Walton, *France and the Crystal Palace: Bourgeois Taste and Artisan Manufacture in the Nineteenth Century* (Berkeley, 1992).

[63] Frébault , 'Curiosités parisiennes. Les industries de la rue', p. 197.

The representation of the *camelot* as a *type* is rooted in the long-standing iconography of *petits métiers* (petty workers) which emphasised visual characteristics, or *cris de Paris*, which classified their sounds.[64] At the *fin-de-siècle* the street continued to teem with innumerable *petits métiers* doing practical services. The *camelot* was identified as a *type* along with the sweeping woman, the door opener, the café caricaturist, the café scavenger who collected cigarette butts, and others such as the commissioner who staked out a street corner and offered a hand to whoever needed help, carrying messages or letters.[65] The representations of the *types* throughout the nineteenth century usually filtered out the workers' individual characteristics and rendered them as picturesque, charming ornaments of the streets fitting well into the boulevard culture that emphasised rapidly registered impressions. In the last decade of the nineteenth century, such depictions had little to do with reality but were based on the middle-class nostalgia of an imagined past. A journalist recounted sitting for an hour at the Café de la Paix on the Grands Boulevards in 1895 when a storm of vendors of the journal *Paris-Sport* passed by, galloping like horses. Subsequently he was solicited by a dog seller, a girl offering flowers, a mother with children trying to sell pencils, a child offering a journal, sketchers and a seller of army uniforms and a 'cloud of *camelots*' who rushed in from all directions.[66]

The Boulevards were the place not only to see, but also to hear. *Camelots*' shouts replaced the disappearing *cris de Paris* and spread the current *nouveautés* (new consumer items) and 'sensational news' through the latest pitches: 'when a new thing appears on the boulevard, after twenty-four hours all shout in unison. They adopt the cry, the voice, or the phrase that had the most success.'[67] A song that ended with 'a series of "Ah!" as if he was about to faint' was sung for a week by a hundred *camelots*.[68] Added to the shouts of the *camelots* were those of newspaper vendors. Vendors literally shouted the news, until an 1889 law prohibited it and allowed only the title, price, indication of editorial opinion, or names of writers to be announced.[69] Their cacophonous cries

---

[64] See V. Milliot, *Les cris de Paris ou le peuple travesti: les représentations des petits métiers parisiens, XVIe–XVIIIe siècles* (Paris, 1995).

[65] See P. Vidal, *Paris qui crie. Petits métiers* (Paris, 1890); G. Chamerot and F. Bloch, *Types du boulevard* (Paris, 1880).

[66] L. Paulian, 'Une heure à la terrasse d'un café', *Le Monde moderne* (1895), pp. 421–5.

[67] Paulian, 'Une heure à la terrasse d'un café', pp. 420–21.

[68] Ibid.

[69] Law of 19 March 1889, cited in G. Le Poittevin, *Traité de la presse* (Paris, 1902), p. 338.

resounded on the Boulevards at three in the afternoon when men and women shouting the latest news rushed onto the street.[70]

A street *type* that was actually an advertising medium was the sandwichman. *The Beautiful Lady* (1905), by Booth Tarkington, starts with a scene on the Grands Boulevards in which a man is kneeling down in the middle of a pavement displaying his shaven head on which is written an advertisement.[71] Passers-by laugh at him. As he sits with his head bowed, he notices the shoes of a woman who is addressing kind words to him, but cannot raise his head to look at her properly. This scene is emblematic of the condition of a sandwichman, reduced to this situation by poverty, and for whom being a living advertisement is a humiliating experience, especially on the Boulevards, where everyone is watching. Although staring at women is a popular pastime on the Boulevards, he is unable to look at the face of a woman who interests him.

The sandwichman provoked more ambiguous sentiment and anxiety than any other street *type*. Christened by Charles Dickens, he appeared in France during the Restoration, only to disappear for the most part until the 1870s.[72] Unlike the *camelot*, the sandwichman was silent. He was often an embarrassment, being neither picturesque nor pleasant. Referring to 'the walking sign, the living advertisement',[73] the term 'sandwichman' (*l'homme-affiche* or *l'homme-sandwich*) was akin to the names for the bizarre human figures shown in circuses and fairs, like monster-man or dog-man. His peculiar condition, at the same time both medium and object, was comparable to that of the prostitute, described by Walter Benjamin as simultaneously the hawker and the wares themselves.[74] Representations of sandwichmen and other *types* seen as further characters on the stage of the Boulevards, reinforced their commercial nature yet also contributed to the preservation of their unique character. Although all the different classes could be seen on the Boulevards, they were divided between spectators and consumers on one hand and the observed and workers on the other.

---

[70] E. Pilon (1901), 'Le crieur de dernières nouvelles', in O. Uzanne et al., *Figures de Paris, ceux qu'on rencontre et celles qu'on frôle* (Paris, 1901), p. 37.

[71] B. Tarkington, *The Beautiful Lady*, in *The Works of Booth Tarkington*, vol. 9 (Garden City, 1922), p. 1.

[72] APP D/b1 203, '*Nos informations. Les hommes-affiches*', *La Liberté*, 19 Sept. 1876.

[73] E. Frébault, *La Vie de Paris. Guide pittoresque et pratique du* visiteur (Paris, 1878), p. 211.

[74] W. Benjamin, 'Paris, Capital of the Nineteenth Century', in P. Demetz (ed.), *Reflections: Essays, Aphorisms, Autobiographical Writings* (New York, 1978), trans. E. Jephcott, p. 157.

## The French strategy: eccentric advertising

In 1886, an 'ingenious businessman' organised an 'altogether singular' advertisement, announced in the major papers as 'a very new invention, very pretty and, what is even better, profoundly humanitarian: the *femmes-réclames* (sandwichwomen)'.[75] Likewise, the advent of the first female billposter was loudly trumpeted.[76] The sandwichwoman and the female billposter were figures of the street scene that provided material for the boulevard press. Such a phenomenon once again underlines the fact that boulevard culture encouraged a focus on the appearance of advertisements rather than its content. Shabby sandwichmen were increasingly replaced by men and women dressed in elegant costumes. This phenomenon is satirised by Albert Robida's caricature from 1888. Titled 'Revolution in Clothes', the image depicts men, women, children and dogs that promenade on the Grands Boulevards as a vehicle for advertising various wares, including those of tailoring shops.[77] Street advertising was a popular theme in Robida's weekly *La Caricature*, which combined a sense of the absurd with keen observations of boulevard culture.

At the beginning of the twentieth century, critics commented that French advertising was distinguished from the Anglo-American variety, which used constant repetition to make a psychological impact on the spectator. French advertising, in contrast, according to the critics aimed to be 'fantastic and amusing'.[78] For example, ten men promenading on the Boulevards 'attracted attention through their rather forced elegance'. At the terrace of each café, they took off their hats and bowed deeply, showing ten shaven heads on which were written an advertisement for an aperitif.[79] In 1905, an American noted that French advertising specialised in 'all kinds of eccentricities' such as magic lantern shows in the street and people promenading and acting theatrically, and recommended a careful study of local colour before launching a campaign in France.[80] The peak years of street advertising as spectacle were those before the First World War. 'People of all countries and all colours promenaded in costumes or paraded on horses and in "superb vehicles"'.[81] Young women wearing 'immaculate shirts' advertised a

---

[75] A. Coffignon, *Paris-vivant. Le pavé parisien* (Paris, 1890), pp. 127–8.
[76] APP D/b1 204, *Etude sur la publicité'*, p. 42.
[77] Anon, 'Révolution dans le costume', *La Caricature*, 21 Jan. 1888, p. 1.
[78] O. Uzanne, 'L'ingénieuse publicité', *La Dépêche de Toulouse*, 28 Dec. 1904.
[79] Uzanne, 'L'ingénieuse publicité'.
[80] *American Advertiser*, 1905, pp. 15–16.
[81] *Breslauer Zeitung*, cited in *La Publicité*, 106, 1912, p. 215.

washhouse, and men in black costumes carried pocket lanterns.[82] A vogue for live mannequins led children and adults to be displayed in the shop windows. Foreign observers saw such practices as a flamboyant and overwhelming feature of the urban decor.[83] Many French experts regarded them as full of 'excess and superfluity' and vainly encouraged the efficient and powerful strategies of American advertising using more transparent means of communication based on the study of human psychology and the principles of suggestion.[84]

After 1900, a reaction against advertising began to set in. This had several causes. French entrepreneurs adopted 'American' strategies of billposting. This coincided with the deterioration in the overall quality of posters, as the most gifted poster artists such as Chéret and Mucha left the trade, thereby causing critics to abandon their support of poster art. At the same time the volume of visual stimuli in the street increased. In the evening the Grands Boulevards blazed with 'an intense illumination … repetitive, hopping, vibrating … catching the gaze, blinding pupils, wringing the optic nerves … tyrannizing attention, breaking through indifference'.[85] It was no longer possible to be a detached flâneur or to adopt a 'blasé attitude' of the kind described by Georg Simmel.[86] Mounting public pressure led to the reduction and even suppression of various forms of street advertising, including the complete banning of handbill distribution.[87]

This essay has examined the way that new forms of advertising attempted to blend into the established visual culture of the Grands Boulevards. Presented as a spectacle, it was therefore more than a simple presentation of images and inspired and reinforced the tendency of French advertising to prefer interesting verbal and visual formats

The Grands Boulevards, as traditional promenade, the principal centre of entertainment, news and shops, the street with the heaviest traffic, and a stage for modern visual experimentation and display, constituted the heart of Paris. A contested and changing realm governed by a complex set of conventions determining what was permissible, the volume and pace of the experiences offered by the Boulevards invited both celebration and criticism. However, despite their controversial status, the Grand Boulevards remained a fundamentally controllable and

---

[82] Ibid.

[83] Comment in *Rund ums Jahr 1911, Jahrbuch fur junge Deutsche, von Dr. Hugo Gruber* (Berlin, 1911), cited in *La Publicité*, 106 (1912), p. 211.

[84] Comment in *Breslauer Zeitung*, cited in *La Publicité*, p. 213.

[85] J. Claretie, 'Les Amis de Paris', 12 (1912), pp. 301–2.

[86] See K. Wolff, ed., G. Simmel, *The Sociology of Georg Simmel* (New York, 1950), trans. K. Wolff, p. 414.

[87] *La Publicité*, 87 (1910), p. 373.

extremely public urban space and ultimately, most Parisians wanted the street to remain a place of pleasantness and amusement rather than of overwhelming stimulation. Perceived as modern par excellence because of their visual culture, in their heyday the Grands Boulevards marked the period when modernity was symbolised by particular forms of absorbable visual and aural stimuli that could be enjoyed during a urban *flâneurie*.

## Further reading

P. Chu and G. Weisberg, eds, *The Popularization of Images: Visual Culture under the July Monarchy* (Princeton, NJ, 1994).

J. Crary, *Techniques of the Observer: On Vision and Modernity in the Nineteenth Century* (Cambridge, Mass., 1990).

J. Crary, *Suspensions of Perception: Attention, Spectacle, and Modern Culture* (Cambridge, Mass., 1999).

V. de Grazia and E. Furlough, eds, *The Sex of Things: Gender and Consumption in Historical Perspective* (Berkeley, 1996).

T. Gronberg, *Designs on Modernity: Exhibiting the City in 1920s Paris* (Manchester, 1998).

R.L. Herbert, *Impressionism: Art, Leisure, and Parisian Society* (New Haven, 1988).

M.B. Miller, *The Bon Marché: Bourgeois Culture and the Department Store, 1869–1929* (Princeton, 1981).

S. Oetermann and D.L. Schneider, *The Panorama: History of Mass Medium* (Cambridge, Mass., 1997).

M. Stafford and F. Terpak, *Devices of Wonder: From the World in a Box to Images on a Screen* (Los Angeles, 2001).

K. Tester, ed., *The Flâneur* (London, 1994).

# PART THREE

# CULTURAL CONTROL AND CULTURAL SUBVERSION

# CHAPTER NINE

# A taste of Vienna: food as a signifier of urban modernity in Vienna, 1890–1930

## Janet Stewart

According to Fodor's guide to *Vienna and the Danube Valley*, Vienna is a city that immediately conjures up images of 'operettas and psychoanalysis, *Apfelstrudel* and marble staircases, Strauss waltzes and Schubert melodies'.[1] By juxtaposing apple strudel with music, architecture and psychoanalysis, this guidebook seems to suggest that food enjoys an elevated cultural status in Vienna. This idea is reiterated in the title of the guidebook's introduction, 'Beyond the Schlag [whipped cream]', which implies that only the most intrepid tourist will experience the city in terms of anything other than layers of sweets, pastries and whipped cream. So pervasive is this image of Vienna that, in modern literature, many descriptions of the city abound with references to the aforementioned whipped cream. For example, John Irving's novel, *Hotel New Hampshire*, which is partly located in Vienna, not only features a detailed description of the Hotel Sacher, home of the *Sachertorte,* but also plays to the stereotypical connection between high culture and food by entitling one of his chapters 'A Night at the Opera: Schlagobers and Blood'.[2]

These examples of the way in which a particular kind of food is associated with a particular location support Roland Barthes's claim that food is a 'real sign, ... the functional unit of a system of communication'.[3] In the case of the sweets, pastries and whipped cream that play an important role in advertising and defining Vienna as an object, not just of the tourists' gaze, but also of their taste, we see an example of the way that food advertising 'permit[s] a person ... to partake each day of the national past'.[4] In his examination of food

---

[1] R. Fischer, *Fodor's Vienna and the Danube Valley* (New York, 1997), p. 5.

[2] J. Irving, *Hotel New Hampshire* (New York, 1981).

[3] R. Barthes, 'Toward a psycho-sociology of contemporary food consumption', in C. Counihan and P. van Esterik, eds, *Food and Culture. A Reader* (London, 1997), pp. 20–27.

[4] Barthes , 'Towards a psycho-sociology', p. 24.

advertising in France, Barthes argues that historical themes are utilised in two main areas: first, the aristocratic tradition and, second, the survival of an old rural society. This is also the case in Vienna where, in focusing the tourist gaze on the city, modern food advertisements tend either to centre on an aristocratic and *haut bourgeois* past (the *Hofpatisserie*, coffeehouses, *Sachertorte*) or on an old semi-rural society (the Viennese wine taverns known as the *Heuriger*, which are the epitome of Viennese *Gemütlichkeit* – a concept which also plays a prominent role in characterising Vienna in Irving's *Hotel New Hampshire*).

While modern tourist narratives of Viennese cuisine focus on the familiar *Sachertorte*, *Apfelstrudel* and *Wiener Schnitzel*, a rather more unfamiliar gastronomic delight, the dumpling (*Knödel*), takes centre stage in the following exploration of the role that food has played in analyses of urban modernity. Although today, the dumpling does not often figure as a signifier of Vienna, it was, historically, a mainstay of traditional Viennese cooking. Perusal of one of the leading instructional cookbooks of the Austro-Hungarian monarchy *Süddeutsche Küche*, by Katharina Prato, reveals recipes for a large range of dumplings, varying widely in filling and substance.[5] And the significance of the dumpling has not been lost on cultural historians such as Otto Basil, whose humorous article on 'Viennese Cuisine' purports to trace the development of the Viennese dumpling as it shrank in size from the Baroque dumpling, which was as big as a child's head and modelled on the Turkish cannonball, to the smaller Rococo version, and the even more modest Biedermeier dumpling.[6] In 1927, apricot dumplings were the focus of a lecture on Viennese cuisine, which provoked many furious reactions in the Viennese press and which provides us with an insight into the many tensions and contradictions characteristic of life in Vienna in the inter-war period.

The lecture was given by Adolf Loos, a well-known Viennese architect and cultural critic, who, in 1924, left Vienna for Paris, thereafter returning only briefly and intermittently to the city in which he had lived and worked since the mid-1890s.[7] On one of these occasions, in the spring of 1927, Loos was in Vienna to give a series of public lectures, including, on 19 February 1927, a talk on 'Viennese Cuisine'.[8] Such was the impact of this lecture that he repeated it in Berlin later in the same

[5] K. Prato, *Süddeutsche Küche* (Graz, n.d.), pp. 388–91, 484–5.

[6] O. Basil, 'Wiener Küche', in P. Zsolnay, ed., *Wiener Cocktail* (Hamburg and Vienna, 1960).

[7] On Adolf Loos's cultural criticism, see J. Stewart, *Fashioning Vienna. Adolf Loos's Cultural Criticism* (London, 2002).

[8] *Neue Freie Presse*, 'Adolf Loos über die Wiener Küche', 20 Feb. 1927, p. 9.

year.[9] Although no known manuscripts for these lectures exist, their content can be reconstructed from a number of reports that appeared in Viennese newspapers at the time. Loos's central theme was the difference between Viennese and French cuisine, and he devoted pride of place to the dumpling and other *Mehlspeisen* (puddings) in his scathing description of Viennese food. Criticising the conflation of food and art in Viennese life, Loos reportedly concluded his Berlin lecture with the comment: 'What do the Viennese think poetry is? A *Mehlspeis*! What do the Viennese think a *Mehlspeis* is? Poetry!'[10]

Never one to mince his words, Loos described Viennese cuisine as the most wasteful, irrational and asocial in the world, claiming that dumplings, strudels and pastries represent the foodstuff of a bygone era which, in the rest of the world, had already been replaced by industrialised foods. Other nations, he argued, only consumed flour in the simple form of bread, and not in the complex form of *Mehlspeisen*, which were so time-consuming to prepare that they had to be made and consumed in vast quantities.

In a humorous fantasy typical of his hyperbolic lecturing style, he claimed that 'Apricot-dumpling Derbies', which were much more popular than the Freudenau horse races, were a regular fixture in many Viennese households. There were, Loos maintained, two stages to the 'Apricot-dumpling Derby'. The first stage involved all available surfaces in a participating home being draped with dough all morning and hundreds of dumplings being rolled by hand, while the second stage consisted of a competition to see who could consume the most dumplings.[11] How different the situation in France was, proclaimed Loos. Here everyone, no matter whether rich or poor, would sit down to a six-course meal, which was much healthier than stuffing oneself with dumplings and nothing else. Anticipating the Viennese reaction that serving six courses would be impossible as the average household did not generally own dinner services with six kinds of plates, Loos explained that neither did the French, as a rule, own such opulent dinner services. Instead, they used bread to clean their plates after every course, which allowed the same plate to be used throughout the entire meal. This piece of bread, stated Loos, was the key to understanding the success of French cuisine.

---

[9] *Neues Wiener Journal* [1927] (1988) 'Das "Marillenknödel-Derby" des Herrn Adolf Loos', in A. Opel, ed., *Konfrontationen. Schriften von und über Adolf Loos* (Vienna, 1988), p. 118.

[10] Loos, cited in the *Neues Wiener Journal*, in Opel, *Konfrontationen*, p. 119.

[11] *Neues Wiener Journal*, 'Das "Marillenknödel-Derby" des Herrn Adolf Loos', p. 118.

Loos's description of Viennese cuisine generated many column inches in the Viennese press and, apart from one report in the *Neue Freie Presse*, all the articles that appeared were critical of Loos. One particularly scathing critic denounced him as a 'Master at insulting Vienna, a giant among grouches' who had committed the sin of 'fouling his own nest'.[12] Meanwhile, in a lecture given at the 'Woman of Today' exhibition held in Vienna later in 1927, Fanny Freund Markus reportedly concluded her contribution by taking issue with Loos's view of Viennese cuisine which, she maintained, was held in high regard in Paris. She then warned that 'maintaining, in a public lecture, that Viennese cuisine is disgusting does not do anything for tourism'.[13] Loos, however, did have his supporters. In his own journal, *Die Fackel*, Karl Kraus took issue with a number of responses to Loos's lecture, arguing that such misguided reactions merely served to demonstrate the widespread failure to comprehend the complexity of Loos's critique. And, in a satirical ditty published in *Die Fackel*, Kraus poked fun at the extreme reactions of the Viennese press:

> Just as Mephisto hid in Faust's poodle,
> So there's more to us than meets the eye.
> For in dumplings, noodles and apple strudel
> Does the pride of the Viennese lie.
> And everyone screamed out loud and in print,
> And the panic was tremendous:
> The last thing that remained of us distinct
> Is snatched away: by the predator, Loos!
> And everyone wants a slice of the action,
> And everyone wants a slice of the action,
> And everyone wants a slice of the action,
> Loos should get lost that's our solution![14]

As Kraus recognised, Loos's satire on the 'Apricot-dumpling Derby' was more than merely an ironic, and potentially harmful, exaggeration of the realities of Viennese food culture. In fact, there are correspondences between his perspective on food and taste, and that of others such as Ludwig Feuerbach, Georg Simmel, Max Weber, Norbert Elias, Roland

---

[12]  Ibid.

[13]  *Neues Wiener Tagblatt*, 'Die Wiener Küche. Ein Vortrag gegen Adolf Loos', 4 Mar. 1927, p. 7.

[14]  K. Kraus, *Die Fackel* (1927), pp. 759–65. (Wie seinen Kern hat jeder Pudel,/ So steckt halt auch in uns was drin./ In Knödel, Nudeln, Apfelstrudel/ Setzt seinen Stolz der Mensch in Wien./ Und alle schrieen laut und schrieben,/ Und die Panik war riesengroß:/ Das Letzte, was uns noch geblieben,/ Wird uns geraubt der Löw' ist Loos!/ Und alles stürzt sich in den Strudel hinein,/ Und alles stürzt sich in den Strudel hinein,/ Und alles stürzt sich in den Strudel hinein,/ Los von Loos soll unsre Losung sein!) I am grateful to Simon Ward and Gundula Sharman for this translation.

Barthes, Michael Foucault and Pierre Bourdieu, who all include gastronomy in their cultural analyses. In 1825, Jean-Anthelme Brillat-Savarin published *The Physiology of Taste,* which included the aphorism: 'Tell me what you eat, and I shall tell you what you are.'[15] A quarter of a century later, Ludwig Feuerbach coined the slogan 'We are what we eat' ('Der Mensch ist, was er ißt').[16] Since then, the development of gastronomy in social anthropology has demonstrated that an examination of food, and related activities, will produce a series of clues to the social structures in which the food is produced and consumed.

Loos utilised the tale of the 'Apricot-dumpling Derby' to criticise a culture of gorging and a failure to exercise control over appetite, which he denounced as 'pre-modern'. Recent historical sociology provides evidence to support Loos's position. Basing his analysis of appetite on the figurational sociology of Norbert Elias, Stephen Mennell traced the development of culinary taste from the Middle Ages, showing that, in the eighteenth century, the first 'truly gastronomic controversies were taking place'. He showed that these controversies, which were driven by the contradictory requirements in court life for social display and refinement, also began to colour bourgeois patterns of eating which in turn, probably accelerated the move towards delicacy and self-restraint that characterised nineteenth-century food culture. In the complex evolution of culinary tastes throughout the ages, then, a move towards the control of appetite can be discerned, which is analogous to the increase in self-control which Max Weber,[17] and later, Michael Foucault,[18] demonstrated to be a marker of modernity. According to Foucault, one of the main areas in which, through the ages, increased levels of self-control could be demonstrated was sexuality. In his 1927 lecture, Loos explicitly alluded to the connections between appetite for food and appetite for sex by likening the desire for soft round dumplings to the desire for soft female curves, and by arguing that Viennese culture was characterised by a lack of self-control in both areas. In other words, his 'Dumpling-Derby' satire can be read as part of his wider critique of the non-modernity of Viennese culture that forms the basis of many of his essays and lectures.

[15] J. Brillat-Savarin, *The Physiology of Taste: Or Meditations on Transcendental Gastronomy,* trans. M.F.K. Fischer (New York, 1971 [1826]), p. 3.

[16] Cited in M. Symons, 'Simmel and gastronomic depth', in *Simmel Newsletter,* 5 (1), 1995, pp. 23–34.

[17] M. Weber, *The Protestant Ethic and the Spirit of Capitalism* (London, 1992 [1904/5]).

[18] M. Foucault, *The History of Sexuality,* vol. 1, *An Introduction* (Harmondsworth, 1986).

The idea of a close connection between the control of appetite for food and the control of sexuality was not lost on Loos's contemporaries. Arthur Schnitzler's drama *Reigen* consists of a series of ten dialogues, which narrate a controversial tale of sexual scandal and the illusion of class distinctions.[19] In this play, written in 1896–7, but not performed in public in Vienna until 1921, issues of control relating to both food and sexuality are revealed through the juxtaposition of two characters: first, the ubiquitous 'sweet girl' (*süße Mädel*) from the inner suburbs (*Vorstadt*), a figure that continually features in the fictional and real-life dramas of Arthur Schnitzler and his ilk, and second, a young, newly-married bourgeois woman. The stage directions indicate that, at the beginning of the scene focusing on the young woman's husband and his *süße Mädel*, the girl is to appear sitting beside him, 'spooning cream from a meringue and slurping with enjoyment'.[20] Her voracious appetite frames her lack of self-control and morals in matters of a sexual nature. The relative sexual freedom enjoyed by the *süße Mädel* is signified by her relative emancipation from the food constraints and controls operative on bourgeois women. While also partaking of forbidden fruit in the shape of an extramarital affair, the young bourgeois wife presented in *Reigen* is unable to show the same unselfconscious delight in food that the *süße Mädel* can. When offered sustenance by her lover, the young bourgeois woman will only consent to a glass of cognac, on the condition that she can first drink a glass of water, eats only half of a candied pear then, towards the end of the scene, quickly snatches a chocolate biscuit.[21] Both food and sex are illicit pleasures and she is only able fleetingly, temporarily and above all, guiltily, to flout the restrictive codes of behaviour by which she is bound.

Further anecdotal insight into the constraints on eating and on enjoying food imposed on bourgeois women in this period, albeit from a different standpoint, is contained in the tale of the Viennese author, Bertha Eckstein-Diener.[22] She apparently believed that she could only prove her status as an emancipated woman by surpassing the normal bodily requirements for the bourgeois woman. Accordingly, she set about starving herself, regularly testing how thin she had become by having water poured between her ribs as she was lying on her back and then observing whether a goldfish had room to swim freely in the space. In the face of such extreme examples of self-denial, it is perhaps not

---

[19]  A. Schnitzler, *Reigen/Liebelei* (Frankfurt am Main, 1960).
[20]  Schnitzler, *Reigen/Liebelei*, p. 59.
[21]  Schnitzler, *Reigen/Liebelei*, pp. 38–50.
[22]  L. Fischer, *Lina Loos oder Wenn die Muse sich selbst küßt* (Vienna, Cologne, Weimar, 1994), p. 50.

surprising to find that the first documented cases of anorexia nervosa are to be found among such upper-middle-class women.[23]

In these examples, the distinction between the social types of *süße Mädel* and young bourgeois woman centres on their different attitudes towards food. It is, however, also possible to look for differences at the level of signification, examining the way in which flavours come to signify class difference. This is an aspect of the cultural history of changing tastes, explored by Barthes in his examination of the semiotics of food,[24] and also used by Pierre Bourdieu in his seminal work, *Distinction*, a study of class difference and taste in late twentieth-century France.[25] In *Reigen*, the *süße Mädel* is characterised above all by her sweet tooth. This play on the word 'sweet' (*süß*) is not fortuitous. In another of Schnitzler's plays, *Liebelei*, first performed in 1895, Mizi, another *süße Mädel*, is charged with the task of procuring the food for an evening's entertainment with two young upper-class men. Her first act is to add a gateau to the list of savoury foods with which the young men have provided her. Here, taste is dependent on class and gender divisions, with 'sweet' signifying the lower-class woman, while 'savoury' denotes the upper-class men. When one of the young men admonishes Mizi for her choice and insists that, before she consumes her cake, she eats 'all sorts of savoury things first', it becomes clear that these divisions are part of an existing social hierarchy.[26] Adopting a position akin to that of the young gentleman in Schnitzler's drama, in his lecture on Viennese cuisine, Loos reflected on the signification of flavours, using the binary opposition between 'sweet' and 'savoury' to argue that a taste for the 'sweet' is linked to the pre-modern, while a preference for the 'savoury' is connected to the modern. In the context of his all-encompassing project to introduce modernity into Austria, he placed himself firmly in the camp of those who, as he saw it, had evolved sufficiently to develop a taste for things savoury.

Perhaps Loos was not entirely wrong in prophesying a change in taste from an emphasis on the sweet to a desire for the savoury. While, at the beginning of the twentieth century, pressure to control appetite and suppress their desire for sweetmeats was felt above all by upper-middle-class women, by the 1920s, all classes were affected, as is demonstrated in Helmut Gruber's analysis of the ideal of the 'new

---

[23] J. Brumberg, 'The appetite as voice', in Counihan and van Esterik, *Food and Culture*, pp. 168–74.

[24] Barthes, 'Towards a psycho-sociology'.

[25] P. Bourdieu, *Distinction. A Social Critique of the Judgement of Taste* (Cambridge, Mass., 1984).

[26] Schnitzler, *Reigen/Liebelei*, p. 120.

woman'.[27] Fully embraced by the socialists in Vienna, she was to be a youthful character with a 'slender *garçon* figure made supple by sports, with bobbed hair and unrestraining garments bespeaking an active life'.[28] Loos's explanation for this change in taste is linked to his analysis of the logic of fashion, according to which the lower classes strive to attain that which, in any given period, the upper classes regard as fashionable.[29] He argues that modernity is characterised by a move from a desire for the sweet to a desire for the savoury, which means that 'sweetness' is left to signify 'pre-modern'.

However, as Gruber points out, the majority of working-class women in the 1920s were unable to attain the ideal of the 'new woman'. This was due, in no small part, to the unsatisfactory nature of the diet available to them, which would have consisted of bread, starchy grains and fat, coffee to keep them awake, and sugar, the cheapest form of energy.[30] Here we see a recognition of sugar's historical position as part of what Sidney W. Mintz has labelled the 'drug-food' complex.[31] Tracing changes in production and consumption over time, Mintz follows the 'career' of sugar in Western Europe, from medicine, to luxury food and preservative, and finally, to cheap 'junk food' or 'proletarian hunger-killer'.[32] In its final incarnation, sugar functions as a kind of drug, masking the potential for disillusionment held by the proletariat in capitalist society. Extrapolating from Mintz's argument, it can be argued that sugar plays a role in creating and maintaining the false but comfortable 'dream world' of modernity as described by Walter Benjamin in his *Arcades Project*.[33]

In his critique of Viennese cuisine, Loos did seem to go some of the way towards grasping the way that certain foodstuffs could be used as 'hunger-killers', and both sugar and flour were the objects of his wrath. Both in his 1927 lecture and in earlier articles on the Settlers' Movement (*Siedlungsbewegung*) in Vienna,[34] Loos criticised the traditional Viennese method of adding flour to vegetable dishes to give them substance and

---

[27] H. Gruber, *Red Vienna. Experiment in Working Class Culture 1919–1934* (New York, 1991), pp. 147–50.

[28] Gruber, *Red Vienna*, p. 148.

[29] G. Simmel, 'Sociology of the meal', in D. Frisby and M. Featherstone, eds, *Simmel on Culture: Selected Writings* (London, 1997), p. 189.

[30] Simmel, 'Sociology of the meal', p. 154.

[31] S.W. Mintz, 'Time, sugar and sweetness', in Counihan and Van Esterik, *Food and Culture*, p. 366.

[32] Mintz, , 'Time, sugar and sweetness', p. 360.

[33] For further discussion of this aspect of Benjamin's work, see S. Buck-Morss, *The Dialectics of Seeing. Walter Benjamin and the Arcades Project* (Cambridge, Mass., 1989), p. 511.

[34] A more detailed description history of the Viennese Settlers' Movement can

make them go further ('strecken') and, of course, in his critique of the dumpling, which consisted largely of flour and sugar, he focused on its ability to sate hunger without providing proper nutrition.[35] However, in his demands that 'healthy' foodstuffs should be introduced into Viennese cuisine without further delay, Loos failed to take real economic hardship into account. This explains the frustrated reaction to Loos's attack on Viennese cuisine from the delegates at the 1927 'Woman of Today' exhibition:

> but, in the last few years, we have come closer to Loos's ideal. The modern woman wants to remain slim and therefore puddings (*Mehlspeisen*) have been banned in many families. Instead we prefer raw foods, fruit, vegetables and a lot of salad! Of course, we cannot afford six courses at one sitting as Loos recommends, otherwise we would happily follow him in this. The delicacies which he extols are indeed delicacies for us and therefore, beyond our means.[36]

The major problem with Loos's analysis, however, is that, in setting up a simple equation, in which flour and sugar are signifiers of the pre-modern, while 'healthy' foodstuffs signify modernity, Loos failed to recognise the modernity of flour, sugar and other 'proletarian hunger-killers'. In fact, sugar and flour, the mainstays of sweet foods, 'were probably the first substances to become the basis of advertising campaigns to increase consumption'[37] and, therefore, to flaunt their modernity.

Nevertheless, Loos's controversial lecture on Viennese cuisine and the 'Apricot-Dumpling-Derby' did make a number of serious points about the way in which food is linked to wider questions of class structure, modernity and control. By identifying the dumpling as a kind of 'proletarian hunger-killer', he embarked upon an exploration of economic matters and, in particular, on a critique of the amount of time and energy expended in making dumplings. In his lecture, he claimed that, in the rest of the modern world, foods such as dumplings and strudel had been superseded by machine-made fare so that people of more civilised nations now only consumed flour in the form of bread. A year later, Loos reiterated his belief in the gastronomic cultural lag of the Viennese in a different public space. As he stood in court on charges of child abuse and was asked to justify himself, he began a long monologue with the following claim: 'Three hundred years ago, the French also ate

---

be found in E. Blau, *The Architecture of Red Vienna 1919-1934* (Cambridge, Mass., 1999), pp. 88–133.

[35] A. Loos, 'The day of the settler', in Opel, ed., *Trotzdem* (Vienna, 1982), p. 162.

[36] *Neues Wiener Tagblatt*, 'Die Wiener Küche', p. 7.

[37] Mintz, 'Time, sugar and sweetness', p. 359.

plum dumplings, you know ...'.[38] From the witness box to the lecture platform, Loos criticised what he regarded as pre-modern forms of food production. Implicitly at least, he was advocating the industrialisation and rationalisation of food which was facilitated by technological developments in preserving, mechanisation, retailing and transport.[39] Despite the tenor of Loos's polemic, the possibilities offered by new technology for both the production and consumption of food had not bypassed Vienna altogether. Indeed, as early as the late 1890s, the theatre director, Gabor Steiner, had an 'automated restaurant' (*Automaton-Buffet*) which he had had specially imported from Naples, installed in the popular amusement park, 'Venice in Vienna' (*Venedig in Wien*).[40] Significantly, it is the example of the vending machine that Simmel seizes upon in his *Philosophy of Money* to illustrate the alienation in the money economy caused by objective culture surging ahead of subjective culture.[41] In contrast, Loos's critique of Viennese cuisine centres on the problems associated with the domination of traditional forms of food production and consumption over new technology. This difference can, however, be partly explained by the fact that complaints from Viennese traders soon brought about the rapid demise of the 'automated restaurant' in the Prater, thereby denying Loos an insight into the industrialisation of food in practice.[42]

Loos's faith in the rationalisation of food production and consumption can be traced throughout his writings and is closely connected to his rejection of ornament in modern architecture. Indeed, the rationalisation of food formed one strand of his famous lecture 'Ornament and crime', which he first gave in Vienna in 1910. In the course of this lecture, he argued that the 'man with modern nerves' would rather eat roast beef than ornamental baroque dishes of peacock.[43] Similarly, in an earlier article, 'The woman and the home', Loos compared the typical German housewife with the typical American housewife in terms of their attitudes to the preparation of food.[44] While the German woman spends all

---

[38] P. Rismondo, 'Vergessenes um Adolf Loos', in A. Opel, ed., *Konfrontationen*, p. 196.

[39] J. Goody, 'Industrial food: towards the development of a world cuisine', in Counihan and Van Esterik, *Food and Culture*, pp. 338–56.

[40] N. Rubey and P. Schoenwald, *Venedig in Wien: Theater- und Vergnügungsstadt der Jahrhundertwende* (Vienna, 1996), p. 82.

[41] G. Simmel, *Philosophie des Geldes* (Frankfurt am Main, 1989 [1900]), p. 634.

[42] Rubey and Schoenwald, *Venedig in Wien*, p. 82.

[43] Loos, 'Ornament and Crime', in Opel, *Trotzdem*, p. 81.

[44] A. Loos, 'The woman and the home' [1898] in Opel, *Konfrontationen*, p. 69.

morning preparing complicated dishes, according to Loos, the more modern American woman cooks steak, which is fast, efficient and leaves her time to pursue other activities. In terms of the rationalisation of food production, Loos's arguments echo his view of modernity, which holds that a simplification in processes and expectations will bring about a reduction in labour time. In this, his critique bears a resemblance to the critique of capitalism contained in Marx's 'labour theory of value'.[45]

Loos was not alone in associating the rationalisation of food production in Vienna in the 1920s with the reduction of labour time. The socialist ideal of the 'new woman' was predicated on the procurement of labour-saving devices, which were to be shared, if buying outright were out of the question.[46] During the First World War and in its immediate aftermath, Loos was involved in initiatives to rationalise food production on a larger scale through his relationship with Eugenie Schwarzwald, or 'Frau Doktor', as she was universally known in Vienna.[47] At this time, Schwarzwald was a member of the 'Association for the Establishment of Community Kitchens', which set up a number of 'community kitchens' in Vienna and Lower Austria, providing up to 20 000 hot meals a day.[48] According to a report contained in *Die Zeit* on 6 June 1917, Loos had been involved in the conversion of one of these 'community kitchens', the Akazienhof.

By the early 1920s, Loos had developed a deep interest in the economy of the *Siedlungsbewegung* and the Garden City Movement, which developed out of desperate struggles to cope with the severe food shortages experienced in Vienna in the aftermath of the First World War.[49] As a result of this new focus for his energies, he produced a series of lectures and articles, in which he distanced himself from the idea of the 'community kitchen', embracing instead the individual living-kitchen. In the 1920s and 1930s, one of the most prominent designers of

---

[45] In part six of the first volume of *Das Kapital, Kritik der politischen Ökonomie*, 1, vol. 23, *Karl Marx und Friedrich Engels. Werke* (Berlin, 1962), pp. 557–8, Karl Marx outlines his controversial labour theory of value, in which he criticises political economists for failing to question the equation of the wage, or price of labour, with the duration of labour.

[46] Gruber, *Red Vienna*, p. 148.

[47] Murray Hall provides an overview of connections between Loos and Schwarzwald, focusing on her charity work: M. Hall, 'Adolf Loos und "Frau Doktor". Die Vereinstätigkeit der Eugenie Schwarzwald', in C. Kreuzmayer, ed., *Aufbruch zur Jahrhundertwende. Der Künstlerkreis um Adolf Loos. Parnaß, Sonderheft 2* (Linz, 1985), pp. 92–9.

[48] B. Rukschcio and R. Schachel, *Adolf Loos. Leben und Werk* (Salzburg, 1982), p. 216.

[49] K. Novy and W. Förster, *Einfach Bauen: genossenschaftliche Selbsthilfe nach der Jahrhundertwende* (Vienna, 1991).

the new high-tech kitchen was the Viennese-born architect, Margarethe Schütte-Lihotsky, who worked closely with Loos in the context of the Viennese *Siedlungsbewegung* in the early 1920s.[50] In her first published article, Schütte-Lihotsky presented a kitchen conceived as an integral part of the living area, which could, however, also be partitioned off from the living area if required.[51] In his work for the *Siedlungsbewegung*, Loos began to design living-kitchens, arguing in a 1921 lecture, entitled 'Learn to live', that this would allow the woman to be involved in all aspects of home life, rather than being isolated in a separate kitchen.[52] He reiterated these demands in Stuttgart in 1926. Lecturing on 'The modern settlement', Loos insisted that unpleasant cooking smells were best avoided, not by separating the kitchen from the living area, but by only cooking foods which have a pleasant aroma – such as ham, eggs and beef steak.[53]

While Loos adopted the living-kitchen for reasons of social integration, Schütte-Lihotsky's kitchen designs concentrated on the use of new technology to enable the rationalisation of food production. Both in Vienna and later in Frankfurt, Schütte-Lihotsky became renowned for designing kitchens based on the reform of home economics, including the 'Frankfurt Kitchen' of 1926, and the variety of built-in kitchens displayed in an exhibition on 'The New House and its Interior – the Modern Household' organised by the City Buildings Department in Frankfurt in 1927. In contrast, Loos sought inspiration for his kitchens in American and English grill-restaurants where food was cooked in the sight of diners, English country houses, and the lifestyle of the Austrian peasant – none of which has an immediate connection with urban industrial modernity. Although rejecting the idea of a return to a romanticised peasant lifestyle,[54] the ideal upon which Loos's view of the *Siedlung* is predicated involves the sublation of the divide between the city and the country which Marx identified as the starting point of the modern division of labour.[55] As such, Loos's view of rationalised food production paradoxically constitutes a critique of the rationalised and industrialised modernity of the city.

Indeed, the Settlement Movement and the Garden City Movement have their roots in the *Lebensreform* ('natural reform') movement, which

---

[50]  M. Schütte-Lihotsky, 'Gedanken über Adolf Loos', *Bauwelt* 72, 42 (1981), pp. 1877–81.

[51]  P. Noever et al. (1996), *Margarethe Schütte-Lihotsky. Soziale Architektur. Zeitzeugin eines Jahrhunderts* (Vienna, Cologne, Weimar, 1996), pp. 44–5.

[52]  Loos, 'Learn to live. Questions of Etiquette', in Opel, *Trotzdem*, p. 16.

[53]  Loos, 'The modern settlement', in Opel, *Trotzdem*, p. 193.

[54]  Stewart, *Fashioning Vienna*, p. 63.

[55]  Marx, *Das Kapital*, p. 373.

offered a platform from which to criticise urban bourgeois modernity in the early twentieth century.[56] It has been suggested that the centrality of the body in the *Lebensreform* movement, which was concerned with food, clothing, exercise and other life style indicators, represented a reaction against bourgeois respectability.[57] Klaus Eder describes the movement in all its many guises as a site of an alternative modernity, embodying a 'counter-cultural relationship to nature linked for the first time to an intentional critique of modernity'.[58] He argues that if, for example, a person accepts that dominant culture is reproduced in culinary culture in the shape of eating meat, then the possibility presents itself of a critique of that culture through vegetarianism.[59] Underlining his thesis, there is evidence that, in Vienna in the early twentieth century, socialists such as Victor Adler, who believed that to advocate peace meant to avoid all shedding of blood, practised political vegetarianism.[60] Other prominent vegetarians at the time included Gustav Mahler, and the bourgeois feminists, Rosa Mayreder and Marie Lang.[61]

In his lecture of 1927, and indeed, in many earlier texts and lectures, Loos touched on similar themes. For example, in his short-lived journal, *Das Andere* (1903), he included, under the rubric 'What we are sold', an article on the aubergine, which, he claimed, is an extremely popular American vegetable. The article included detailed instructions on how to prepare the aubergine, as well as an invitation to taste one cooked properly in a vegetarian restaurant (Spiegelgasse 8) with which Loos claims to have made special arrangements.[62] Elsewhere in his writings on the *Siedlungsbewegung*, he attempted to instruct his readers in the value of other 'American' foodstuffs such as oatmeal.[63] However, Loos rejected suggestions that he was a *Lebensreformer* and, although he criticised the consumption of roast peacock, he advocated eating roast beef instead, a mainstay of bourgeois carnivorous culture.[64] Moreover, in *Das Andere*, the main aim of which is to introduce Western culture into Austria, he

---

[56] The wide variety of groups and beliefs encompassed by the umbrella term 'Lebensreform movement' are explored in detail by E. Barlösius, *Naturegemässe Lebensführung: zur Naturgemässe Lebensführung. Zur Geschichte der Lebensreform um die Jahrhundertwende* (Frankfurt, New York, 1997).

[57] G. Mosse, *Nationalism and Sexuality: Respectability and Abnormal Sexuality in Modern Europe* (New York, 1985).

[58] K. Eder, *The Social Construction of Nature* (London, 1996), p. 149.

[59] Eder, *The Social Contruction of Nature*, p. 152.

[60] F. Eckstein, *'Alte unnennbare Tage!' Erinnerungen aus siebzig Lehr und Wanderjahren* (Vienna, 1936), p. 185.

[61] Fischer, *Lina Loos oder Wenn die Muse sich selbst küßt*, Loos, p. 41.

[62] Loos, 'What we are sold', in Opel, *Trotzdem*, pp. 31–2.

[63] Loos, 'Learn to live', p. 167.

[64] Loos, 'Ornament and crime', p. 81.

does not criticise, but rather affirms the dominant bourgeois–aristocratic culture, as is made clear in his expositions of modern fashion, contemporary work practices and table manners.

In *Das Andere* and elsewhere, Loos, in a move later employed by Norbert Elias in *The Civilising Process*,[65] used the development of table manners as an index of civilisation and, therefore, of modernity. His concern with the form of food consumption also demonstrates affinities with the work of Simmel, since it involves understanding the meal as a 'sociological matter' that 'arranges itself in a[n] . . . aesthetic, stylised and supra-individually regulated form', and in which formal norms are valued above the needs of the individual.[66] Simmel specifically identifies the regulation of table manners as a class issue, illustrating his point by comparing the form of eating in a farmhouse or at a workers' festival with a highly stylised dinner in educated circles. In 'Learn to live', Loos criticised the mode of food consumption and failure to regulate table manners prevalent amongst the Viennese urban proletariat, stating that 80 per cent of the city's population did not sit down together around a table to eat, but remained instead scattered around the kitchen. This situation is exacerbated, he argued, in the case of the typical Viennese breakfast, which consisted of a sip of coffee taken at the stove and a piece of bread, half of which was consumed on the staircase, the other on the street. Loos focused on the economic consequences of this form of breakfast, which necessitated the purchase of a so-called *Gabelfrühstück* (literally 'fork breakfast', usually consisting of goulash) at 10 am, washed down with beer. Continuing his critique of table manners, Loos suggested that calling this meal a *Gabelfrühstück* could only be a joke, since most Viennese ate it with their knives, demonstrating that they were not familiar with the norms of culinary etiquette.[67]

In 'On salting', Loos claimed that the Viennese custom of helping oneself to salt by dipping one's knife into the communal salt cellar, rather than using a spoon kept solely for that purpose, illustrates the lack of Western culture in Vienna.[68] 'On salting' was not published until 1933, but the tale upon which this article was based was first related in *Das Andere*, where Loos described his embarrassment at a fellow countryman who, during a journey to America by ship, used his knife to

[65] N. Elias, *The Civilising Process*, vol. 1, *The History of Manners* (Oxford, 1978).

[66] Simmel, 'The sociology of the meal', pp. 131–2.

[67] Loos, 'Learn to live', pp. 166–7.

[68] Loos, 'On salting', in A. Opel, ed., *Der 'potemkinishe', Stadt* (Vienna, 1983), pp. 231–2.

help himself to salt, thereby upsetting the modern etiquette of the other passengers (and especially of the Germans and the Americans).[69] Loos concluded this tale by comparing the Austrian who insists on using his knife to eat sauce with the Turk who uses his hand to eat his food. Although both practices are acceptable in their respective cultural contexts, Loos argued, the fact that they are not acceptable in the Anglo-American world demonstrates their lack of modernity.

The admiration for Anglo-American table manners and cuisine, which is reiterated throughout Loos's writings, is, interestingly, also a marker of the *Lebensreform* movement in the late 1920s. For example, the journal, *Die Lebensreform*, regularly included articles with titles such as 'What the American eats in May' and 'What the Englishman eats in May'.[70] However, while both Loos and a number of *Lebensreformer* were enthusiastic about intercultural influence on Viennese cuisine in the shape of Anglo-American culinary habits, they would appear to have ignored the actual multicultural nature of traditional Viennese cooking. This was certainly the impression of those who voiced their opposition to Loos's lecture on Viennese cuisine. In a report that appeared in the *Neues Wiener Tagblatt* on 4 March 1927, the writer sought to diffuse Loos's polemic by emphasising the eclectic nature of Viennese food, pointing out, for example, that dumplings originated in Czechoslovakia, and goulash in Hungary. Six years earlier, however, in an article entitled 'The day of the settler', Loos had already addressed the question of the eclectic nature of Viennese cuisine, arguing that, with the dissolution of the multicultural Habsburg Empire in 1918, certain foodstuffs became difficult to procure.[71] Using the example of the plum dumpling, he asserted that, since the flour needed to make this dish came from Moravia, Poland and Hungary, the plums were grown in Southern Hungary and Bohemia, and the sugar was produced in Bohemia and Moravia, it no longer made economic sense to eat dumplings. He suggested that the dumpling, a signifier of the multicultural Austro-Hungarian Empire, was out of place in the tiny post-1918 Austria. Instead, in line with the socialists' search for new symbolic forms for the new era,[72] a new Viennese cuisine that would signify the new Republic of Austria was called for. Ironically, however, while rejecting the signifiers of Vienna's pre-modern imperial past, Loos invoked a view of modernity which utilised signifiers connected to the pre-modern life style

---

[69] Loos, 'Learn to live', pp. 38–9.
[70] B. Schaeble, 'Was der Amerikaner in Mai ißt. Was der Engländer in Mai ißt', *Die Lebensreform*, 7, 4 (1930), p. 181.
[71] Loos, 'The day of the settler', pp. 161–2.
[72] See Gruber, *Red Vienna*, p. 84.

of the English gentleman, such as the roast beef mentioned in 'Ornament und Verbrechen'.[73]

Nevertheless, in his writings on the *Siedlungsbewegung*, Loos did indeed develop a detailed prescription of a new Viennese cuisine, based on 'healthy' foodstuffs such as oatmeal and home-grown vegetables and fruit, which included instructions for its consumption in the home. However, it becomes clear that this apparently altruistic ideal actually masked a desire to control and regulate the potentially disruptive excesses of the lower classes. The *Siedlungen*, located on the edges of the city, were conceived as sites in which family values would be upheld as a way of overcoming the economic and moral problems associated with *Gasthäuser*. The ideal was, then, class-specific. It was not designed to affect the life style of the urban bourgeoisie who inhabited the centre of Vienna and in whose life style, particularly in the period before the First World War, eating out played a central role.

The urban bourgeoisie's predilection for dining out was well provided for in Vienna at the turn of the last century. The multicultural nature of traditional Viennese cuisine was supplemented by a fascination with other, more exotic foods catered for in a variety of restaurants. The Prater, described by Crankshaw as the primary meeting place in Vienna, 'where rich and poor can both mingle and cultivate their own preserves',[74] housed a large array of restaurants, especially in the bounds of Gabor Steiner's amusement park, 'Venice in Vienna'. Working on the juxtaposition of *Alt-Wien* (old Vienna) and *Neu-Wien* (new Vienna), home and abroad, known and unknown, the exotic foods available in many of these restaurants signify a desire to know the 'Other', a marker of modernity. 'Venice in Vienna', itself an attempt to bring the 'Other' to Vienna, housed not only Venetian restaurants, but also an 'international city', featuring an Arabic coffeehouse located in the 'Cairo Street',[75] the 'Restaurant Français',[76] and, neatly illustrating the complex nature of the illusion upon which 'Venice in Vienna' was built, the restaurant 'Vienna a Venezia' situated on the 'Campo Zobenico', which Markus Kristan describes as representing 'a piece of Viennese cultural life in the middle of Venice'.[77]

However, in the midst of the multicultural nature of the restaurant provision in Vienna in the early twentieth century, one institution

---

[73] Loos, 'Ornament and Crime', p. 81.

[74] E. Crankshaw, *Vienna. The Image of a Culture in Decline* (London, 1976), p. 38.

[75] Rubey and Schoenwald, *Venedig in Wien*, p. 90.

[76] Rubey and Schoenwald, *Venedig in Wien*, p. 80.

[77] M. Kristan (1996), *Oskar Marmorek: Architect und Zionist, 1863–1909* (Vienna, Cologne, Weimar, 1996), p. 188.

appears today to be essentially Viennese: the coffeehouse. Yet, despite the typically Viennese aura of the coffeehouse, it too has multicultural origins and actually forms part of the city's Turkish legacy. According to tradition, the Viennese coffeehouse originates from the immediate aftermath of the Turkish siege of 1683. A certain Georg Franz Koltschitzky had been able to slip through the Turkish lines and deliver messages from Vienna to armies waiting to come to the city's rescue. After the siege, he asked that, as his reward, he be given the coffee beans that the Turkish army had left behind. He was given both the beans and premises in the Domgasse, where he set up the first Viennese coffeehouse.[78]

Notwithstanding its multicultural heritage, the Viennese coffeehouse has today become a ubiquitous culinary signifier of the city, illustrated in the painstaking restoration of the Café Griensteidl and the Café Central, both now important objects of the modern tourist's gaze. Further evidence for the centrality of the coffeehouse in narratives of the city can be found in the rich literature which explores the character of the Viennese coffeehouse, focusing in detail on aspects such as the private public space of the coffeehouse as a location of modernity, a place of literary production, a glasshouse of ideas.[79] It falls to Peter Altenberg, however, to provide the most typical snapshot of the institution (*c*. 1900) in his poem entitled simply, 'Coffeehouse':

> You are SPIRITUALLY on the threshold of suicide — — —
> THE COFFEEHOUSE!
> You hate and disdain people and yet cannot do without them — — —
> THE COFFEEHOUSE!
> Nobody extends you any more credit anywhere — — —
> THE COFFEEHOUSE![80]

The Viennese coffeehouse was, and is, more than merely a comfortable place in which to consume coffee, cakes and *Schlagobers*. At the end of the nineteenth century, coffeehouses were the prime locations to observe the patterns of urban bourgeois sociability theorised by Simmel in the 'Sociology of the meal'.[81] They represented urban locations necessary to the circulation of individuals in the city and, indeed, between cities, and were the favourite haunts of the *flâneur*, Benjamin's (1973) archetypal modern figure, who spent his time collecting impressions of modern life.

---

[78] H.B. Segel, ed., *The Viennese Coffeehouse Wits: 1890–1938* (West Lafayette, 1993), p. 7.

[79] H. Veigl, *Lokale Legende. Wiener Kaffeehausliteratur* (Vienna, 1991); Segel, *The Viennese Coffeehouse Wits.*

[80] Altenberg, cited in Segel, *Viennese Coffeehouse*, p. 1.

[81] Simmel, 'The sociology of the meal', pp. 130–35.

One of the most modern Viennese coffeehouses, in terms of the use of space in its interior, was the Café Museum, designed by Loos in 1899. The art critic, Ludwig Hevesi, described it as 'nihilistic',[82] not least because of the simplicity of its design and because Loos 'had not created a cosy coffeehouse full of nooks and crannies, but rather an open-plan space designed to facilitate intellectual communication'.[83] Its open interior created a space conducive to large-scale discussion and the ever-changing constellations constituent of urban modernity.

It is significant that this series of gastronomic snapshots of Vienna in the early decades of the twentieth century has not only demonstrated the importance of food as a signifier of a particular place, but also led us to a consideration of the locations in which the tensions of urban modernity are played out. The strength of a gastronomic analysis lies in the double role of food which, as is demonstrated in Simmel's 'Sociology of the meal' is simultaneously a physical requirement and a cultural construct.[84] In this, it is similar to architecture. Thus modern guidebooks, which describe Vienna in terms of '*Apfelstrudel* and marble staircases', food and architecture, are perhaps closer to the mark than might first appear to be the case. There is a world of difference between the marble staircases of pre-modern Vienna and the nihilistic urban space of Loos's Café Museum and yet both are constitutive of 'Vienna'. In exploring the resonances of Loos's lecture on 'Viennese cuisine' we arrive at a new perspective from which to consider the character of urban modernity. The 'Taste of Vienna' revealed in this process is, above all, paradoxical. Based on a series of binary oppositions such as Viennese/French, Viennese/Anglo-American, traditional/modern, sweet/savoury, carnivorous/vegetarian, a gastronomic analysis underlines the paradoxes and tensions typical of the experience of inhabiting the modern city.

## Further reading

J. Brillat-Savarin, *The Physiology of Taste: Or Meditations on Transcendental Gastronomy*, trans. M.F.K. Fischer (New York, 1971 [1826]).
C. Counihan and P. van Esterik, eds, *Food and Culture: a Reader* (London, 1997).
N. Elias, *The Civilising Process*, vol. 1, *The History of Manners* (Oxford, 1978).

---

[82] L. Hevesi, *Acht Jahre Sezession* (Klagenfurt, 1984), p. 174.
[83] B. Rukschcio and S. Schachel, *Adolf Loos, 67. Leben und Werk* (Salzburg and Vienna, 1982), p. 67.
[84] Simmel, 'The sociology of the meal', pp. 130–35.

S. Mennell, *All Manners of Food: Eating and Taste in England and France from the Middle Ages to the Present* (Oxford, 1985).

G. Simmel, 'The sociology of the meal', in D. Frisby and M. Featherstone, eds, *Simmel on Culture* (London, 1997), pp. 130–35.

H. Veigl, *Lokale Legende. Wiener Kaffeehausliteratur* (Vienna, 1991).

# CHAPTER TEN

# Seeing Imperial Berlin: Lesser Ury, the painter as stranger

*Dorothy Rowe*

> The stranger will thus not be considered here in the usual sense of the term, as the wanderer who comes today and goes tomorrow, but rather as the man who comes today and stays tomorrow.[1]

The centrality of sight and vision to a construction of gendered metropolitan culture is, by now, a well established trope of modernity, the origins of which can be found in Baudelaire's 1859 essay, 'The painter of modern life', Walter Benjamin's interpretation of it and recent feminist analyses of these texts.[2] In addition, Peter Fritzsche has compellingly demonstrated the ways in which *Berlin 1900* was a city of consuming spectators whose versions of metropolitan life were structured and reinforced via the burgeoning feuilleton culture of the daily press in the city.[3] However, contrary to this, Jonathan Crary has recently commented that 'to assert the centrality or "hegemony" of vision within twentieth-century modernity no longer has much value or significance' and that 'within modernity, vision is only one layer of a body that could be captured, shaped, or controlled by a range of external critiques'.[4] As a way of substantiating this, he provides an enriched historical account of perception and attentiveness within French modernity between 1879 and 1907 that seeks to re-embody historically the detached spectator of urban modernity. As his narrative unfolds, Crary reveals the palpably historically determined origins of his dismissal of the visual as the dominant *modus operandi* of the embodied subject.

---

[1] G. Simmel, 'The stranger', in D. Levine, ed., *Georg Simmel: On Individuality and Social Forms* (Chicago and London, 1971), p. 143.

[2] For further details, see C. Baudelaire, 'The painter of modern life', in *Selected Writings on Art and Literature*, trans. P.E. Charvet (London, 1972); W. Benjamin, *Charles Baudelaire: A Lyric Poet in the Era of High Capitalism* (London and New York, 1990); J. Wolff, 'The invisible *flâneuse*', *Feminine Sentences* (Cambridge, 1990), pp. 34–50; and S. Weigel, *Body-and-Image-Space: Rereading Walter Benjamin*, trans. G. Paul (London and New York, 1997), amongst others.

[3] See P. Fritzsche, *Reading Berlin 1900* (Cambridge, Mass., 1996).

[4] J. Crary, *Suspensions of Perception: Attention, Spectacle and Modern Culture* (Cambridge, Mass., 1999), p. 3.

Nevertheless, I should like to suggest in this essay that, during the Wilhelmine and Weimar eras in Germany, the co-option of vision into a position of privilege within the discursive formations of urban modernity in which the role of the metropolis was a key site in the struggle for social control, was one of the most powerful strategies of cultural discourse that actually bears witness to Crary's comments that 'so much of what seems to constitute a domain of the visual is an *effect* of other kinds of forces and relations of power'.[5]

Thus, whilst Crary argues for a more nuanced consideration of the field of the visual as ultimately only an end-product of a host of other historically significant perceptual apparatuses that he investigates, I would argue that it is still appropriate to consider the ways in which cultural commentators of modernity attempted to secure the visual as a dominant sign of cultural stability, irrespective of the slippages in signification that Crary so adeptly reveals.

Indeed, it was precisely the dominance of the visual–technological experience of modernity during the first three decades of the twentieth century that the National Socialist ideologue, Oswald Spengler, used as the lever for his notorious and irrational critique of modern culture in the apocalyptic rhetoric of his 1931 publication, *Der Mensch und die Technik: Beitrag zu einer Philosophie des Lebens*, where he asserts:

> The act of fixation by two eyes ... is equivalent to the birth of the world, in the sense that Man possesses a world – that is, as a picture, as a world before the eyes as a world of perspective distance, of space and motions in space ... This way of seeing ... implies in itself the notion of domination. The world-picture is the environment insofar as it is dominated by the eyes ... The world is the prey, and in the last analysis human culture itself has arisen from this fact.[6]

As Jonathan Rée has observed, for Spengler the 'thought of the eye' cultivated a 'proud, solitary and resolute subjectivity' that fixed itself upon the optical details of mechanical invention at the expense of inner spirituality. This meant for Spengler, and other right-wing supporters of his point of view, that humanity in the twentieth century was heading for an imminent crisis.[7] Having lost its capacity for a full range of sensual experience that included having a voice and the ability to hear, human life 'was destined to go downhill *seeing*'.[8]

---

[5] Crary, *Suspensions of Perception*, p. 23.

[6] O. Spengler, *Der Mensch und die Technik: Beitrag zu einer Philosophie des Lebens* (Munich, 1931), pp. 19–20.

[7] J. Rée, *I See a Voice: A Philosophical History of Language, Deafness and the Senses* (London, 1999), p. 4.

[8] Spengler, cited in Rée, *I See a Voice*, p. 4.

As Crary's arguments imply, Spengler's position on vision was extreme and radically overstated, yet, as I shall demonstrate below, during the twentieth century Spengler's, Crary's, Rée's and Georg Simmel's analyses of vision all point, with radically different outcomes, to the undeniable trajectory in modernist epistemology, that the sense of sight, however dubiously placed or insecurely produced, was central to the discursive formations of urban industrial technological modernity.

In this essay, then, I explore a metropolitan discourse of vision in which Berlin is iconographically structured for the purposes of looking and in which such acts of looking serve to smooth over 'the infinite variety of the most divergent moods, emotions and thoughts' that, for Georg Simmel (1858–1918) at least, could more readily be found in the oral and olfactory senses.[9] Although one of Simmel's most celebrated considerations of urban modernity in recent revaluations of his work is the by now familiar 'Metropolis and mental life' essay (1903), what is less often noted is that this piece was published in the same year as two further essays by Simmel, entitled, respectively, 'On the spatial projection of social forms', and 'The sociology of space'.[10] The appearance of these three works in the same year is undoubtedly linked to Simmel's interest in the modern metropolis as a major site of differentiation of the individual personality. These two essays on space were also published with three further appendices, on 'The social boundary', 'The sociology of the senses' and 'The stranger'.[11] What connects the individual essays is their focus on the sociological relations engendered by issues of proximity and distance in the modern metropolis.

Simmel's writings on space and on the senses offer an interesting framework for this essay in terms of a consideration of the dialectic between Berlin as a city of sight structured through a selection of Berlin street paintings produced by the artist Lesser Ury (1861–1931), who employed optimal painterly strategies in his rendering of some of the key visual tropes of urban modernity, and Berlin as a city of sounds, smells, tastes and touch that often, though not always, were used to secure the

[9] G. Simmel, 'The sociology of space', in D. Frisby and M. Featherstone, eds, *Simmel on Culture* (London, 1997), p. 155.

[10] The two essays on space later formed Chapter 9 of Simmel's major work, *Soziologie* (Leipzig, 1908), pp. 614–708, when they were published under the generic heading 'Space and the spatial ordering of society': G. Simmel, 'Über räumliche Projektionen sozialer Formen', *Zeitschrift für Sozialwissenschaft*, 6 (1903), pp. 287–302; 'Soziologie des Räumes', *Jahrbuch für Gesetzgebung, Verwaltung und Volkswirtschaft*, 27 (1909), pp. 27–71.

[11] 'The sociology of the senses' was also subsequently republished in *Die Neue Rundschau* (1907); see also G. Simmel, 'The sociology of the senses', in Frisby and Featherstone, eds, *Simmel on Culture*, pp. 109–20; 'The stranger', in Levine, *Georg Simmel*, pp. 143–9.

'magisterial gaze' constructed and maintained through the move towards modernist visual culture in both Ury's work and in its critical reception during the Wilhelmine and Weimar eras.[12]

Berlin of the Imperial era underwent rapid growth and transformation as a result of the relatively late unification of Germany in 1871. By the mid-1890s, Berlin was successfully transforming itself from an ordinary *Großstadt* (big city) to a thriving new *Weltstadt* (world city).[13] The significance of this achievement and the desire to celebrate it can be more properly understood when one compares the city at this time with some of its European counterparts, especially London, Paris and Vienna.[14] In relation to these capital cities, Berlin was an extremely late starter, yet it managed to catch up with them in a dramatically short space of time in terms of size, status and proportional demography. The new status of Berlin as a *Weltstadt*, although firmly established in the discourses of the popular press only after the success of the 1896 Berlin Trade Exhibition, was something that was already being debated during the 1880s by optimistic proponents of the new growth city.[15]

Whilst for many commentators, *Weltstadt* status was a desirable position for the city to occupy, for others it was also a source of incredulity and anxiety that elicited a number of conflicting reports about the city, symptomatic of the growing tensions between new

---

[12] There appears to be some unfounded confusion over the exact date of Ury's birth. Robin Lenman lists Ury's dates as 1862–1937, yet my research from various German sources and from the National Art Library clearly identifies his dates as 1861–1931. See R. Lenman, *Artists and Society in Germany 1850–1914* (Manchester and New York, 1997), p. 6. For just two comparisons amongst many others, see R. Bothe, 'Stadtbilder zwischen Menzel und Liebermann', in Berlin Museum, *Stadtbilder*, exhibition catalogue (Berlin, 1987), p. 220, and A. Donath, *Lesser Ury: Seine Stellung in der modernen deutschen Malerei* (Berlin, 1921) (edn 40 of a limited edition set of 110), 'Anmerkungen' 3a,' ... Ury ist nicht 1863, sondern 1861 (7. November) geboren'. I am confident that 1861 is correct since his sixtieth birthday was marked specifically in 1921 with several published reappraisals of his work, including Donath's, cited here. I borrow the term 'magisterial gaze' from G.H. Bender, 'Chapter two: magic spectacles and city spaces: thrill, freedom and the magisterial gaze'; paper presented at the 89th College Art Association Annual Conference, Chicago, 2001.

[13] For further details on the distinction between the terms *Großstadt* and *Weltstadt*, see G. Masur, 'World City? Perhaps', in G. Masur, *Imperial Berlin* (London and New York, 1971), ch. 5, pp. 125ff.

[14] For the development of London and Paris, see A. Sutcliffe, ed., *Metropolis 1890–1940* (London, 1984). For Vienna, London and Paris, see D. Olsen, *The City as a Work of Art* (New Haven and London, 1986).

[15] D. Rowe, 'Georg Simmel and the 1896 Berlin trade exhibition', *Journal of Urban History*, 22, 2 (Aug 1995), p. 31.

advocates of modernity and more cautious guardians of tradition.[16] Examples of the perceived crisis of urban culture in Berlin specifically during this era are too numerous to delineate in any great depth, but a flavour of the tone of debates can be seen in the comments of the art critic Karl Scheffler, one of the editors of the influential art journal *Kunst und Künstler.*

Scheffler's negative position with regard to Berlin's modernity remained fairly consistent throughout his publishing career and is found at its most concentrated in his 1910 publication, *Berlin: Ein Stadtschicksal (Berlin: A City's Destiny)*, as well as in his contributions to the journal *Die Neue Rundschau*. Specifically, Scheffler deplored the city's absence of any urban traditions, as well as its lack of physiognomic character and aesthetic unity. The city was thought to offer the modern urbanite 'no home, nothing symbolic and no morally elevating sense of community'.[17] It was specifically this opposition between community and society articulated here by Scheffler but formulated more thoroughly in the sociological writings of Ferdinand Tönnies in 1887 in *Gemeinschaft und Gesellschaft (Community and Society)*, and based on the earlier nineteenth-century ideals of Gottfried Fichte, that established the paradigms for much of the criticism levelled at city cultures generally but at Imperial Berlin in particular.

The standard terms of the Imperial urban debate that raged around Berlin as *Weltstadt* referred to its rootlessness, ugliness, disorder, chaos and lack of community pitted against an image of Berlin as aspirational, exciting, proud, open and full of potential; they were the standard terms of the Imperial urban debate that raged around Berlin as *Weltstadt*. It is in the nexus between these oppositional binaries that the singular art of Lesser Ury emerged during the 1880s and 1890s as one symptom of a peculiar 'German encounter with modernism' that played out many of the tropes of modern metropolitan culture, using techniques of surface impressionism initially borrowed from Paris but specifically adapted for Berlin.[18]

Ury's works contribute to a visual construction of a specific set of masculinist tropes that laid the ground for representations of urban modernity that were to persist well into the Weimar era in terms of the preferred subject matter of Berlin-based metropolitan male artists: city squares, public parks, the zoo, the central railway station, the interiors

---

[16] D. Rowe, *Representing Berlin: Sexuality and the City in Imperial and Weimar Germany* (Aldershot, 2003), pp. 30–33; Masur, *Imperial Berlin*, p. 125.

[17] K. Scheffler, *Berlin: Ein Stadtschicksal* (Berlin, 1910), p. 885.

[18] See Donath, *Lesser Ury*; P. Paret, *German Encounters with Modernism 1840–1945* (Cambridge, 2001).

SEEING IMPERIAL BERLIN: LESSER URY, PAINTER AS STRANGER    203

of specifically named cafés and, more particularly, the Leipzigerstraße, the Friedrichstraße and the Potsdamer Platz by night – those spaces of self-consciously fabricated cosmopolitan consumerist culture in the heart of the newly established *Berlin-Mitte* after the *Gründerzeit*. As Marsha Meskimmon has consistently demonstrated throughout her research on the gendered biases of German visual modernism, 'the structures of modernism as conceived through the masculine imaginary delineate ... the urban environment ... as no place for a lady' and Ury's art is no exception.[19] Women in Ury's metropolis are reified signs of bourgeois leisure, presented on the arms of their top-hatted male partners, depicted in pairs, or displayed frontally as signs of urban modernity corralled into signifying a fragile stability for a social order that was undergoing rapid and radical social transformations on all fronts but especially in terms of the transformation of gender roles, the demand for women's suffrage and the cultivation of a specifically new and urban *Frauenkultur* (women's culture).[20]

Ury's series of city scenes of Berlin date initially from the years of his return to the city after a six-year extended study period in Düsseldorf, Brussels, Paris and Volluvet (Flanders), that had begun when he was eighteen, during the late 1870s.[21] In many standard accounts of German modernism, Ury's role in the Berlin art world is shown to be somewhat marginal, yet it is clear both from his position as an early member of Paul Cassirer's stable of artists and from the not insignificant number of reviews and monographs devoted to him during his lifetime, that he did achieve a measure of popular success in the period leading up to the First War as well as during the Weimar years. The popular explanation for the perceived marginality of his status concerns the frequently cited troubled

---

[19] M. Meskimmon, 'No place for a lady: women artists and urban prostitution in the Weimar Republic', in S. Spier, ed., *Urban Visions: Experiencing and Envisioning the City* (Liverpool, 2000), p. 38.

[20] There are a number of publications of both primary material and secondary analysis that consider the transformation of the Imperial social order, the 'woman question' and the rise of women's culture as a direct result of the changes wrought via industrial capitalism and the founding of the nation state, but, for a general historical overview that ranges from the late eighteenth century to the late 1980s, see U. Frevert, *Women in German History* (Oxford, 1989). For a very specific analysis of the role of women during the Imperial era, see R. Orthmann, *Out of Necessity: Women Working in Berlin at the Height of Industrialization 1874–1913* (New York, 1991).

[21] Although not born in Berlin, Ury had arrived in the city aged ten in 1872, one year after unification, and had been brought up there by his widowed mother. They had moved to Berlin from Posen after the death of Ury's father. For more biographical details, see K. Schwarz, *Lesser Ury* (Berlin, 1920).

relationship he had with Max Liebermann, the leading figure of the Secessionist artists of the 1890s, who went on to become a dominant establishment figure in Berlin artistic circles until his death in 1935.[22] However, a further possible explanation, and one that I propose in more detail below, concerns the specific configuration of the relationship between the artist and his subject matter. If Berlin's rise to *Weltstadt* status was riven with anxiety and ambivalence, even from those enthusiastic advocates of urban cosmopolitanism, then the earliest artist to produce such an abundance of celebratory and aestheticising representations of the emergent *Weltstadt* is also likely to have been regarded with some caution. As I shall demonstrate, the stress upon Ury's *wanderlust*, and the constant reminders that 'he had to see the world with his own eyes' before he could settle down in one place, all contribute to his positioning as an 'outsider' figure who was said to be able to appreciate the worldly charms of Berlin only because he had 'seen the world' and crucially because he was 'not a native Berliner'.[23]

Nevertheless, despite his apparent marginal status, Ury did enjoy success as the capital city's first chronicler in paint in a series of oil paintings and graphic works that spanned most of his career until the late 1920s. Adolph Donath, in a text published to mark the occasion of Ury's sixtieth birthday in 1921, described the Berlin of Ury's art as follows:

> Ury was the first to paint Berlin city scenes: the modern streets with their hunting and their hissing, their busy people, their solid horse-drawn carriages, their old-fashioned taxis, the city streets at dusk with all the wonderful sunlit reflections on the houses and pavements, the city streets in the evening and at night with the play of yellow gas light and the sparkling radial glow of the electric arc lamps, the big city café in the evening and at night, with its overpowering atmosphere of light and smoke. Yes, Ury was the first to paint modern Berlin and to uncover its inner nervousness, as though at the beginning of the 1880s he saw the newness of the territory set out before him.[24]

What distinguishes Ury's scenes of the city from those of his more familiar contemporary, Hans Baluschek (1870–1935), is Ury's consistent focus on a small trajectory of Berlin-Mitte, ranging from the topography

---

[22] For more information regarding Liebermann's (1847–1935) dominance of the Berlin art scene, see P. Paret, *The Berlin Secession. Modernism and its Enemies in Imperial Germany* (Cambridge, Mass. and London, 1980) and Paret, *German Encounters with Modernism*.

[23] Donath, *Lesser Ury*, p. 8; L. Briegar, *Graphiker der Gegenwart: Lesser Ury*, vol. 9 (Berlin, 1921), p. 5.

[24] Donath, *Lesser Ury*, p. 14. Unless otherwise indicated, all translations from the original are mine throughout.

of Unter den Linden to the Tiergarten, the Leipzigerstraße, the Friedrichstraße and Potsdamer Platz, which set the scenes for his modernist visions of the city as a spectacle of middle-class leisure based on watching and being watched, looking and being looked at.[25] In Baluschek's work, on the other hand, the viewer is presented with scenes of proletarian Berlin in which the modernist city is shown to be a city of labour, of toil and of social inequity.[26] Ury stages the city as 'a landscape' bathed in light, steam, rain and atmosphere, in a style that echoes the aestheticising impressionism of August Endell's infamous 1908 account of *Die Schönheit der großen Stadt (The Beauty of the Metropolis)*.[27] However, whilst Endell celebrated the newer technological and mechanistic aspects of Berlin, deliberately avoiding the picturesque areas around the city's parks and gardens in order to foreground his perceptions of the beauty of industrialised modernity facilitated from his privileged position of *flânerie*, Ury frequently focuses his attention on the more visually appealing sites of the bourgeois city in which he worked.

In 1888, Ury held his first exhibition at Galerie Gurlitt alongside other modern German painters, including Wilhelm Leibl, Fritz Uhde and Max Liebermann. The gallery was a small art dealership owned by Fritz Gurlitt (1853–93), which was located on the Behrenstraße one block south of Unter den Linden and was central to the early introduction of French and German Impressionism to an otherwise resistant Berlin art scene at this time.[28] Ury's exhibition there was swiftly followed by two more and in 1889 his third show (together with works by Wilhelm Leibl and Hans Thoma) represented at least a dozen of his city paintings produced between 1888 and 1889 and depicting a selection of central sites of urban modernity in Berlin, ranging from the railways to well known cafés and squares, painted at various times of day and night and under different atmospheric conditions.[29]

---

[25] The one other main site of his focus in Berlin is the area around the Nollendorfplatz in Berlin-Schöneberg, where he eventually had his studio, from 1920 until his death in 1931.

[26] For further details and an excellent chapter concerning Hans Baluscheck's city scenes, see J. Czaplicka, 'Pictures of a city at work, Berlin c.1890–1930: visual reflections on social structures and technology in the modern urban construct', in C. Haxthausen and H. Suhr, eds, *Berlin: Culture and Metropolis* (Minneapolis, 1990), pp. 3–36.

[27] For further details, see L. Müller, 'The beauty of the metropolis', in Haxthausen and Suhr, *Berlin*, pp. 37–57, and Rowe, *Representing Berlin*, p. 15.

[28] See Lenman, *Artists and Society in Germany*, p. 112; D. and R. Glatzer, eds, *Berlin Leben 1900–1914. Eine historische Reportage aus Erinnerungen und Berichten* (Berlin, 1997), p. 210.

[29] For a full list of Ury's city scenes painted between 1888 and 1889, see Bothe, 'Stadtbilder', p. 198.

It was during this 1889 exhibition that the art historian Cornelius Gurlitt (1850–1938) first saw Ury's Berlin pictures and the following year, in February 1890, he published an extensive review of Ury's work (together with that of Thoma), in the journal *Die Gegenwart*. It is worth recalling an extract from the review at some length here since within it is located a significant moment of interplay between the constructed vision of the city as foregrounded in Ury's paintings and the sensual evocation of the city as experienced by Gurlitt and transmitted in his description of wandering the city streets outside the gallery immediately after seeing Ury's works for the first time. Gurlitt's opening remarks are designed to convey to the reader the experience of shock and confusion on his first glimpse of Ury's two paintings, *Unter den Linden* (see Figure 10.1) and *Leipziger Platz*, both painted in 1888. On viewing *Leipziger Platz*, Gurlitt is horrified by 'a series of white daubs on a predominantly black stew of colours' and he concurs with the overheard remarks made by another gallery visitor that the works were *verrückt* (insane). He continues to bemoan the lack of formal pictorial principles in Ury's work, the lack of accuracy in the drawing, the lack of rhythm in the composition and the lack of colour harmony in comparison with 'the true beauty of the Old Masters'. He comments that 'these pictures and other similar works by Ury are painted in such a way that they are not easily forgotten from one's thoughts. They have something powerfully brutal about them. They remain fixed in the field of vision'.[30] In order to recover from his shock, he decides to wander a little through the city so that he can gather his thoughts for the ensuing task of critical analysis:

> It had become evening. I don't have to describe for the first time the weather of the last few days. A grey sky; a heavy downpour just finishing. The streets were wet through. Then, as I strolled along the Linden, a peculiar picture revealed itself to me. The still light, white sky was now only visible in one strip between the tall houses and the leafless trees. But still lighter and shining brightly like white-hot metal, lay the street before me, the damp surfaces of which had absorbed all of the sky's light and appeared to be reflecting it back into my bedazzled eyes. Carriage after carriage rolled along. The shining surfaces of their tops created a restless line of traffic against the Brandenburg Gate, the powerful lead grey mass of which rose up against the sky ... An acquaintance tapped me on the back: 'Berlin is amazing isn't it?' We walked on together and night fell as we came to the Potsdamer Platz and saw the Leipzigerstraße ahead of us. The lamps burned, the rain had begun again. It was a deep black night, its darkness clearly struggling against the brutal bright whiteness of the streetlights and the shop window displays ... Even more than in

---

[30] The last sentence reads in the original, *Sie bleiben einem in den Augen haften* (C. Gurlitt, 'Von den Kunstausstellungen Lesser Ury und Hans Thoma'), *Die Gegenwart*, 37 (22 Feb. 1890), p. 125.

Fig 10.1    Lesser Ury, *Unter den Linden*, 1883

the earlier twilight, everything was covered in uncertain half-tones
... This was the Berlin of the pedestrian, every shimmer of gas and
electricity, every quick recognition and even quicker forgetting – the
big city, with its nervous appeal, its haste, its fast pulsating life. 'The
hustle and bustle is fantastic' my friend shouted over to me, 'Berlin
really has become a beautiful city' ... The next day, I saw Ury's
pictures with different eyes. There I saw an artist who ... takes
seriously what nature has taught him ... [and who] ... paints what
he sees ...[31]

What is particularly interesting about this extended passage is the
privilege that Gurlitt assigns to the power of the artist's eye to report
what he [sic] sees. As Gurlitt understands it, such reportage can no
longer be determined by conventional structures of pictorial form, colour
harmonies and composition and therefore he needs to find a new
language and set of concepts with which to account for this emergent art
form. In order to contextualise such a radical departure from the
academic rules of painting for his readers, Gurlitt constructs an urban
discourse based upon the sensory impressions of the city that he has
experienced while walking the streets. Here, the visual construction of
the urban *Weltstadt* in Ury's work is dependent on the critical language
of its reception upon the sensual evocation of the city that its critics
regularly constructed around the work.[32] Hence, certainly in terms of
this critical context, it is the role of vision in consolidating the sensual
experiences of the city (particularly the auditory but also the olfactory
senses – the noise of the carriages and the smell of 'damp air', for
example – that produces a comprehensible experience of the work for
viewers and readers in the 1890s and beyond.

The noise of the city was a recurrent theme in much of the critical
discussion of the experience of Berlin during the Imperial era and was
even the subject of a painting by Fritz Gehrke in 1893, *Die Sprengung
des alten Doms* (*The Explosion of the Old Cathedral*), (see Figure 10.2),
in which the noise of the explosion in the background startles the
pedestrians in front and causes a horse to rear up and almost throw its
uniformed rider. A few years later, in Paul Lindenberg's 1895 assessment
of different aspects of *Berlin in Wort und Bild*, an essay devoted to life
'On the Streets', opens with an extended evocation of the life and noise
of the city streets:

---

[31] Gurlitt, 'Von den Kunstausstellungen Lesser Ury und Hans Thoma',
pp. 125–6.
[32] The contextualising of Ury's work within a discourse concerning Berlin's
identity as a *Weltstadt* is an issue that is still centralised in Lothar Briegar's
monograph published 31 years later, for example.

Fig 10.2    Fritz Gehrke, *Die Sprengung des alten Doms*
[*The Explosion of the Old Cathedral*], 1893

> Berlin life shows itself to be constantly changing and always different as it rolls along the countless arterial roads of the immense city, from the earliest hour to the latest, filling it with its noise and its racket and leaving its mark of haste and restlessness, which only the daily and hourly self-renewing chaos of a world city can create. Yes, Berlin life is full of restlessness and haste, noise and tumult, weaving and pushing ... yet it fills the Berliner with pride.[33]

Over a decade later, Hans Ostwald, editor of the fifty-volume series, *Die Großstadt Dokumente* (1905–8) and author of numerous publications on the sexual underside of Imperial Berlin, also commented on the sounds of the city in order to evoke the atmosphere of cosmopolitan leisure and sexual consumption that he recreated for his readers in his text *Berlin und die Berlinerin* (*Berlin and the Berlin Woman*): the noise of trams and of the electric railway, the loud laughter of prostitutes and the music of the casinos, cafés and dancehalls all contribute to his evocation of Berlin's sexualised nightlife.[34]

However, whilst the *visual* construction of urban modernity in Berlin as constructed in the relationship between Ury's art and its critical reception from 1889 through to the late Weimar years works its effects via the evocation of other senses, it does so by suppressing the imminent moral dangers of sensual excess, suggested frequently through Ostwald's coupling of city experience with the activities of the *demimonde*, for example, in a controlled visual narrative constructed around specific sites of the bourgeois consumer city. Prostitution, labour, domestic hardship, social inequity and deprivation play little or no part in Ury's visual celebration of the modernist *Weltstadt*. The eye of the painter secures the dominant public tropes of bourgeois modernity in an aesthetic celebration of the city as landscape that suppresses the urban underside prevalent in Ostwald's more licentious evocation of the urban experience for the bourgeois *flâneur* of modernity.

Gurlitt's 1890 mapping of his temporal and mobile experience of Berlin-Mitte, over the course of the transition from dusk to nightfall over a few hours one evening in 1889, is translated for the reader of the appropriately entitled *Gegenwart* (*The Present*) into a spatially static description of that experience via Ury's paintings. In *Unter den Linden* (1888) and in Gurlitt's description of it (1890) the experience of time and motion (1889) have been solidified into a vision of space and atmosphere that bestows perspectival order on the disorder of metropolitan life in a

---

[33] P. Lindenberg, *Berlin in Wort und Bild* (Berlin, 1895), p. 150.
[34] H. Ostwald, *Berlin und die Berlinerin* (Berlin, 1911), pp. 399–431. For a list of Ostwald's many publications concerned specifically with the nightlife of Berlin, see Rowe, *Representing Berlin*.

deliberate strategy of control that is nevertheless introduced to the reader initially in the language of shock, chaos and disharmony. The perceived disorder of metropolitan urban life prevalent in the critical debates of the era, already demonstrated towards the beginning of this essay and as Peter Fritzsche and Richard Evans have also illustrated via their accounts of the sensationalising fantasies prevalent in the popular press and reportage during the period, is brought into check for the bourgeois art lover and consumer of modern urban leisure, through the authority of the painter and his professional interpreters.[35]

In terms of the pictorial format of *Unter den Linden*, the initially perceived disorder stems, I think, from the lack of a significant middle-ground focus to the scene. The vista of the street spreads out in front of the viewer without a central anchor of vision. A small dog standing low to the ground in the middle distance, a horse-drawn carriage and a tiny figure of a girl crossing in the further distance are all that draw the viewer's centrally directed gaze into the scene before the entire composition converges on the monumental structure of the Brandenburg Gate at its vanishing point. Sky and road meet at this central monument, which, although tiny in its distance, still towers above the horizon-line of the buildings on the left-hand side and remains pivotal to the pictorial arrangement of the composition as the site of convergence. The more the eye surveys the apparent emptiness of the broad street, the more regimental and structured the topography of the scene becomes. The buildings descend in scale towards the central vanishing point in an ordered line, intermittently dotted with the rounded shapes of the glowing electric arc lamps. The only interruption to our line of vision is situated close to the frontal plane, in the figures of the bourgeois couple about to cross the street in front of the viewer. The woman returns our gaze, while the top-hatted man continues in his path, striding onwards with walking stick outstretched, heedless of the viewer or of the oncoming traffic of the metropolis.

The position of these two frontal figures to the left of our line of vision immediately recalls the pictorial principles of the Golden Section that Ury has carefully employed here. Although the cut-off view of the horse-drawn carriage on the left, in front of the Café Bauer, is an obviously borrowed device of French Impressionism knowingly staged to concoct the illusion of the random snapshot that complicitly becomes one of Cornelius Gurlitt's sites of 'insanity' and 'disharmony' within this modern scene, the pictorial principles of mechanistic order, harmony and rationality embedded in the use of the Golden Section and single point

---

[35] P. Fritzsche, *Reading Berlin* (Cambridge, Mass., 1996); R. Evans, *Tales from the German Underworld* (New Haven and London, 1998).

perspective ultimately cannot be disavowed.[36] The mechanistic operations of the painter's eye have subjected the organic animation of the city
street to a manipulated trope of bourgeois modernity that masquerades
as a casual scene of modern everyday life. Painter and critic collude in
securing the spectators' position within the nexus of hegemonic visuality
that structures the masculine experience of metropolitan modernity
played out in these city scenes.

The mechanistic aspects of Ury's pictorial constructions were not lost
on a hostile contemporary reviewer of his work, published in the Berlin
art journal *Das Atelier* in 1891, in which the author reveals the emphasis
on optics in Ury's work. He writes that 'impressionism has to be the art
of the shortsighted. Liebermann and Ury are less painters than people
who know how to apply the laws of optics to colours in an admirably
mechanical way'.[37] Consistently, it is the role of the eye and of vision that
is privileged in the critical discourse that structures the context, reception
and understanding of Ury's city scenes of Imperial Berlin.

The role of vision as the dominant sense in the structuring of social
relations of urban modernity is an issue that was explored at some length
by Georg Simmel in 1903 in a pertinent analysis of 'The sociology of
space' and one of its accompanying appendices, 'The sociology of the
senses'. In 'The sociology of space', Simmel explores a range of different
perspectives from which space can effect the operations of social,
political, institutional and historical structures as well as individual
human interaction. In particular he observes that physical distance
between people has a tendency to objectify relations between them and
he comments:

> the significance of the spatial interval is merely that it eliminates the
> stimulations, frictions, attractions and repulsions which sensory
> proximity calls forth ... With respect to a spatially close person,
> with whom one has contact in the most mutually varied situations
> and moods without the possibility of caution or choice, there tend
> to be only decisive emotions, so that this proximity can be the basis
> both for the most effusive joy and the most unbearable constraint ...
> [However] in the modern metropolis, complete indifference and the
> exclusion of all emotional reactions can occur even between next
> door neighbours ... because the incessant contacts with countless
> people produce the same effect through the dulling of the senses.
> Here the indifference to that which is spatially close is simply a
> protective device without which one would be mentally ground
> down and destroyed in the metropolis.[38]

---

[36] Gurlitt, 'Von den Kunstausstellungen Lesser Ury und Hans Thoma', p. 25.
[37] *Das Atelier*, 1, 18 (1891), p. 2.
[38] Simmel, 'The sociology of space', p. 154.

The notion of the potential destruction of the individual in the over-stimulating environment of the modern city is a familiar *leitmotif* in Simmel's writings on metropolitan culture and is an issue to which he frequently turns his attention, particularly in his considerations of the divisions between what he terms subjective (inner) and objective (outer) culture.[39] The concept that the individual cultivates a 'paralysis of the senses' as a subliminal strategy for coping with the excess of modern urban stimulation is significant in this context since it suggests precisely the repression of sensual experience under the mastery of the controlling gaze of spectacular modernity that is at stake in my analysis of Ury's paintings of Berlin.[40]

Simmel goes on to argue the further point that, in those cities that contain especially lively populations, usually of distinct ethnic origins, segregation is frequently introduced in order to 'prevent conflicts between neighbours' and to maintain the metropolitan social order (for example the regular ghettoisation of the Jews within European cities). He elaborates on this more specifically in a brief mention of the role that the senses also play in terms of proximity or distance between people and hints that this is an issue that requires further investigation, resulting in the accompanying appendices on 'The sociology of the senses' and 'The stranger', both of which are considered below. In relation to the role of the senses in this essay however, he comments:

> In comparison to the optical image of a person or persons, which always shows only a relatively stable content that can only be varied within narrow limits, the ear transmits an infinite variety of the most divergent moods, emotions and thoughts – in short the entire polarity of subjective and objective life ... Conversational proximity creates a much more individual relationship than does visual closeness ... where only the sense of sight exploits proximity, more of a feeling of a general conceptual and unspecific unity or of a mechanical concurrence will result, whereas the possibility of speaking and hearing will produce individual, animated, organic feelings of unity ... Of a much greater significance for the association or repulsion among human beings is the sense of smell ... The sense of smell has a great influence at least on the sociological relationship of different races living on the same territory. The reception of Negroes into the higher social circles in America is excluded simply because of the odour of the Negro; the often instinctive aversion between Germans and Jews has been

---

[39] For more information and a more detailed analysis of this aspect of Simmel's thought, see Rowe, *Representing Berlin*, pp. 63–80.

[40] For examples of other essays by Simmel in which the notion of the 'dulling' or 'paralysis' of the senses is postulated as the main outcome as a result of the perceived excess of stimuli on offer within modern metropolitan consumer culture, see Rowe, *Representing Berlin*, pp. 52–62.

ascribed to the same factor. Personal contact between the educated
class and the workers, often so vigorously advocated for modern
social development ... fails simply because of the insuperability of
the sensory impressions in this area.[41]

Clearly for Simmel, as elaborated here, the sense of sight performs an
inadequate smoothing away or levelling out of differences that cannot be
denied when the other senses are brought into play. If vision structures
the discourses of urban modernity played out in the images produced by
city painters such as Lesser Ury, it seems that, for Simmel, as suggested
by this essay, it may well be at the expense of a more nuanced sensual
perception of the city offered via alternative phenomenological urban
experiences.

In 'The sociology of the senses', Simmel's analysis of the powerful
operations of the sense of sight is elaborated more fully and he focuses
on its centrality in the structuring of human social relations and social
interaction between individuals. While many of the key aspects of his
analysis of the senses in this essay are a repetition of almost identical
observations in the essay on space, the main distinction is a more
detailed consideration of the significance of sight and vision. For Simmel,
in line with many modernist thinkers, the experience of inter-subjectivity
as outlined in this essay is predicated on sight and on an investment in
the look between individuals. In a particularly telling statement, he
comments that, in relation to all of the other senses, 'in general, one can
possess only the "visible", whereas that which is only audible is already
past in the moment of its present and provides no "property".'[42] Vision
is clearly aligned with the power of ownership and in this instance is
privileged, although not without the further recognition that the other
senses, in particular smell, also have the subversive potential to disrupt
the dominant form of unity that is manufactured through sight and
vision as Simmel identifies it here.

Simmel's essays on space and on the senses offer a significant contemporary commentary on the role of vision within the epistemologies of
urban modernity. They serve to strengthen the hegemonic role of vision
and the visual in the structuring of spatial tropes of urban modernity and
they offer an interesting correlation to the way in which city spaces are
structured through the visual iconography of Ury's Berlin street scenes
and contemporary critical readings of them. However, where Simmel's
analyses offer a significant point of departure from many other
modernist attempts to secure vision as the structuring principle and
founding moment of subjective recognition and identity is in his

---

[41] G. Simmel, 'The sociology of space', pp. 155–6.
[42] G. Simmel, 'The sociology of the senses', p. 116.

consideration of the unique effects that the other senses can also produce within what he terms 'the sociation' and interaction between individuals. For Simmel, unlike the irrational position that can be read in the later apocalyptic writings of Oswald Spengler, the dominance of the sense of sight is not all-consuming and, although other senses may at times appear subordinate to it, their peculiar effects are not considered to have been lost by Simmel, rather they remain to be properly considered within emergent theories of sociological analysis. In his conclusion to 'The sociology of the senses', he advises fellow sociologists that 'one will no longer be able to consider as unworthy of attention the delicate, invisible threads that are spun from one person to another if one wishes to understand the web of society according to its productive, form-giving forces'.[43] A focus on the role of the senses in the structuring of social life is one way amongst others that he identifies as being a productive mode of enquiry for a future microsociological analysis of urban modernity.

Finally, one further significant feature in the critical reception of Ury's work from the 1890s onwards and for which Simmel's essay on 'The stranger' offers an interesting parallel, was the replication of the tensions between tradition and modernity that characterised so many of the concurrent debates about Berlin. The success of Ury's artistic development was regularly aligned with the perceived success and development of his most notorious subject, the Imperial *Weltstadt*, and since, as I have already indicated, the achievement of *Weltstadt* status was conceived in terms of a dialectical tension between those who mourned the loss of community and those who celebrated the cosmopolitanism of urban society, Ury's role in relation to his subject matter is also situated as part of the same dialectic.

In 1921, the same year as his sixtieth birthday, volume 9 of a small series of monographs devoted to a consideration of *Graphiker der Gegenwart* was published by Lothar Briegar with Ury as its subject.[44] As

---

[43] G. Simmel, 'The sociology of sociability', in Frisby and Featherstone, eds, *Simmel on Culture*, p. 120.

[44] Other volumes in the series included individual books on Emil Orlik, vol. 2, Ernst Stern, vol. 3, Käthe Kollwitz, vol. 6, Hans Meid, vol. 7 and Max Liebermann, vol. 8, amongst others, all of whom were considered together again in a further publication of the same name published seven years later in 1928, towards the end of Ury's career, in M. Liebermann, H. Meid, A. Zorn, M. Slevogt, E. Orlik, E. Stern, L. Ury, K. Kollwitz and H. Zille, eds, *Graphiker der Gegenwart* (Berlin, 1928). It would seem that this later publication, although produced by a different publisher than for the earlier nine-volume series, was essentially a slightly edited reprint of the series but within a single volume instead. The same artists feature in both publications and the 1921 essay on Ury by Briegar, although not accredited in the later volume, bears very close resemblances apart from a few minor editorial changes, additions and amendments.

a context and background to his consideration of Ury's work, Briegar opens his text with an analysis of the history of the recently formed *Weltstadt*. Having considered how unfairly critics of Berlin have treated the city's development, given its need to create itself as the heart of a new empire 'without a natural centre', he considers the achievements of the city in terms of how it also had to overcome the difficulties that 'arose when the new Berlin had to build itself over the extremely outspoken style of the old Berlin, a magnificent style, full of character'.[45] However, as he comments, 'Berlin as the centre of Germany strode its way into the world and brought the world back to it.'[46] The main reason for Briegar's fairly extended consideration of the difficulties that Berlin had in achieving its *Weltstadt* status is so that he can contextualise its struggle for development alongside the parallel 'hard won development of Berlin impressionism by his subject, Lesser Ury'.[47] He comments:

> Ury was equipped to connect the development of Berlin to world art before many others were: he was not a native Berliner. He belongs to that type of immigrant who feels at home with Berlin under his feet but who must first travel the world in order to gain the soul of the world for the world city.[48]

The positioning of Ury as global outsider, able to bring worldliness to bear on the emergent capital, transforming it from a provincial *Fisherdorf* to a cosmopolitan *Weltstadt,* is a recurrent trope in the Weimar literature about the artist. In the 1928 reprint of the Briegar essay, along with other essays about Ury's contemporaries, the artist was said to be the first painter to capture 'the new world spirit of the new world city'.[49] The position of the cosmopolitan outsider figure is a useful trope for the kind of emergent cultural modernity that was being analysed and celebrated in these accounts and recalls Simmel's analysis of the outsider figure in his essay on 'The stranger', one of the appendices to the 1903 publication on 'The sociology of space' which, together with the other 1903 essays on space, the metropolis and the senses, were reprinted in 1908 under the generic title *Soziologie*.[50] The essay, 'The stranger' is worth considering here in the context of the other two related essays, 'The sociology of space' and 'The sociology of the senses', since they were all engaged with the same general theme of the sociological effects of spatial proximity and distance between people and how this

[45] Briegar, *Graphiker der Gegenwart*, pp. 3–4.
[46] Briegar, p. 4.
[47] Briegar, p. 5.
[48] Briegar, p. 5.
[49] Liebermann, Meid, et al., *Graphiker der Gegenwart*, p. 110.
[50] The translation that I am relying on here can be found in Levine, *Georg Simmel*, pp. 143–9.

was enacted, whether through physical or psychological boundaries or through the effects of intimacy or repulsion generated in varying degrees by the different effects of the five senses.

Simmel's analysis of the stranger seeks to offer an impartial sociological account of what constitutes the status of an outsider within a community and in this respect it offers an interesting parallel with the ways in which Ury's outsider status was articulated in critical attempts to position him as 'cosmopolitan other' to the native 'norm'. According to Simmel, the position of the stranger 'within a group ... is fundamentally affected by the fact that he does not belong in it initially and that he brings qualities into it that are not, and cannot be, indigenous to it' and moreover that 'the state of being a stranger is of course a completely positive relation; it is a specific form of inter-action'.[51] In the terms in which Simmel conceives it, the membership of the stranger to a group is predicated upon the stranger's ability to be 'both outside it' and to confront it and, with regard to this 'objectivity of the stranger', he also comments:

> Because he is not bound by roots to the particular constituents and partisan dispositions of the group, he confronts all of these with a distinctly 'objective' attitude, an attitude that does not signify mere detachment and non-participation, but is a distinct structure composed of remoteness and nearness, indifference and involvement.[52]

While Ury's visions of Berlin as the modern Imperial *Weltstadt* of the leisured classes helped to build up a long-term critical admiration for his boldness in tackling a subject that was still so raw for many early commentators and that remained a source of incredulity right through to the 1920s, they also articulated a space of marginality in terms of his ability to objectify optically the sensuous dynamism of the pulsating rhythms of urban life that for many native critics was a source of anxiety and fear. By positioning Ury as a stranger to the city within much of the critical assessment of his work with all the attendant associations of global experience, worldly knowledge and dispassionate objectivity, both the cosmopolitan *Weltstadt* and its visually cohesive representation could be properly secured and simultaneously admired. The mechanical eye of the painter as stranger smoothes out the disruptions, smells and sounds of the unruly city and coheres it in a controlled visual fiction for the masculine bourgeois spectators of modernity.

---

[51] Levine, p. 143.
[52] Levine, p. 145.

## Further reading

J. Crary, *Suspensions of Perception: Attention, Spectacle and Modern Culture* (Cambridge, Mass., 1999).

R. Evans, *Tales from the German Underworld* (New Haven and London, 1998).

U. Frevert, *Women in German History* (Oxford, 1989).

D. Frisby and M. Featherstone (eds), *Simmel on Culture* (London, 1997).

P. Fritzsche, *Reading Berlin 1900* (Cambridge, Mass., 1996).

R. Lenman, *Artists and Society in Germany 1850–1914* (Manchester and New York, 1997).

P. Paret, *German Encounters with Modernism 1840–1945* (Cambridge, 2001).

J. Rée, *I See a Voice: A Philosophical History of Language, Deafness and the Senses* (London, 1999).

D. Rowe, *Representing Berlin: Sexuality and the City in Imperial and Weimar Germany* (Aldershot, 2003).

S. Spier, *Urban Visions: Experiencing and Envisioning the City* (Liverpool, 2002).

# CHAPTER ELEVEN

# Street noises: celebrating the Liberation of Paris in music and dance[1]

*Rosemary Wakeman*

In the Liberation newspaper *Combat*, Jean-Paul Sartre described the chaos on the Left Bank on 14 July 1944, the first national holiday of the deliverance:

> The church bells of Saint-Germain rang out ... an immense clamour spilled out from the houses and streets. In the middle of the *carrefour*, a man sang 'the *Marseillaise*'. He only knew a few stanzas that the crowd repeated again and again ... Someone lit a fire at the corner of the Boulevard Montparnasse and, just as July 14 had been celebrated before the war, the crowd danced the farandole around the flames. Suddenly someone screamed: 'Tanks, Tanks!' You could hear gunfire and people scrambled for refuge under cars. There were still Germans in Paris. The crowd dissipated into the night and the *carrefour* was plunged once more into obscurity and silence.[2]

The Liberation of Paris was perhaps the ultimate urban spectacle, one in which military frays blended with the carnavalesque in an outpouring of public emotion. In his book *Libération, fête folle*, Alain Brossard argues that, as spectacle, the Liberation took place outside modern time and place, that its tone was more like that of pre-modern celebrations and the tomfoolery once associated with seasonal cycles or public festivals rejoicing at springtime rebirth.[3] Yet one could argue that its appropriation of dramatic spectacle, its plurality, its self-conscious reflexivity and explicit use of celebrity, its contentious quality, all made the performance of the Liberation overtly modern. The event translated the public arena of Paris into a theatrical stage set of adversarial scenes and tableaux, that is, a cultural performance, a meta-narrative of song and dance in a distinctively modern genre.

Public space is, of course, an arena of lavish representation. It provides

---

[1] Many thanks to Alex Cowan and my colleagues at Fordham University for their suggestions and critical readings of this text.

[2] *Combat* (2 Sept. 1944).

[3] A. Brossat, *Libération, fête folle* (Paris, 1994), p. 20.

a symbolic context for public activities and a mechanism for their accomplishment. They become particularly readable when this scenographic or theatrical dimension is underscored. Public space becomes a stage on which to study the city as dramatic culture in which a variety of actors and choruses move forward and backward, become visible and invisible.[4] This is a particularly useful projection when a city's public space is reclaimed after being abandoned or severely restricted, as was the case during the Occupation. Retaking the street takes on a symbolic context of immense proportions. Like other rituals, people used this street theatre as a tool to confront power relations. Parades, public ceremonies and spectacles and ritual singing all became ways of reconstituting civility – they were a political instrument. Paris re-emerged from the war at the prow of a reconstituted nation, a showcase for reconstruction and the new France,[5] yet its theatre of public space had a dynamic, socially contentious quality. It was a space of serendipity, of a freedom of spirit and action marked heavily by the Occupation and Liberation. This essay argues that music and dance guided access into this uncertain, multi-form public space. They were a 'machinery of communication' and part of the social and political conflicts shaping events. Public space was reclaimed in a cacophony of sounds and practices that were impulsive, reflexive, in search of celebrity. They belied any rational delivery, were performed amid danger, and amounted to a collective ritual for reappropriating the city. Song and dance acted as a liturgy for resanctifying space and the civic realm. Yet, in doing so, these performances dramatised the profound social divisions in a city traumatised by defeat and occupation, and then freed in a moment of ritual deliverance.

The German Occupation and the war had drastically altered the traditional urban fabric of Paris. The war isolated the city almost

---

[4] On the scenographic dimension of urban space, see I. Joseph, ed., *Prendre place, espace public et culture dramatique*, Colloque de Cerisy (Paris, 1995), especially the series of articles on 'La règle du visible'. On singing and popular urban culture, see A. Cohen, *Masquerade Politics. Explorations in the Structure of Urban Cultural Movements* (Berkeley, 1993); S.G. Davis, *Parades and Power. Street Theatre in Nineteenth-Century Philadelphia* (Philadelphia, 1986); L.A. Waxer, 'In the city of musical memory. Salsa, record grooves, and popular culture in Cali, Colombia', in G. Lipsitz, ed., *Music/Culture* (Middletown, 2002).

[5] On Paris and French reconstruction, see the excellent analysis in 'Images, discours et enjeux de la reconstruction des villes françaises après 1945', *Les Cahiers de L'IHT*, 5, June 1987 and 'Région parisienne, approches d'une notion 1860–1980', *Les Cahiers de L'IHT* 12, Oct. 1989, both by D. Voldman, as well as her *La Reconstruction des villes françaises de 1940–1954* (Paris, 1997). See also A. Kopp, F. Boucher, D. Pauly, *1943–1955: France, architecture de la reconstruction, solutions obligées ou occasions perdues?* (Paris, 1980).

completely. No trains or subways ran. The statues that graced the city's great public spaces were secreted behind earthworks. Nightly blackouts, curfews and strict public regulation curtailed any and all 'suspicious', that is public, activities. Public dancing and the traditional *bals publiques* were officially prohibited in 1940, especially to corrupt 'Jewish–American', or 'black–American' (as it was alternatively called by the authorities) jazz music. However, the German censors were surprisingly lenient and there was no blanket prohibition of the music itself. The city's cabarets and music-halls continued their celebrated variety shows featuring entertainers Charles Trenet, Tino Rossi, Edith Piaf and Maurice Chevalier, willing to skirt the political compromises made in order to perform. With an average of two performances a month, the jazz or swing craze in occupied Paris surpassed that of the 1930s. The December 1940 jazz festival featuring the Hot Club de France sold out in 24 hours, while fans lined up in the freezing cold of January 1941 to hear the Orchestre du Jazz de Paris and Django Reinhardt and his Hot Club de France at the Pleyel Music-Hall.[6] The American tunes they played were given French titles as subterfuge. Although tolerated by the authorities, jazz was nevertheless a symbol of personal freedom and defiance. One early form of youthful anti-conformism to the reality of Occupation was clandestine 'surprise-parties', covert dancing, and listening to Radio London music broadcasts. Swing was adopted as political parody to become the 'anti-music' to the official military marches and folkloric hymns. The craze was most closely identified with the rebellious and very public *zazous*. With pompadour hairdos, long jackets over tight trousers or short skirts, multi-colour socks and platform shoes, they mocked the New Order, especially when they promenaded the Boul'-Mich and the Boulevard Germain-des-Prés flaunting conspicuous 'yellow stars' on their chests emblazoned with the words 'swing' or 'zazous'.[7] Their idols were singer Johnny Hess and his *Je suis swing* and *Ils sont zazous,* and singer–actress Irène de Trébert, with her *Elle était swing* and *Mademoiselle Swing.* (These songs, written principally by Pierre Dac and Maurice Van Moppès, were played on the BBC as a direct rebuff to Nazi-controlled Radio Paris.) Hess ridiculed the moralists of the New Order and their absorption with racism. *La musique nègre et le jazz hot / Sont déjà de vieilles machines / Maintenant pour être dans la note / Il faut être swing.*

---

[6] For an excellent discussion of jazz during the Occupation, see L. Tournès, 'Le Jazz: Un espace de liberté pour un phénomène culturel en voie d'identification', in M. Chimènes, ed., *La vie musicale sous Vichy, histoire du temps présent* (Paris, 2001). Also useful is H. Le Boterf, *La vie parisienne sous l'occupation, 1940–1944*, vol. 1 (Paris, 1974).

[7] See J–C. Loiseau, *Les zazous* (Paris, 1990).

This kind of playful, daring defiance was looked upon as a public threat and did not long survive the brutality of Nazi Occupation. As the 'black years' settled over the city, the mood became sombre and bleak, particularly from February 1943, when the *Service du travail obligatoire* began claiming young men for work duty in Germany. Yet daring public performances continued. In June 1943, students on the Left Bank ended their exams by parading through the streets, singing traditional 'student songs', and staged a sitdown demonstration at the Panthéon until the police arrived.[8] Regardless of this unruliness, in the midst of war, it was food that obsessed the majority of Parisians. Ration books were guarded with desperation and most people learned to rely on the fiendish services of the black market dealers who raised prices to exorbitant levels. By 1944, rumour had it that the hulls of the American Liberty Ships landing in Normandy were bursting with provisions. Even after the arrival of the Allied troops, vast areas of the city that had functioned as traditional public space were still deserted, les Halles most prominently among them. Only the open spaces used as military depots remained active. The Invalides esplanade, the city's parks at Vincennes and Boulogne were covered with army equipment, vehicles and 'kaks'.[9] Liberated they may have been, but Parisians faced a desperate winter in 1944–45. Bitter cold joined hunger as the new enemies. The city's electricity and water functioned sporadically. Stores were open only a few hours a day. The arrival of coal was the only news worth hearing.

Public space was the theatre for the poverty, helplessness and destitution that the war left in its wake. Documentary photographs taken in Paris immediately after the Liberation, as well as numerous memoirs, are a continuous parade of searing images: the inevitable queues of needy people waiting for food, clinics filled with pneumonia victims, charity drives for the most desperate, returning prisoners arriving by train to be met by distraught crowds. Fear, pity, fate were all embodied in the tragic dramas unfolding in the streets. These were the sacrificial spaces of the city, those that represented the destruction of the war and the urban world as a void of hopeless casualties. The marginalised social groups who had always existed at the boundaries of urban life became a veritable torrent of suffering humanity, spilling out into the public world, a parade of destitution whose presence consecrated the symbolic spaces

---

[8] Archives de Police, Etudiants, Manifestations, partis, groupes, 1946–1957, BA2134.

[9] Two of the best known memoirs of the Liberation years are Jean Dutourd, *Au bon beurre* (Paris, 1952) and Marguerite Duras, *The War, a Memoir* (New York, 1994). The Paris Municipal Archives contains a vast collection of statements, affidavits and interviews taken after the Liberation. See also Le Boterf, *La Vie Parisienne*; G. Perrault, *Paris sous l'occupation* (Paris, 1987).

of an inhuman dystopia. 'Each night, the city's garbage cans were searched painstakingly by legions of poor people. Everything was rubbed, cleaned, checked.'[10] The reception centres for returning refugees at the Gare d'Orsay and the Gare du Nord, at the Hôtel Lutetia, at Vel' d'Hiv' and the Gaumont Theatre were 'incredible spectacles of haggard, wasted people garbed in striped costumes'. Each morning at 8:15 the trains of prisoners and deportees would arrive at the Gare du Nord. 'There were people, so many people ... Inside, Red Cross doctors and nurses were everywhere, surrounded by stretchers and wheelchairs. There were barriers that formed a kind of column through which the arrivals would pass. On either side were the crowds of parents and friends hoping that their loved ones would suddenly materialize.'[11] These 'scenes' acted as a way of absorbing the most traumatised victims of the war back into the national fold. Destitution and hopelessness were centre-stage, a ritual atonement for an extraordinary tragedy that was all the more important because of the French ambivalence and friction concerning the war's memory made traditional forms of commemoration inappropriate.

As Henri Ruosso has pointed out, there were relatively few official public ceremonies memorialising the Second World War and its end. A single grandiose ceremony was staged on Armistice Day, 11 November 1945, when fifteen French citizens who had died during the war were brought to the tomb of the Unknown Soldier.[12] The void was filled at the unofficial, urban level, in which the street and public spaces became the theatre for outpourings of public emotion. In *Rabelais and His World*, Bakhtin pointed to the ceaseless battle between official and unofficial sociocultural forces, the latter identified with popular or 'folk-festive' culture of the people, the 'eternally living element of unofficial speech and unofficial thought' that appears under specific circumstances.[13] Alongside the visible tragedy, the public spaces where this battle was played out were filled with the clamour of an uncontrollable, zany joy that also functioned as ritual and performance. This might, at first glance, appear to be individual, typically spontaneous and superfluous forms of release. Yet, as a collective popular event, it represented the public mechanism for absorbing the incomprehensible and for

---

[10] J-L. Babelay, *Un An* (Paris, 1946), p. 76.

[11] These two testimonies are from Madeleine Louradour and Monique Bauzou, as related in Mairie de Paris, *C'était Paris dans les années 50* (Paris, 1997), p. 14.

[12] H. Ruosso, *The Vichy Syndrome, History and Memory in France since 1944* (Cambridge, Mass., 1991), pp. 23–5.

[13] M. Bakhtin, *Rabelais and his World* (Cambridge, Mass., 1994), trans. H. Isolowsky.

reinitiating popular public life. For the majority of Parisians, secluded in their apartments and rooms, the first inkling of the Liberation was *heard* on the evening of 24 August 1944 and the morning after.

> As night fell, the church bells, all the church bells of Paris began ringing. In tears, I ran out onto the balcony with my neighbours ... what joy, this incredible concert of over a hundred church bells ringing out in the warm evening sky ... Then suddenly we heard this one bell. It was grave, splendid: the great bell of Notre Dame.[14]

> All the church bells in Paris started ringing ... The bells were ringing out under a sky in which the guns still thunder while the smoke rises from the burning Grand Palais. People are singing the *Marseillaise* in the street, cheering, and it's delirious.[15]

The music of the church bells, especially the great bell of Notre Dame Cathedral, awakening the city from the dark night of Nazi occupation, was the symbolic liturgy for the re-emergence of public culture. The deliverance of Paris took on powerful religious overtones. As they had traditionally called the people to prayer, the 'song of the liberated bells' called the people out into the public realm, there to sanctify the city with song, dance and rejoicing.

Along with the religious symbolism, a carnivalesque dimension acted as an ironic–comic component that 'made the serious ridiculous' and disclosed the potentiality of an entirely different world, another way of life. It was a form of irreverent, nervy political theatre against the savagery perpetrated by those in power. Claude Roy's description of the crowds on the Champs Elysées waiting for De Gaulle on Saturday 26 August illustrates this sense of spontaneous theatre in which everyone was a star:

> The crowd is pouring, piling, pushing, pressing ... looking for something to cheer. They cheer the stretcher-bearers. Bravooooo. The FFI. Bravooooo. Some fine-looking officers go by. Bravooooo. What else is there to cheer? Three cheers for the sparrows. Three cheers for the newsreel planes overhead. Three cheers for the bicycles. Three cheers for the chestnut trees. Three cheers for everything ... A hurricane of shouts breaks over us, beats down on us. Vive De Gaulle! Vive la France! ... The crowds, thousands, hundreds of thousands of voices singing the *Marseillaise*. I think De Gaulle is embracing a war cripple.[16]

---

[14] C. de Saint-Pierre (1945), *Des ténèbres à l'aube, journal d'une Française* (Paris, 1945), p. 54.

[15] B. and F. Groult (1965), *Diary in Duo* (New York, 1965), trans. Humphrey Hare, p. 351.

[16] C. Roy, *Eight Days That Freed Paris* (London, 1945), pp. 50–51, 54.

Max Douy and his Resistance colleagues participated in the festivities by flinging open the windows of his apartment and playing recordings of the *Marche Lorraine* and other patriotic hymns at full volume into the streets.[17] On 26 August a reporter for the daily *Le Figaro* described the streets:

> As soon as I left the Hôtel de Ville, I was stopped, submerged by an enormous crowd that was everywhere, on the streets, the quays, the avenues, the passage ways. They applauded. They shouted. They stamped their feet. They cried. On one of the tanks, surrounded by the din of motors and smoke, a cat, a minuscule little cat, calmly sat surveying the scene. The crowd roared their approval. That was what this unique day was like: one part exuberant celebration, exalted, delirious, an incredible lightheartedness that poured out in song, kisses, in bounding joy; the other part, a climate of civil war.[18]

Throughout 1944 and 1945, the first anniversaries of wartime victory and Liberation were celebrated with immense popular acclaim. Most of these gatherings were turned immediately into charity events for some desperate group of castaways (of which there were many), for the homeless, the FFI, for orphans, for deportees, for refugees, the wounded and the dead. Singer–comedian Pierre Dac, who had been one of the best known voices on Radio London during the war, performed at a Red Cross benefit at Luna Park in September 1944. A few days later, the Jazz Symphonique de Paris inaugurated a concert series at the Palais de Chaillot as a tribute to the allies. Then it was an open-air music-hall extravaganza to benefit prisoners and war victims. The same month, Fred Astaire and a cavalcade of French music-hall stars entertained the allied troops.[19] The music pouring out from Luna Park, from the Théâtre des Champs-Elysées, the Palais de Chaillot, the city's churches, the place de la Concorde, the Tuileries and Luxembourg gardens and from neighbourhood squares all signalled the resurfacing of collective life and public space. Many of the concerts were broadcast on RDF (Radiodiffusion française) which began operation on 22 August 1944. Liberated radio provided an enhanced venue for song. Music shows such as *Ploum ploum tralala*, inaugurated in 1945, with its title melody *On chante dans mon quartier*, proliferated.

VE Day, 8 May 1945, elicited an outpouring of public marching and ceremony. American journalist Janet Flanner described it as 'an

---

[17] *L'Ecran français,* 7 (15 Aug. 1945).

[18] *Le Figaro* (26 Aug. 1944).

[19] Descriptions of these events can be found in daily newspapers such as *Combat* (September 1944). See also P. Gumplowicz and J–C. Klein, eds, *Paris 1944–1954. Artistes, intellectuals, publics: la Culture comme enjeu,* Série *Mémoires No. 38* (Paris, 1945).

occupation of Paris by Parisians. They streamed out onto their city's avenues and boulevards and took possession of them ... They paved the Champs Elysées with their moving, serried bodies ... [They] drowned out the sound of the church bells that clanged for peace'. Food was scarce, everyone was hungry, but 'All anyone cared about was to keep moving, to keep shouting, to keep singing snatches of the *Marseillaise*'.[20] This was the discourse of the Liberation, a tragic–ecstatic cacophony that permeated public space. *La Vie Ouvrière* reported, 'From the République to the Concorde, the streets and pavements were jammed with men, women, children. Everywhere singing and cries of joy ... *Le Madelon* alternated with the *Chant des Partisans*, the *Jeune Garde*, and the *Internationale*.'[21] There was an inventory of time-honoured tunes, verses and refrains that were transmitted through memory or readily available in song sheets sold by itinerant singers. This musical stock took on renewed meaning and symbolism as it was appropriated to the dislocated world of 1944–45. It was not just a mark of civic life, but a depiction of consensus and unity, shared pride and patriotism. For three days in July 1945, Bastille Day was saluted with massive street parades and dances replete with orchestras, choral performances and street theatre. They were represented as a re-emergence of the traditional 'open-air festivities' associated with Parisian popular culture. Their character was spontaneous, irreverent and disruptive of everyday normalities, a 'bursting' of the personal into the public domain. Normally private people drank themselves into silliness, grabbed partners and danced into the streets, interrupting traffic and bringing their neighbourhoods to a standstill. They joined in with the music and burst into song.[22]

Yet public space was a complex social domain. It absorbed those who had indeed fought for Paris, and those in need of a formula for inserting themselves back into the national fold because they had stayed silent or collaborated. Thus the 'play-acting' and musical performance of social roles could be genuine or spurious, valid or phoney. Consequently, in the context of the extraordinary social conflicts of these years, the political theatre of the Liberation was both conservative and revolutionary in content. After years of tight control, the public spaces of Paris were suddenly the arena for encounters once again, where various social classes could interact in unknown, undefined and dangerous ways. Scenes and actors shifted; sometimes they were ebullient, at other times threatening. Women known to have been involved with German soldiers

---

[20] J. Flanner, *Paris Journal 1944–1965* (London, 1996), pp. 26–7.
[21] *La Vie Ouvrière, Hebdomadaire de la CGT* (10 May 1945).
[22] *L'Humanité* (17 July 1945).

were publicly stripped, beaten and paraded through the streets with shaven heads. Collaborators were hunted down. The civic rituals and communal song of the Liberation created traditional rules of social engagement amid this disorder. They reached back into customary popular urban practices and oral traditions to re-knit the fabric of urban civility and retrieve the nation, artificially, from disaster. During the annual *fête nationale* celebrations of the late 1940s, the symbolic sites of the city, the great squares of the Hôtel de Ville, Châtelet, the Bourse and the place de la Concorde, hosted huge choral performances of the *Marseillaise*, with thousands of citizens patriotically joining in song 'to celebrate their freedoms'.

Walter Benjamin argued that this type of 'aestheticization of politics' represented the abyss of appearances that would vanish into nothing.[23] And indeed the rewoven cloth of civic life had a distinctively rebellious, disputatious pattern. Collective song represented the 'voice of the people', refound and politicised. Songs had always echoed through Parisian streets and enjoyed a long genealogy as political protest and community practice. Festival practices were steeped in the everyday. Political or labour union activities in the city's neighbourhoods were structured around ritual celebrations: buying 1 May lilies of the valley, the open-air dance parties of the *fête nationale* on 14 July, renewing party membership on 6 January, accompanied by communal singing at the local café. These oral traditions and popular performances set mocking and current political messages to old, familiar tunes. This political aspect of song was particularly critical for the Communist Party, which emerged from the war as the most popular and triumphant 'voice', and the principal political party in France. During the 14 July national holiday in 1945, the National Entertainment Union and the Communist Party daily newspaper *L'Humanité* organised open-air 'spectacles' at symbolic hubs of working-class life: the place de la République, the porte Saint-Martin and the porte Saint-Denis in the northern districts. Enormous crowds listened to massive assembled choirs singing and reciting from the historic texts of the French revolutionary tradition.[24] In September 1945, *L'Humanité* sponsored the reappearance of the Fête de l'Humanité, the pre-war working-class celebration that had drawn all of eastern Paris and the 'red' suburbs into great festivals of public solidarity. Over a million people streamed from the métro stations into the Bois de Vincennes, singing the *Marseillaise*,

---

[23] On Benjamin's aesthetics, see in particular R. Nägele, *Theater, Theory, Speculation. Walter Benjamin and the Scenes of Modernity* (Baltimore and London, 1991).

[24] *L'Humanité* (17 July 1945).

the *Internationale* and the *Chant des Partisans*. 'It is the people, singing!', *L'Humanité* reported. Over the course of the day, a traditional music festival was staged as well as a theatrical re-enactment of the 'Resistance, Victory and Liberation' with full chorus and ballet. By the evening, a star-studded regalia of singers (Paule Morin, Olga Adabache) and dancers (Loinard, Romand Jamet) performed on a fully illuminated stage (a 'fantasy' after years of blackouts) draped in tricolours.[25]

Working-class festivals such as the Fête de l'Humanité championed the revival of working class song and dance, such as that practised by *sociétés orphéoniques* and neighbourhood music societies, by accordionists and brass bands. The French had shared a distinctive vernacular song culture since the days of the 1789 Revolution. Open air concerts and impromptu sing-alongs given in the local public square were a traditional feature of working-class life.[26] Both at the neighbourhood level and at the citywide level sponsored by the Communist Party, musical performances such as the Fête de l'Humanité consecrated the public realm and acted as theatrical devices for inaugurating patriotic citizenship and reviving the myth of 'the people'. In January 1946, a journalist for *L'Humanité* reported wistfully that, despite freezing temperatures, the place Wagram in the working-class district of the 17th arrondissement was filled with 'seamstresses and shop girls, students, bicyclists, housewives with flutes in their arms, people at their windows' there to sing with Saint-Granier and his accordionist: 'It's difficult to choose between the amateurs who take their turn at the microphone. The cobblers and carpenters sing as they work ... I vote for the métro driver. And suddenly, despite my voice, I find myself singing along with the chorus, me too! An excellent idea, this "singing in my neighbourhood."'[27]

Although the national anthem was the song most associated with the Liberation, others were frequently sung in the streets or played at open-air concerts: the *Hymn of the FFI* and *Goodbye Adolf*, for example, or *Ma Voiture contre une Jeep*, inspired by Leclerc's victorious entry into

---

[25] *L'Humanité* (4 Sept. 1945).

[26] See in particular L. Mason, *Singing the French Revolution: Popular Culture and Politics, 1789-1799* (Ithaca, NY, 1996); R. Sweeney, 'Singing our way to victory. French cultural politics and music during the Great War', in Lipsitz, ed., *Music/Culture*. See also P. Gumplowicz, *Les travaux d'Orphée: 150 ans de vie musicale amateur en France, harmonies, chorales, fanfares* (Paris, 1978); C. Rearick, *The French in Love and War: Popular Culture in the Era of the World Wars* (New Haven, 1997).

[27] *L'Humanité* (16 Jan. 1946). Saint-Granier was a French singer–actor and songwriter of the 1930s, best known for 'Ramona' and 'C'est jeune et ça ne sait pas'.

the city.[28] Spontaneous sing-alongs with street performers accompanied by accordion or banjo music enjoyed a long tradition in Paris. Street-singers hawking cheap sheet music for the latest ballads had still been a familiar sight before the war, especially at weekends and during holidays. Sociologist Henri Lefebvre remembered that, in 1937, 'Everywhere in Paris music reigned in the streets and on the squares. On certain corners, such as at the Barbès métro, there were always singers accompanied by accordions or violins, surrounded by a large circle of people listening to the popular songs of the day.'[29] Sheet music for the *Internationale* and the *Chant des Partisans* sold with great success, as did the nostalgic old-fashioned waltz, *Le Petit Vin Blanc*.[30]

Lily Lian, one of the city's last street-singers, recalled 'selling pounds of them' on street corners in late 1944 and 1945, and singing with the crowds at the Mur des Fédérés outside the Père-Lachaise cemetery, the métro stations at Barbès-Rochechouart and La Motte-Picquet, at the place de l'Opéra and on the Champs Elysées. As Laura Mason has argued in her work on singing in the French Revolution, a song came to life only in being sung. Street performers made songs their own with vocal inflections and gestures, and by the particular circumstances in which they sang. Song lyrics functioned as allegories about events. It was through the performance of those lyrics that singers and audience 'discussed' and adapted them to their own experiences.[31]

Anna Marly had sung the *Chant des Partisans* over the BBC during the Occupation years as the theme song of the Free French programme 'Honour and Country' (*Ami, entends-tu le vol noir des corbeaux sur nos plaines? / Ami, entends-tu ces cris sourds du pays qu'on enchaîne? / Ohé, partisans, ouvriers et paysans, c'est l'alarme*). From August 1944, it became a national standard, openly performed in the streets, associated with the myths of the French Revolution, the revival of the 'people', and the victory of the Resistance. Singing practices such as these reveal the extent to which 'everyman' contributed to the appropriation of revolutionary tradition to the war and its aftermath, and made singing a metaphor for defiance. A January 1946 editorial in the communist *L'Humanité* on the reappearance of street singers disparaged the ban on street music during the black years as too frivolous 'for the hardness of

---

[28] See G. and G. Martz, 'La Chanson sous l'occupation et à la libération', *Histoire et Sociétés*, 51 (1994), pp. 5–34.

[29] Henri Lefebvre , in Centre Georges Pompidou, ed., *Paris 1937–1957* (Paris, 1981).

[30] The sheet music for *Le Petit Vin Blanc* sold 1·5 million copies in 1943 (the year it was released), making it among the most popular songs of the war era. See P. Saka, *La chanson française à travers ses succès* (Paris, 1988), p. 152.

[31] Mason, *Singing the French Revolution*, p. 2.

war, work, and the austerity. Song expresses the rebellious spirit of Paris. The indignation against the *munichois*, against the Nazis, and the traitors streamed out from song. That's why we were deprived of it. They feared the song of the French people'.[32]

*Le Petit Vin Blanc* and songs such as *On Boit l'Café au Lait au Lit* and *Fleur de Paris* (*C'est une fleur de Paris / Du vieux Paris qui sourit / Car c'est la fleur de retour / Du retour des beaux jours / Pendant quatre ans dans nos cœurs / Elle a gardé ses couleurs / Bleu, blanc, rouge / Avec l'espoir elle a fleuri / Fleur de Paris*) represented a far more nostalgic genre of popular favourites sung throughout Paris as part of the resurrection of public culture. Among Lily Lian's 'corners' were the gates of the Renault and Citroën factories in the suburbs. During the lunch hour, thousands of workers streamed out to accompany her in rounds of *Le Chant des Partisans, Le Petit Vin Blanc* and *On Boit l'Café au Lait au Lit*: 'They beat all records. Everyone knew them by heart. It was like I was accompanied by a chorus each time. Yes, it was like a celebration.'[33] The reappearance of street performers at the Liberation, along with street singing and dancing, the open-air concerts, all symbolised the re-emergence of historic custom and memory. This recovery of public memory and culture was an essential mechanism for re-imagining the collective life of the city. It was both antithetical to and expressive of the social and class conflicts of the 1930s and the war years. The 'performance' of the Liberation, in song and dance, acted to make what had been invisible and unlawful visible once again. Music and song acted as a momentary symbolic code of social unity and a nostalgic vision of urban cohesiveness. In the 1951 *Portrait of Paris*, a collection published for the city's 2000th anniversary, Robert Garric described the 'people of Paris', recruited from every corner of the country. 'They have their gatherings, their holidays ... their music, their songs, their newspapers. And Paris is the melting pot, it absorbs them all.'[34]

Yet public life was a drama of contestation and there was a competitive 'disharmony' among the musical forms and practices performed in the public realm. While working-class associations, for example, promoted patriotic song together with customary choral and

---

[32] *L'Humanité* (9 Jan. 1946). See also S. Dillaz, *La chanson française de contestation de la Commune à Mai 68* (Paris, 1973).

[33] L. Lian, *Lily Panam, mémoires de la dernière chanteuse des rues* (Paris, 1981), p. 104. See also R. Carré, 'Chanteurs et chansons des rues', *Gavroche, Revue d'histoire populaire*, 69–70 (1993), pp. 27–30, and the photographs of Robert Doisneau: B. Cendrars, *La Banlieue de Paris* (Paris, 1949), p. 55.

[34] R. Garric, 'Le Peuple de Paris', in J. Romains, ed., *Portrait de Paris* (Paris, 1951), p. 150.

instrumental forms derived from the *quartier*, there were other sounds that permeated space and the popular imagination. Hélène Brunschwig was in the Latin Quarter in late August 1944, 'where on every street corner there was dancing. It was incredible to see all of Paris dancing the tango, the waltz … the be-bop, the rumba'.[35] Radios tuned to Radio France, spontaneous combinations of street musicians and hurriedly purchased sheet music all provided a mélange, a round robin of melodies. Rumba lines of soldiers, young men and women, snaked through the place de la Madelaine. On the Blvd. Montmartre, crowds circled to cheer a soldier performing the jitterbug. Men stripped to their shorts danced in the city's fountains, waving French flags.[36] The lunacy and drunkenness plunged officialdom and the war's sobriety into disorder. They danced in the public squares and neighbourhood spaces traditionally used for congregation and celebrations around bonfires, tanks, orchestras and jeeps. The place Denfert-Rochereau, for example, which was the historic focal point of the 14th arrondissement and the location of traditional festivities of the *fête nationale* and *fêtes foraines*, was the site where people ventured out to parade with Leclerc's tanks as they rumbled up the avenue d'Orléans and arranged themselves around the great statue of the *Lion de Denfert*. The images were both extraordinary and complex. Gabriel Gallice remembered that 'It was disturbing to see these tanks arranging themselves in a star [around the statue]. I thought the Russians had arrived. These soldiers with crepe soles that made no noise … it upset me … It reminded me of images of the war of '14, the parades, the trumpets, the hobnail soles. And now there was another army here, another atmosphere, another époque.'[37]

Banned throughout the Occupation, the traditional neighbourhood dance halls, known as *bals populaires* or *bals publics*, reopened immediately after the Liberation. On 13 September 1944, British Major Palfred had officially authorised dancing and opened the doors of the city's dance halls and cabarets, announcing that Paris should once again become 'the merriest city on the continent'.[38] The most popular were on the rue de Lappe near the place de la Bastille and the numerous *bals musette* around the edge of Paris, where performers were offered free room and a meal for an evening of tunes. Various neighbourhoods (such as Saint-Germain, Robinson, Nogent) organised dances, as did regional

---

[35] Mairie de Paris, *C'était Paris*, p. 12. See also J–P. Dorian, *Jours et nuits de Paris, 1948–1949* (Paris, 1953); A. Beevor and A. Cooper, *Paris After the Liberation 1944–1949* (New York, 1994).

[36] R. Doisneau, 'Libération de Paris', p. 2, BHVP.

[37] Retold in S. Bonin and B. Costa, *Je me souviens du 14ᵉ arrondissement* (Paris, 1993), p. 14.

[38] *Combat* (14 Sept. 1944).

associations such as the 'Auvergnats de Paris'. The next level up were *les dancings*, including the more sophisticated dance halls and nightspots such as the Moulin de la Galette. At the war's end, many of these spots featured two dance rooms, one for dancing the traditional waltzes and tango to the accordion, and one for swing.

The tomfoolery was temporarily stopped by the Provisional Government in January 1945 when a press campaign complained that too many families were in mourning to permit such levity and the 'known' cabarets were closed. But this did little to stop the explosion of free-for-all dancing out into the public domain, especially among the young who boogie-woogied the wartime memories away anywhere they could. Musicians set up shop in the favourite haunts of the young crowds, particularly in the Latin Quarter, Saint-Germain-des-Prés and around the Place de la Bastille, where dancing went on spontaneously in the streets and around métro stations, often accompanied simply by a singer and an accordionist. Lights were strung across a neighbourhood square, a radio set up and dance parties spontaneously organised. Colette Bouisson remembered, 'after four years of immobility an explosion of dance shook the city. There had never been so many evenings of dance, places to dance, clubs, studios, get-togethers, parties ... here the waltz, there the tango or even the charleston, while from neighbourhood to neighbourhood there were outbursts of be-bop'.[39] Public dancing, especially be-bop and the jitterbug, was the ultimate expression of a freeing, a liberating of the civic body from the imprisonment of Occupation. It was anti-conformism, irrational and free form, a reversal of personal and public confinement.

American swing, arriving with the GIs in a city suddenly filled with Allied soldiers, most embodied the moment. Glenn Miller's *In the Mood* was the unofficial American anthem, the GI's march played by military bands, on the radio, in the clubs of Saint-Germain. In September 1944, Glenn Miller and his orchestra descended on the newly liberated city and played *In the Mood* and *Tuxedo Junction* to an enthralled audience at the Olympia Theatre. Clubs and hotels hosting American and British soldiers organised Franco-Allied dances. 'Franco' meant women, 'Allied' meant men, but the conditions were propitious. Benoîte Groult was 'Hostess No.129' at Rainbow Corner: 'We danced, we laughed, we drank coffee with thick milk, deliciously over sugared, ate doughnuts dripping with butter ... How easy life seems with the Americans! ... most of the G.I. girls are really handpicked. And we dance and dance!'[40]

---

[39] *C'était Paris dans les années 50* (Paris, 1997), p. 116.
[40] Groult, *Diary in Duo*, p. 361. On American cultural influence, see R. Kuisel, *Seducing the French. The Dilemma of Americanization* (Berkeley,

The Groult sisters 'clubbed' their way around the gala evenings at the Rainbow Corner, the Independence Club at the Hôtel Crillon, the Weber American Club, the Canadian Club as part of a 'collection of girls *de luxe*' chasing a good meal, good times and handsome men.

In the aftermath of the war and Liberation, young people dominated the public spaces of Paris, fleeing into the streets as a sign of their newfound freedom, and staying there day and night. A new generational dissonance fed into the complexities of traditional social and class divisions. By the Liberation, the J3s, as they were often called after the name of the food ration category for fifteen to twenty-one-year-olds, were defining themselves on the basis of new clothes and hairstyles. The rebellious wartime *zazous* had largely disappeared. The demand now was for genuine American clothes, especially beach shirts with cut-off trousers and tennis shoes, sent by American relief agencies and then sold at the flea market at Saint-Ouen for almost nothing. The J3s sported crew cuts and khaki pants in emulation of the GIs. For the young, this became the definition of NEW STYLE and they paraded it on the streets of Paris, zipping along on roller-skates, once the curfews were lifted. The undergraduates at the Sorbonne took up ski clothes as required fashion, the costume worn by the *maquis* fighting in the countryside during winter. There was an unending repertoire of 'found objects', in the sense that Marcel Duchamp gave to the term, introduced into the space of everyday life. For the *midinettes*, or working girls, short dresses made from parachute silk, sheets and bedclothes were in vogue at the war's end because there was no material. Straw shoes with wooden soles substituted for leather. Public life became a momentary 'zone' of spontaneous mood and invention.

Parisians took their first post-war 'vacations' in the summer of 1945. They travelled in makeshift vehicles and invented 'campers' to the surrounding parks, woods and beaches (still infested with millions of mines) as a great parade of war-weary gypsies. When the news of the 6 August atomic bomb attack on Japan reached Paris, nearby vacationers immediately held a beauty contest to crown 'Miss Atomic'.[41] Sardonic humour and grotesque images negated contemporary realities. For the young, retaking the street, infusing it with song, dance and spontaneous invention was a right of passage. Paris was a 'school of life' after the war in which anything and everything could happen. Public festivities were youthful 'rites of inversion' in which the ridiculous, the unseemly, the wildness negated the trap of wartime existence. This

---

1993). See also F. Kupferman, *Les premiers beaux jours 1944–1946* (Paris, 1985).

[41] Babelay, *Un An*, p. 194. See also A. Bony, *Les années 40 d'Anne Bony* (Paris, 1985).

serendipitous quality to urban existence was a continuous projection of the Liberation, an explosion of freedom, out into the public world. Paris 'was a whirlwind of places, partners, surroundings'.

The Left Bank was a musical landscape of experimentation associated with the young generation emerging from the war. Music and dance were instruments for the development of a new social collectivity of youth, and acted to mobilise their newly found freedom. Anne-Marie Deschodt remembered that her musical education had been 'honourable' up to 1947 when she 'became old enough to go out alone', left behind the Edith Piaf records in her family's apartment and headed for a jazz festival in the streets of Saint-Germain-des-Prés to hear Boris Vian, Jacqueline François and Gilbert Bécaud.[42] Immediately after the Liberation, Henri Leduc, a well known Montmartre and Saint-Germain-des-Prés impresario, opened Le Bar Vert on the rue Jacob, the first café-restaurant to play American music, while Claude Luter and his jazz combo set up the first basement club in the Hotel de Lorient in May 1946 (in this case devoted to the New Orleans style of Jelly Roll Morton and King Oliver). The basement clubs and pavements of Saint-Germain-des-Prés pulsated to the sounds of a growing admiration of jazz musicians and devotees. For writer Olivier Merlin, their horns trumpeted the 'pure spirit of Paris'.[43] The battle raged between the clubs that remained loyal to traditional jazz and those like the Tabou and the Caveau de la Huchette that became 'be-bop heavens' with boogie-woogie and jitterbug dance exhibitions that spilled out into the street.[44] There was immense informality and spontaneity to these performances that continued the revelry and carnival formula of the Liberation. They were open-ended and continually unpredictable, ridiculing officialdom and hierarchy, a violation of decorum and proportion. The carnivalesque strategy of 'provoking' and destabilising accepted standards was intentionally appropriated, for example, for suggestive beauty contests to elect 'Miss Tabou' and students seduced from their classes by all-night jam sessions, beat poetry readings and wild dancing. The jazz landscape of the Left Bank contributed to the image of youth as deviant, exotic, celebratory and entertaining. In 1948, Duke Ellington played the Club Saint-Germain-des-Prés and over a thousand admirers jammed into the narrow rue Saint-Benoit to catch a glimpse of their idol.

---

[42]  A–M. Deschodt, 'Variétés', in Bony, *Les années 40 d'Anne Bony*, p. 275.

[43]  O. Merlin, *Une belle époque, 1945–1950* (Paris, 1986).

[44]  On Saint-Germain-des-Prés and the post-war jazz era, see J–P. Caracalla, *Saint-Germain-des-Prés* (Paris, 1993) and G. Latour, *Le Cabaret Théâtre 1945–1965* (Paris, 1996). See also the works of Boris Vian, such as *Chroniques de jazz* (Paris, 1998), or *Jazz in Paris* (Paris, 1997). The revue *Jazz Hot* of the late 1940s provides excellent material on jazz music.

By the spring of 1946, some 53 theatres and five music halls were going full blast in Paris, the most celebrated on the Right Bank. The Olympia and the ABC were packed with fans listening spellbound to Yves Montand and Edith Piaf crooning *Dans les Plaines du Far West*, *La Vie en Rose* and *L'Hymne à l'amour*.[45] Exotic Italian and Spanish melodies were mixed with American tunes. Movie houses began showing American films. The racetracks, the opera, the theatres and museums, the bars and restaurants were continuously packed. The city's amusement park at the Porte Maillot, Luna Park, was re-opened after the war and became an instantaneous hang-out for young people. The Vel' d'Hiv' sports arena on the rue Nélaton (15th arrondissement) took on a celebrity that made it a metaphor for Parisian public life in the years after the war. Its 'six day' bicycle races, ice skating and ice hockey games, boxing matches and, especially, its roller-derbies for both men and women, were immensely popular, as were its 'spectaculars', among which were an American rodeo and a battle staged by 'Arabs' on camels and 'Spahis' on horses. As the Liberation years receded into the past, in a real sense public life became increasingly associated with staged performances and facile spectacles produced and choreographed by professionals. However even a good portion of these were initially staged within the context of usual public space. Here they acted as a transition between the dynamic theatre of 'the people' derived from the Liberation and the compliant theatre of modern mass-produced entertainment that functioned as festive forms of social control.

The greatest spectacle of all, however, was Paris itself. From 1946, the municipal government began using it as the ultimate urban backdrop for carefully controlled, professionalised 'open air' entertainment and performances in which 'the people' withdrew from the stage and functioned largely as spectators. The traditional *Bal des Petits Lits Blancs* (which had been a small-time, amateur affair before the war) was resurrected in 1946 along the Pont d'Argent with eight orchestras, the Champs-Elysées Ballet, and a star-studded cast that included Rita Hayworth, Roland Petit, Edith Piaf and Yves Montand. Its preparation was riddled with discord over whether receipts were to be donated to the Paris Opera or to Resistance orphans. This was a sign that the theatre of the Liberation was fading. In June 1948, the city staged the *Grande Nuit de Paris* during which the Eiffel Tower was floodlit, with great ceremony, for the first time since the war. The gala was arranged under the guidance of the prefecture of police, which strictly controlled the crowd of some

---

[45] On the evolution of the music industry in France, see J–C. Klein, *La chanson à l'affiche, Histoire de la chanson française du café–concert à nos jours* (Paris, 1991).

150 000 along the Champ de Mars. Vaudeville shows were staged. The Cirque Bouglione performed under the tower with appearances by Rita Hayworth, Hedy Lamarr, Charles Boyer, Ingrid Bergman, Lana Turner, Edward G. Robinson and musical skits by Yves Montand, Lily Pons and the Folies Bergères. At 2 a.m. fireworks were launched, and the historic monuments along the Seine were illuminated once again. For the first time since the Occupation, city buses and the *métro* stayed open for revellers, as did restaurants and cafes.

Paris became the ultimate stage set for a public culture progressively constructed as a place of passive enjoyment, a kind of theatre for adult gregariousness. Rather than 'lived space', the central districts were turned into spectacles of dramatic urban beauty. The breathtaking views and cityscape endlessly claimed the rebirth of the city after the long night of war. In this sense, the great urban scenography that Paris represented was the Liberation revisited. It was in part derived from the memory-numbing festivals of freedom and rejoicing at the war's end. But there was little civic community or shaped politics on this stage. The 'actors' had become professionalised (Hollywood stars Edward G. Robinson and Ingrid Bergman were the invited guests for a gala dinner in the upper reaches of the Eiffel Tower on the *Grande Nuit de Paris*). However, the ironic–comic carnivalesque of public life was not easy to vanquish. On the night of the *Grande Nuit de Paris*, event organiser Alain Duchemin hurried past the iron grill fence around the Tuileries Garden, where public lavatories had been set up, only to find hundreds of people laughing hysterically at the spontaneous spectacle of a line of commodes in full use, the back walls of the cabins having been inadvertently left open.[46] The Liberation translated the public arena of Paris into a theatrical stage set of adversarial tragic–comic scenes; that is, a cultural performance or modern meta-narrative written in song and dance. It encapsulated the festival qualities of popular political activism and dramatised both the quest for patriotic unity and the profound social divisions in Paris in the wake of defeat and occupation, and in the freedom of the Liberation's deliverance. The exceptional moment also captured the struggle between official and unofficial voices, the shifting visibility and invisibility of social actors on the stage of the city's public sites. The 'people', the working classes, the 'nation', the young performed in the quest for legitimacy. Celebrity was equated with political empowerment, and guaranteed recognition and respect. The landscape of Paris became the musical theatre of these social and political struggles of the Liberation.

---

[46] A. Duchemin, *Paris en Fêtes* (Paris, 1985), p. 49.

## Further reading

A. Beevor and A. Cooper, *Paris after the Liberation 1944–1949* (New York, 1994).

A. Brossat, *Libération, fête folle*, séries mémoires, no. 30 (Paris, 1994).

A. Brossat, *Paris 1937–1957* (Paris, 1994).

M. Chimenes, ed., *La vie musicale sous Vichy, histoire du temps présent* (Paris, 2001).

A. Cohen, *Masquerade Politics. Explorations in the Structure of Urban Cultural Movements* (Berkeley, 1993).

S. Dillaz, *La Chanson française de contestation de la Commune à Mai 68* (Paris, 1993).

P. Gumplowicz and J.C. Klein, eds, 'Paris 1944–1954', *Artistes, intellectuels, publics: la culture comme Enjeu*, séries mémoires no. 38 (Paris, 1995).

J. Isaac, ed., *Prendre place, espace public et culture dramatique*, Colloque de Cerisy (Paris, 1995).

L. Mason, *Staging the French Revolution: Popular Culture and Politics, 1789–1799* (Ithaca, NY, 1996).

O. Merlin, *Une Belle Epoque, 1945-1950* (Paris, 1986).

C. Rearick, *The French in Love and War: Popular Culture in the Era of the World Wars* (New Haven, 1997).

J.L. Robert and M. Tsikounas, eds, *Imaginaires parisiens*, number 17 of *Sociétiés & Représentations (2004)*.

R. Sweeney, 'Singing our way to victory: French cultural politics and music during the Great War', in G. Lipsitz et al., eds, *Music/Culture* (Middletown, CT, 2001).

# Index